European Roma Integration Efforts – A Snapshot

Morag Goodwin
Paul De Hert
(eds)

European Roma Integration Efforts –
A Snapshot

Brussels University Press

Institute for European Studies – publication series, nr. 21

The Institute for European Studies is a Jean Monnet Centre of Excellence. It promulgates European Studies in general, and studies of European and Comparative Law, Environment, Media, Migration and Regional (European) Integration specifically. The IES is an education and research centre, carrying out research on various European issues relating to the EU in international affairs, and responsible for the Masters of European Integration and Development, and for the internationally renowned LL.M of International and European Law (formerly PILC programme).

Institute for European Studies (IES)
Vrije Universiteit Brussel
Pleinlaan 2
B-1050 Brussels
ies@vub.ac.be
http://www.ies.be

Cover design: Koloriet, Leefdaal
Book design: theSWitch, Antwerpen
Print: Flin Graphic Group, Oostkamp

© 2013 VUBPRESS Brussels University Press
VUBPRESS is an imprint of ASP nv (Academic and Scientific Publishers nv)
Ravensteingalerij 28
B-1000 Brussels
Tel. + 32 (0)2 289 26 50
Fax + 32 (0)2 289 26 59
E-mail info@vubpress.be
www.vubpress.be

ISBN 978 90 5718 157 3
NUR 747 / 740 / 828
Legal deposit D/2013/11.161/072

Table of contents

Acknowledgements   7

Chapter 1: An Introductory Essay – Contextualising Romani
Integration Efforts in the European Union
    Morag Goodwin   9

SECTION 1: EXAMINING INSTITUTIONAL APPROACHES   25

Chapter 2: Is the European Court of Human Rights' Case-law on
Anti-Romani Violence 'Beyond Reasonable Doubt'?
    Mathias Möschel   27

Chapter 3: Proving the Invisible: Addressing Evidentiary Issues in
Cases of Presumed Discriminatory Abuse against Roma before the
European Court of Human Rights through *V.C. v. Slovakia*
    Jasmina Mačkić   51

Chapter 4: The Roma and the Framework Convention for the
Protection of National Minorities: A Tool to Disentangle the
Dichotomy between a Socially Disadvantaged Group and a National
Minority
    Roberta Medda-Windischer   77

Chapter 5: Enforcing Fundamental Rights in the European Union
After the Treaty of Lisbon: What Can the Roma Case Tell Us?
    Elise Muir and Mark Dawson   99

SECTION 2: COUNTRY PERSPECTIVES   127

Chapter 6: Great Ideas – Bad Practice: On Implementation of
Policies and Programmes for Roma
    Ada Ingrid Engebrigtsen   129

Chapter 7: Anti-Roma Hate Speech in the Czech Republic, Hungary
and Poland
   Uladzislau Belavusau   141

Chapter 8: Roma as a Discrete and Insular Minority in Poland:
In a Quest for Effective Rights Protection Mechanisms
   Anna Śledzińska-Simon   183

Chapter 9: Roma in Romania: From Law to Practice
   Emanuela Ignatoiu-Sora   211

Chapter 10: Positive Action for Roma in Belgium
   Jozefien Van Caeneghem   227

Annex: Extract from *The Situation of Roma in 11 EU Member
States: Survey Results At A Glance*
   Fundamental Rights Agency (FRA)   251

Acknowledgements

This collection of papers is the product of a workshop held in Brussels on 16 March 2012 under the title 'Europe and the Roma: Where do we stand now?'. The workshop was organised by Paul De Hert and Emanuela Ignatoiu-Sora on behalf of, and funded by, the Institute for European Studies and the Fundamental Rights and Constitutionalism Research Group of the Vrije Universiteit Brussel. Our thanks to Emanuela and to the Institute for European Studies and the Fundamental Rights and Constitutional Research Group for making it happen. Our thanks, too, to the speakers and participants at the workshop for the fruitful discussions that resulted. Jozefien Van Caeneghem and Julia Muraszkiewicz have provided valuable editing assistance and we are grateful for their efforts.

Sections of *The Situation of Roma in 11 EU Member States. Survey Results at a Glance* (Luxembourg: Publications Office of the European Union, 2012) have been reproduced in the annex to this volume with the kind permission of the European Union Agency for Fundamental Rights Agency (FRA). © FRA – European Union Agency for Fundamental Rights, pp. 14-29. Our thanks to the FRA, and to Michael Beis in particular for his facilitating role.

Morag Goodwin & Paul de Hert, Tilburg and Brussels 2013

Chapter 1

An Introductory Essay –
Contextualising Romani Integration Efforts in the European Union

*Morag Goodwin**

I. Introduction

This collection of papers is the product of a workshop organised by Paul De Hert and Emanuela Ignatoiu-Sora on behalf of, and funded by, the Institute for European Studies and the Fundamental Rights and Constitutionalism Research Group of the Vrije Universiteit Brussel. The workshop was held in Brussels on 16 March 2012 under the title *Europe and the Roma: Where Do We Stand Now?* We have given this collection of papers the slightly different title of *European Romani Integration Efforts – A Snapshot.* This title reflects not only that the papers collected here present a specific moment in time but that each individual contribution reflects upon a particular country or institution. What the new title also hopes to make clear was that this volume makes no claim to comprehensiveness in reflecting upon Romani integration efforts in Europe. Instead, this book provides a series of snapshots offering the reader a detailed view of particular integration efforts at a given moment. When taken together, these essays offer a fascinating collage of where we are now.

Such reflection comes at a critical time. Understanding past efforts, knowing where we are now, is of course essential to moving forward towards one's desired destination. The last few years have been particularly busy with regard to European Romani integration efforts. The large international furore in the summer and early autumn of 2010 over media reports of the on-going French practice of collective expulsion of Romanian and Bulgarian Roma[1]

---

* Morag Goodwin is Associate Professor of European and International Law, Tilburg Law School; m.e.a.goodwin@uvt.nl
1 See Muir and Dawson in this volume for a description and analysis of the events in France and the European Commission's response.

gave impetus to a process already underway. The EU has in its own words 'stepped up' efforts for Romani integration.[2] This is visible in numerous recent efforts at the European level, such as the launch of the European Roma Summits in 2008 to provide decision-makers at the highest levels of the EU and Member States with the opportunity to meet and discuss Romani issues;[3] the creation of the European Roma Platform in 2007, at the first meeting of which in April 2009 the '10 Common Basic Principles on Roma Inclusion' were adopted;[4] the publication of the Commission report on the social and economic integration of Roma;[5] the formation of a Roma Task Force in September 2010, a body internal to the European Commission and charged with streamlining, assessing and benchmarking the use of EU funds by Member States for Romani integration;[6] and, certainly not least, the adoption of the EU Framework for National Roma Integration Strategies in the spring of 2011.[7] Roma have never been higher on the EU's agenda.

This renewed focus on the Roma seems to bear witness to a shift in approach by the institutions and agencies of the European Union. In a recent article, Sobotka and Vermeersch suggested that we are witnessing a transition from a minority rights approach in the context of Enlargement to a focus on social and economic integration; from Roma as an issue that fell under Enlargement to a topic high on the EU's internal agenda.[8] Such a shift in focus befits both the new social agenda of the Lisbon Treaty and the EU's 2020 Strategy. A change in emphasis from separation in the form of minority rights with a focus on the countries of Central and Eastern Europe to an emphasis on inclusion, coupled with the recognition that Roma suffer discrimination and exclusion

---

2   See the Fundamental Rights Agency report, *The situation of Roma in 11 EU Member States. Survey results at a glance* (Luxembourg: Publications Office of the European Union, 2012); parts of this report are reproduced in as an Annex to this volume.

3   First European Roma Summit, Brussels, 16 September 2008; http://ec.europa.eu/social/main.jsp?catId=88&langId=en&eventsId=105&furtherEvents=yes.

4   See http://ec.europa.eu/justice/discrimination/roma/roma-platform/index_en.htm

5   European Commission, *The social and economic integration of the Roma*, COM(2010) 133 final, Brussels, http://eur-lex.europa.eu/LexUriServ/LexUriServ.do?uri=COM:20 10:0133:FIN:EN:PDF.

6   Press Release, Roma Integration: First Findings of Task Force and Report on Social Inclusion, European Commission, MEMO/10/701, 21 December 2010.

7   European Commission, *An EU Framework for National Roma Integration Strategies up to 2020*, COM(2011) 173/4 final, Brussels, http://eur-lex.europa.eu/LexUriServ/LexUriServ.do?uri=CELEX:52011DC0173:en:NOT

8   Eva Sobotka & Peter Vermeersch, *Governing Human Rights and Roma Inclusion: Can the EU be a Catalyst for Local Change?* 34 HUMAN RIGHTS QUARTERLY 800-822 (2012).

right across the EU-27 is to be welcomed. Yet, the flurry of initiatives over the last few years appears to represent the formation of a new orthodoxy in relation to Roma. This new orthodoxy consists in a shared approach across a number of institutions[9] on how Roma are to be viewed within the European space, what purposes integration should serve and how that integration should be achieved if we are indeed witnessing the creation of an orthodox approach to questions of Romani exclusion, this is a particularly apposite moment to reflect upon the achievements and failures to date of integration efforts aimed at Europe's Romani populations.

While the European Union is altering its approach to Roma – driven by the logic, momentum and demands of its own integration project – it is not acting in isolation. The Council of Europe has long taken a leading role on questions of Romani exclusion and discrimination, both through the European Convention on Human Rights and the Framework Convention for the Protection of National Minorities. The European Court of Human Rights in particular has played a significant role over the last two decades in setting the tone for how Roma are viewed within the realm of national spaces as well as within the European sphere. The anticipated accession of the European Union to the European Convention on Human Rights, and early indications that the Strasbourg Court see their new position within the European hierarchy as akin to that of a European constitutional court, make assessments of its record to date on dealing with questions of Romani exclusion and discrimination particularly timely.[10] A number of the essays here focus on the Strasbourg Court's contribution to our understanding of Romani exclusion and integration and, by so doing, provide a window onto broader questions of European (self-)identity.

What this introductory essay attempts to do is briefly sketch a broad outline of recent trends in European policy towards Roma so as to provide the reader with a context from which the snapshots that follow can, hopefully, be better viewed.

---

9   Other institutions of relevance here include the World Bank, the Open Society Institute, the UNDP and the OSCE.

10 See Eur. Court H.R., *M.S.S. v. Belgium and Greece*, Judgment of the Grand Chamber of 21 January 2011, Application no. 30696/00; and the response of the European Union to the earlier Chamber decision in ECJ Press Release of 22 September 2011, Opinions of Advocate General Trstenjak in Joined Cases C-411/10 N.S. v Secretary of State for the Home Department and C-493/10 M.E. and Others v Refugee Applications Commissioner and Minister for Justice, Equality and Law Reform.

II. From Minority Rights to Individual Rights

The 2011 EU Framework for National Roma Integration Strategies begins by stating that many of Europe's Romani population of 10-12 million people face prejudice, intolerance, discrimination and social exclusion in their daily lives – a situation it labels 'unacceptable'.[11] This statement on the realities of the lives of many of Europe's Romani citizens was confirmed by a 2012 study conducted by the Fundamental Rights Agency in 11 countries across the European Union; this research found that the situation of Roma in relation to education, employment, health and housing was markedly worse than that of the non-Romani majority with whom they lived in close proximity.[12] Roma are, by a considerable margin and in the words of a 2012 Amnesty International report, the "poorest and most reviled people in Europe".[13] The UNDP, used to working with the very poorest of the world's poor, has labelled the socio-economic challenges that many Roma face within Europe as 'grave'.[14]

These assessments of the socio-economic situation of Roma in today's Europe come despite twenty years of efforts at the national and at the European level to protect and integrate Roma since the end of Communism. As the European Commission acknowledges, "there is a widely shared assumption that the living and working conditions of the Roma have not much improved over the last two decades".[15] Such recent efforts are themselves only a small part of a long history of attempts to integrate or assimilate Roma within the European space.[16] Many of these efforts have caused enormous suffering; most have been unsuccessful in achieving their goals. How, then, should we understand the recent efforts of the last twenty years?

European policy in relation to the Roma in the 1990s was largely guided by the immediate concerns of protection against widespread violence that

---

11   European Commission, An EU Framework for National Roma Integration Strategies up to 2020, COM(2011) 173/4, 2.

12   FRA report (2012), *supra* note 2.

13   Amnesty International Annual Report 2012; available at http://www.amnesty.org/en/annual-report/2012.

14   UNDP, http://www.undp.org/content/undp/en/home/presscenter/pressreleases/2012/05/23/widespread-roma-exclusion-persists-find-new-surveys.html; last accessed 28 February 2013.

15   See, Commission Staff Working Document, Community Instruments and Policies for Roma Inclusion COM(2008) 420 (Brussels, SEC(2008)XXX), 4.

16   See, for an excellent account of the history of Roma in Europe, ANGUS FRASER, THE GYPSIES (1992).

followed in the wake of the events of 1990. As Sobotka and Vermeersch have noted, early concern for the Roma within the EU institutions was guided by Enlargement policy, itself steered by the 1993 Copenhagen Criteria laying down the conditions for EU membership.[17] These Criteria are most well known for the political conditions they contained, namely a commitment to democracy, the rule of law, human rights and minority rights. The focus of early EU policies towards the Roma was thus a mix of human rights and minority rights but with the emphasis on the latter: efforts related to protection from violence, combined with concern for cultural protection, such as the right to use minority languages, or to respect for cultural diversity. This line is visible, too, in the approach of the European Court of Human Rights; in the case of *Buckley v. UK* from 1996, the Court recognised that English Gypsies have a distinctive way of life and placed an obligation upon State Parties to take account of that difference in the application of seemingly neutral law.[18] This approach achieved one of its greatest successes in the Court's statement of general principles in a follow-up case, *Chapman v. UK*. Here, the Court – although still refusing to find a breach of the Convention – in reference to the Council of Europe Framework Convention for the Protection of Minorities, noted:

> "that there may be said to be an emerging international consensus amongst the Contracting States of the Council of Europe recognising the special needs of minorities and an obligation to protect their security, identity and lifestyle, not only for the purpose of safeguarding the interests of the minorities themselves but to preserve a cultural diversity of value to the whole community".[19]

However, this minority rights approach came to be largely over-shadowed as the 1990s became the 2000s by the shift in focus away from minority rights towards non-discrimination law. The 1992 Treaty of Maastricht and the 1997 Treaty of Amsterdam enabled EU institutions to take measures to combat discrimination based upon racial or ethnic origin – a move which culminated in Directive 2000/43 ('the Race Directive') in June

---

17   Sobotka and Vermeersch, *supra* note 8, 802-803.
18   Eur. Court H.R., *Buckley v. UK*, Judgement of 25 September 1996. The Court, however, granted the UK a large margin of appreciation and Mrs. Buckley was unsuccessful in her claim.
19   Eur. Court H.R., *Chapman v. UK*, Judgment of 18 January 2001, para. 93.

2000.[20] This Directive represented a huge advance on the existing state of law throughout Europe in relation to racial discrimination, enshrining standards on indirect discrimination and on the burden of proof shift, requiring sanctions to be effective, proportionate and dissuasive and in mandating the creation of equality bodies to provide assistance to victims of discrimination in pursuing their complaint. Moreover, the Directive has an unexpectedly wide scope, prohibiting discrimination in access to employment and training, social security, education, healthcare, and to all goods and services, including, for example, housing.[21] As part of the European *acquis* that all prospective Member States were required to adopt prior to accession to the Union, the Directive set a pan-European standard for how complaints of racial discrimination are to be handled within national legal systems. This has been a major step forward given the studied resistance of many national courts to taking complaints of racial discrimination by Roma seriously.[22]

It is possible to see this shift within EU thinking towards the Roma being echoed by the Strasbourg Court. Although the Court acknowledged that Romani communities enjoy a distinctive way of life, it has been notably reluctant to find that breaches of the Convention have had a racial motive. Indeed, it has shown an unwillingness to even examine Article 14 complaints and was, for many years, out of step with the developments within anti-discrimination law at the EU level.[23] However, in cases such as *Nachova v. Bulgaria* and in *D.H. and Others v. Czech Republic*, the European Court showed itself not only willing to place an obligation upon states to investigate allegations of a racial motive to Convention claims – expressed as a procedural requirement under Article 14 – and to require a shift in the burden of proof in relation to claims of indirect discrimination, but found

---

20 Treaty on European Union, 29 July 1992, 1992 O.J. (C 191); Treaty of Amsterdam Amending the Treaty on the European Union, 10 November 1997, 1997 O.J. (C 340); Council Directive 2000/43, Implementing the Principle of Equal Treatment Between Persons Irrespective of Racial or Ethnic Origin, 2000 O.J. (L 180) 22.

21 Cf Directive 2000/78/EC of 27 November 2000, establishing a general framework for equal treatment in employment and occupation, 2000 O.J. (L 303), offering protection against discrimination on the grounds of religion or belief, disability, age or sexual orientation but only in the area of employment.

22 For numerous examples, see the European Roma Rights Center website: http://www.errc.org. Within this volume, the paper by Uladzislau Belavusau presents a number of such examples.

23 See Morag Goodwin, *D.H. and Others v. Czech Republic: A Major Set-Back for the Development of Non-Discrimination Norms in Europe*, 7 German Law Journal 421-432 (2006) in response to the Chamber decision in that case.

violations of Article 14 in both these cases.[24] Yet the Court's continuing hesitations to see the allegations of racial discrimination before it remain subject to fierce criticism, the developments in *Nachova* and *D.H. and Others* notwithstanding.[25]

The shift in focus to non-discrimination law away from the language of minority rights has, somewhat paradoxically, been accompanied by an emphasis on a human rights approach to policy-making.[26] This is reflected in the EU Charter of Fundamental Rights becoming, with the 2009 Treaty of Lisbon, directly enforceable before European courts and in national courts in application of Union law.[27] While minority rights are, of course, a sub-set of the human rights canon, there is a fundamental distinction between the two types of rights. Although minority rights are in fact expressed as individual rights, they lay emphasis on the importance of participation in and enjoyment of community life and culture. In contrast, human rights and non-discrimination law stress the identity of the human being as an individual and regulate her movement within society as an individual rather than as a member of a community. It is the focus on Roma as individuals that is the common thread linking the human rights and non-discrimination approach to Romani exclusion with the major shift identified by Sobotka and Vermeersch in European policy-making towards Roma: the turn to social inclusion.

---

24 *Nachova v. Bulgaria*, Judgement of the Grand Chamber of 6 July 2005; *D.H. and Others v. Czech Republic*, Judgement of the Grand Chamber of 13 November 2007.

25 See the contributions by Mathias Möschel and Jasmina Mačkić in this volume.

26 Sobotka and Vermeersch, *supra* note 8, 803. This can be seen as paradoxical in effect (if not in theory) because human rights speak a language of togetherness or sameness – we all have the same entitlements by virtue of being human – whereas a non-discrimination approach actually works to emphasise distinction and difference. See Morag Goodwin, *Multidimensional exclusion: Viewing Romani marginalisation through the nexus of race and poverty* in EUROPEAN UNION NON-DISCRIMINATION LAW. COMPARATIVE PERSPECTIVES ON MULTIDIMENSIONAL EQUALITY LAW (Dagmar Schiek & Victoria Chege eds, 2009), 151-154.

27 The Charter of Fundamental Rights of the European Union, 18 December 2000, 2000 O.J. (L 180) 22; Treaty of Lisbon Amending the Treaty on the European Union and the Treaty Establishing the European Community, 13 December 2007, 2007 O.J. (C 306) 1.

III. Social Inclusion as the Isolated Individual in the Marketplace

With the first two waves of Enlargement completed by 2007, Roma moved from being an item on the external relations agenda to a key priority of internal EU policies. Indeed, Sobotka and Vermeersch date the launch of a social inclusion approach towards the Roma to 2007, and to the European Council of December of that year.[28] This Council called for a co-ordinated approach to the problems that Roma face. Similarly, the Conclusions of the Council of Ministers of Employment, Social Policy, Health and Consumer Affairs of 8 June 2009 reflected the gathering belief in the need for Romani integration via an inclusion approach.[29] The European Commission has likewise increasingly adopted a social inclusion approach towards the Roma. This is marked in the publication of a number of documents – notably *The social and economic integration of the Roma in Europe* and *Roma in Europe: The Implementation of European Union Instruments and Policies for Roma Inclusion* – and has culminated, at least for now, in the 2011 EU Framework for National Roma Integration Strategies.[30] The social inclusion approach, as Sobotka and Vermeersch have observed, builds upon but does not replace a human rights-based approach that emphasises the use of anti-discrimination law as a tool in achieving social inclusion.[31]

---

28 Sobotka and Vermeersch, *supra* note 8, 801. See, Presidency Conclusions, Brussels European Council, 14 December 2007. See also Eva Sobotka, *Targeting and Mainstreaming the Integration of Roma at the EU and European Level*, EQUAL VOICES, 16 June 2005; available at http://infoportal.fra.europa.eu/InfoPortal/ publicationsFrontEndAccess.do?id=15335.

29 Press Release, Council of the European Union, 2947th Employment, Social Policy, Health and Consumer Affairs Council Meeting, Council Conclusions on the Inclusion of the Roma, 8 June 2009, 2. The Ministers issued a strong call to the Commission and to the Member States to co-operate to address questions of Romani integration and to take into account the Common Basic Principles of Roma Inclusion when doing so. Sobotka and Vermeersch, *supra* note 8, 806.

30 Communication from the Commission to the Council, the European Parliament, The European Economic and Social Committee and the Committee of the Regions, *The Social Integration of Roma in Europe*, COM(2010) 133 final; Commission Staff Working Document, *Roma in Europe: The Implementation of European Instruments and Policies for Roma Inclusion – Progress Report 2008-2010*, SEC(2010) 400 final; Communication from the Commission to the Council, the European Parliament, The European Economic and Social Committee and the Committee of the Regions, *An EU Framework for National Roma Integration Stratgies up to 2020*, COM(2011) 173/4 (the 'Framework').

31 Sobotka and Vemeersch, *supra* note 8, 808-809.

This change in emphasis towards the Roma can be viewed in the light of a wider re-orientation of EU policy, in which the primarily economic language of European integration is apparently moderated by a shift towards viewing economic growth and social cohesion as mutually conditioning and sustaining. This is reflected in the 2020 Strategy in the language of 'smart, sustainable and inclusive' growth,[32] as well as in the notion of a 'social market economy'.[33] What this approach laid down in these documents shares with the human rights-based approach is the emphasis on the individual. However, they also reflect another, related, shift that marks a decisive break with the minority rights approach of previous decades: social inclusion within EU policy is to be driven by economic integration. At the 2009 EU Platform for Roma Inclusion, the EU Commissioner for Employment, Social Affairs and Equal Opportunity, Vladimír Špidla, openly stated: "Roma inclusion is in the economic interest of the EU member states, by increasing productivity and state revenues. Furthermore, Roma inclusion will help develop a qualified workforce in conditions of an ageing society".[34]

This equation of Romani social inclusion with economic integration is most clearly visible in the 2011 EU Framework for National Roma Integration Strategies. In describing the economic and social integration envisaged, the Framework puts forward what amounts to an 'integration spiral'. As Goodwin and Buijs have suggested, this positive spiral of integration looks something like: equal access → education → participation in the labour market → economic benefits → social acceptance.[35] The spiral begins by majority communities providing Roma with non-discriminatory access to services and jobs, complemented by policies to ensure equal access and investment in

---

32   Europe 2020: A strategy for smart, sustainable and inclusive growth, COM(2010) 2020 final, 3 March 2010. Commitment to eradicating poverty and social exclusion is at least a decade older, however; these efforts were addressed using the Open Method of Co-ordination approach. See, Hugh Frazier & Eric Marlier, *Social Inclusion in the European Union: Where do we stand, where are we going?* DEVELOPMENT AND TRANSITIONS, 15 June 2010; available at www.developmentandtransition.net (last accessed 3 March 2013).

33   See Catherine Barnard, *The Protection of Fundamental Social Rights in Europe after Lisbon: A Question of Conflicts of Interests* in THE PROTECTION OF FUNDAMENTAL RIGHTS IN THE EU AFTER LISBON (Sybe de Vries, Ulf Berniz & Stephen Weatherill eds., 2013).

34   Press Release, European Network on Social Inclusion and the Roma under the Structural Funds, Second Meeting of the Integrated European Platform for Roma Inclusion, 28 September 2009; quoted in Sobotka and Vermeersch, *supra* note 8, 807.

35   Morag Goodwin & Roosmarijn Buijs, *Making Good Citizens of the Roma: A Closer Look at the EU Framework for National Roma Integration Strategies* (forthcoming, GERMAN LAW JOURNAL (2013)).

education. In this way, Roma can thus be integrated into the formal labour market. Such economic integration will improve economic productivity and increase the taxation base, and thus deliver economic benefits to the majority. As the majority see themselves benefiting from Romani economic integration, social acceptance will follow.[36] Social inclusion is redefined in the Framework into integration, which is itself conceived as participation in the formal labour market. Economic integration as participation in the wage economy both precedes social integration or inclusion and is a precondition for it, not only in raising Romani living standards but by enabling Roma to gain the acceptance of the general public.

Such a vision of integration is far removed from the language of minority rights, with its ideas of cultural protection, of rights to use minority languages, or respect for cultural diversity. In this economic vision of Romani integration, culture is almost entirely absent. What the lack of reference to cultural differences entails is a complete silence on what the consequences or costs of integration are likely to be for Romani communities. This suggests that the marketplace is either viewed as a culturally-neutral realm; or the supreme importance accorded to participation in the formal economy in the EU's vision of a European society entails that cultural diversity that clashes with such participation must be 'overcome'. Such an understanding of integration – in which majority norms in relation to work become the default, non-negotiable standard – brings integration, and this model of social inclusion, awfully close to assimilation.[37]

What the emphasis on participation in the market economy, and, related, the importance of education, reveals is the individualization of integration. The focus of and the responsibility for integration in the EU social inclusion model is and falls upon the individual. It is the same individual, but in relationship to society more broadly, that has largely been the focus of Strasbourg jurisprudence. While a famous recent case has seen the European Court of Human Rights attempt to situate individuals within their cultural milieu and understand their claim from that perspective – notably *D.H. and Others v. Czech Republic* – this is the notable exception.[38] Instead, the

---

36   The Framework, *supra* note 28, 2-3.

37   For arguments in this regard to the formulation of integration in the Framework, see Goodwin and Buijs, *supra* note 35.

38   One could argue that this is not without good reason; it is open to question whether the Court is the best institution to engage in such exercises. See Morag Goodwin, *Taking on Racial Segregation: the European Court of Human Rights at a Brown v. Board of Education moment?*, 170(3) RECHTSGELEERD MAGAZIJN THEMIS 93-105 (2009).

Court displays a marked reluctance to see individual claims from within a pattern of racial discrimination;[39] this, as several of the contributions here suggest, leads to a blindness to the reality of the lives of individual Roma and Romani communities within Europe. Such de-contextualisation of Romani individuals and claims appears to be one of the consequences of this shift to individualized rights and market participation. Another consequence appears to be the transformation of Roma from a European minority into a 'European problem' that needs to be solved through integration.[40]

I suggested in the introduction to this essay that a new orthodoxy on how to approach Romani issues appears to be forming: what I have attempted to suggest is that this orthodoxy is integration rather than diversity, and integration that is predicated upon individual rights and individual participation in society and in the marketplace – in short, an approach that is both rights-driven and economically defined. If indeed such a trend exists and is cementing itself as the new norm for understanding the place of Roma within Europe, it is important to question not only the presuppositions underpinning it but also what the consequences will be.

This, however, is an indication of the direction in which future research may lay. Before we embark on a new journey, it is important to know where we are starting from. The essays in this collection are reflections of an understanding of Romani issues at a turning point. Yet, while the papers collected here may together provide a map of where we are now, told from the perspective of the respective authors, they do not reflect a shared understanding of what the destination is or should be. Indeed, a number of the authors collected here precisely challenge the idea that there is a shared destination or that it is possible to have one at all. This volume, then, is a critical reflection on integration efforts to date but one that challenges the idea that such efforts have or should have a clear *telos*.

---

39 For example, Eur. Court Human Rights, *V.C. v the Slovak Republic*, Judgement of 8 November 2011.

40 The suggestion is Huub van Baar's; see Huub van Baar, *Europe's Romaphobia: problematization, securitization, nomadization*, 29 Environment and Planning: Society and Space 203-212, (2011), 204. See also Huub van Baar, The European Roma. Minority Representation, Memory and the Limits of Transnational Governmentality (2011).

IV. The Snapshots

The collection of essays brought together here analyse the approach to date of European institutions and of various Member States towards the Roma; assess the success of various protection mechanisms, such as rights, and or integration efforts, both historical and contemporary; and, taken together, provide a deeper understanding of how Romani identity has been and is being constructed within European discourses. They highlight the multi-faceted nature of the discrimination and marginalization that Roma face within the European space. At the same time, they address two central questions. The first is how the 'Romani issue' is defined; for example, as a minority rights problem or as individual acts of discrimination or as a civilising quest. The second question addressed in these essays concerns the parameters of the integration debate: our authors analyse different examples of integration efforts, reflect upon the design of those efforts, consider what has been excluded from consideration and draw conclusions about the success or failure of those efforts.

The first section of this collection brings together four papers that focus on the concern for discrimination and violence against Roma within European institutions. The collection begins with a paper by Mathias Möschel, a version of which was published in the 2012 volume of the *Human Rights Law Review*, in which he examines in detail the track record of the European Court of Human Rights in addressing violence against Roma. Möschel highlights the struggles within the Court to accept claims that violence has been racially motivated and analyses the shift by the Strasbourg Court from the 'beyond reasonable doubt' standard to a vaguer requirement of 'racial elements'. By its unwillingness to label violence as racially-motivated, Möschel makes a compelling case that the Court is contributing to the construction of a European self-image as a place of tolerance, in which violence against racial or ethnic minorities are isolated acts.

This critical reading of the European Court of Human Rights' jurisprudence is continued in the second paper in this collection. In her essay analysing the Court's finding in *V.C. v. Slovakia*,[41] Jasmina Mačkić also focuses on the difficulties in proving claims of racial discrimination before the Court, here in the specific context of sterilization. While the Court has come a long way in recent years in bringing its jurisprudence on indirect

---

41   Eur. Court H.R., *V.C. v. Slovakia*, Judgement of 8 November 2011, Application no. 18968/07.

discrimination into line with other European standards, notably in the context of education claims, in cases where the allegation concerns physical violence, it remains unwilling to accept general evidence of discriminatory intent. *V.C.* offered the Court the opportunity to examine a Europe in which attitudes towards Roma are so hostile that, even where it has been made illegal to sterilize individuals without their consent, individual medical staff take it upon themselves to carry on such practices. By treating the case as an isolated incident, the Court thereby gives us permission to believe that racially-motivated sterilization is a horror that belongs to our shared past – a past which European integration was designed to overcome. Instead, *V.C.* becomes simply the victim of a bungled consent procedure.

From the European Court of Human Rights, our third paper turns to another protection mechanism within the Council of Europe structure: the Framework Convention for the Protection of National Minorities. In her paper, Roberta Medda-Windischer assesses the impact of the Framework Convention on the attitudes and policies of state parties towards their Romani populations. She identifies common attitudes to the Roma across the Convention's State Parties, as evidenced by comments by the Framework Convention's Advisory Committee on State reports, as well as problems and positive developments on a country specific level. In contrast to the trend suggested above, Medda-Windischer argues that the operation of the Framework Convention has been relatively successful in urging states to view the Roma as a national minority rather than merely as a socially disadvantaged group. Moreover, in stressing the importance of balancing the two key principles of diversity and inclusion, the Framework mechanism has successfully pushed states towards adopting comprehensive national strategies for improving the socio-economic conditions in Romani communities, and has led to a general increase in the awareness at the level of the national authorities of the diversity among Romani communities and of respect for that cultural diversity.

A paper by Elise Muir and Mark Dawson, originally published in the *Common Market Law Review*, rounds off this section. Muir and Dawson take the row within the EU over the French expulsion of Bulgarian and Romanian Roma from France in the late summer of 2010 as a starting point from which to examine the mechanisms for enforcing fundamental rights within the Union. The paper systematically lays out the strengths and limitations of existing individual and institutional enforcement procedures within the EU for the protection of fundamental rights, and concludes by suggesting a need for enhanced collective vigilance in this area. Enhanced collective vigilance

21

requires, according to Muir and Dawson, a hybrid approach that combines a judicial strategy that empowers and enables vulnerable groups to speak out – by, for example, creating enhanced opportunities for collective action within the EU judicial machinery – and a non-judicial approach that focuses on integration. In sum, the authors argue for a commitment within the EU to a multi-dimensional legal and political approach towards vulnerable groups, including the Roma.

is this different from what's being done

In the second section of this collection, we examine Romani integration and/or protection efforts from a country specific or country comparison perspective. The first paper here, by Ada Ingrid Engebrigtsen, examines two historical examples of failed integration programmes directed at Vlach Roma and analyses them from an anthropological perspective. The first example concerns the integration efforts of the Hapsburg Archduke Jozef to assimilate a group of nomadic Vlach Roma on one of his Hungarian estates between 1891 and 1893; Engebrigtsen draws her second example from an integration programme set up by the municipality of Oslo almost a hundred years later. Despite taking different approaches – notably that the Norwegian effort consulted with the Roma concerned and involve them in the implementation of the plans – both programmes failed. Engebrigtsen draws shared lessons from those failures that should be read by everyone working on Romani integration efforts today if similar failures are to be avoided or at least minimised in the future.

The contribution by Uladzislau Belavusau is also comparative in nature and examines the protection against anti-Romani hate speech provided by the Czech Republic, Hungary and Poland, in particular the legal avenues of redress available to victims. Belavusau combines an analysis of the legal framework with its functioning in practice, and situates both in a country-specific social and historical context. His analysis suggests that all three legal systems take similar approaches to freedom of expression protection, notably that the systems of all three countries attempt to balance the US libertarian approach to freedom of speech with the traditional restrictive European continental method. At the same time, his analysis reveals strong traditions of anti-Romani hate speech in all three countries and a reluctance on the part of lower courts to extend hate speech protection to anti-Romani speech.

The third paper in this section stays in the same geographical region, and examines the effectiveness of rights protection mechanisms for Roma in Poland. In her essay, Anna Śledzińska-Simon takes as a starting point that a rights-based approach to integration is the preferable strategy and she attempts to understand why the legal system in Poland has failed to deliver for

Roma. Her conclusion is that the situation of Roma – both geographically and socio-economically – is such that they face additional hurdles in accessing the protection of the law. The conclusion is equally stark in relation to the ability of Romani groups to access the political process or government support programmes; here, Śledzińska-Simon notes the frequent ineffectiveness and irrelevance of such processes or programmes for Romani citizens and warns of the tendency of supposedly favourable treatment to generate additional tensions within society. However, her final conclusion is upbeat and concerns the need to strengthen legal protection and to design such protections with the needs of the Roma in mind.

Taking a similar approach, Emanuela Ignatoiu-Sora presents the situation of Roma in Romania. The actions of the French authorities in the late summer of 2010 in expelling large numbers of Romanian and Bulgarian Roma threw the spotlight back on the treatment and living conditions of Roma in these countries. Ignatiou-Sora notes how Romania has been ten years ahead of the European turn to social inclusion, having adopted a national strategy for Romani inclusion already in 2001. Indeed, Romania's approach towards the Roma mirrors precisely the swing from cultural protection under minority rights legislation to individual rights under non-discrimination law and a focus on social inclusion. However, while noting some successes, Ignatiou-Sora highlights the difficulty in implementing social inclusion policies, despite the best will in the world. Her analysis of integration in the context of education policy suggests the need to situate education in 'the whole social experience'.

The final paper in the volume turns the spotlight on western Europe, in particular, Belgium. In her contribution, Jozefien Van Caeneghem begins with the hypothesis that positive action may be the tool to break the poverty cycle in which many Romani families and communities are trapped. Van Caeneghem provides an overview of what positive action is generally understand to mean and the scope for introducing positive action measures within the international arena, the Council of Europe and the European Union. An introduction to the common difficulties that Roma face in Belgium, and the approach of the Belgian authorities towards Roma, leads into an analysis of policies towards Roma or affecting Roma at the federal level and within Flanders and Wallonia, and the extent to which positive action is used. Van Caeneghem concludes that the biggest hindrance both to the introduction of positive action and to integration efforts more generally is the unavailability of ethnic data. She notes that within Belgium, a lack of ethnic data entails that there is little good information on how many Roma are resident in Belgium and on the nature and extent of the difficulties that they face.

Finally, we reproduce as an Annex to the volume, with the kind permission of the Fundamental Rights Agency, four extracts from their latest report on Roma that present in stark graphics the nature of the poverty and the scale of disadvantage and discrimination that Roma face. While it is necessary that we continue to critically examine efforts to protect and include Roma within European society, we should not lose sight of why these efforts matter so much.

SECTION 1:
EXAMINING INSTITUTIONAL APPROACHES

Chapter 2

Is the European Court of Human Rights' Case-law on Anti-Romani Violence 'Beyond Reasonable Doubt'?

*Mathias Möschel**

I. Introduction

During the past 10 years the European Court of Human Rights (ECtHR or the 'Court') has ruled on more than 40 cases involving anti-Romani violence.[1] Most of those cases claim Article 2 (right to life), Article 3 (prohibition of torture, or inhuman or degrading treatment or punishment), and Article 14 (non-discrimination) violations. The Court repeatedly ranks the former two provisions amongst the most fundamental of the European Convention for the Protection of Human Rights and Fundamental Freedoms (ECHR or the 'Convention'). With regard to the latter, it often highlights that racial discrimination is a particular affront to human dignity which requires special vigilance from the authorities and a vigorous reaction. The recognition of the fundamental importance of all three involved Convention rights and freedoms has not led to a general acknowledgement of the racial motivations

* Post-doctoral researcher at the Université Paris Ouest Nanterre; mmoschel@u-paris10.fr. A longer version of this chapter has been published in the Human Rights Law Review (2012), vol. 12, no. 3, 479-507. The author wishes to thank Ruth Rubio-Marín, Lourdes Peroni, Alexandra Timmer, Elisa Novic, the participants of the European University Institute's Human Rights Working Group and of the conference "Europe and the Roma: Where do we stand now?" for their helpful comments on earlier versions of this chapter. Any errors or omissions are the author's alone.
1   The reference to the "Roma" throughout this chapter includes individuals and groups as different as the Roma, the Sinti, Travellers, gitanos or the Jenische and the different names under which they might respectively be known in various European countries (e.g. manouches, Ashkali). While aware of the risk of essentializing by using this overarching term, at the same time it reflects the way in which these individuals groups are discriminated, positioned before and disadvantaged before and through the law in uncannily similar ways.

and background to the violence against Romani individuals. Whereas in practically all such cases the ECtHR found an Article 2 and/or Article 3 violation, the track record looks much less flattering when looking at Article 14 violations.

This chapter intends to demonstrate why and how the ECtHR's case law on racially motivated violence against Roma is disappointing and thus contributes to the legal construction of a Europe without, or with very few and isolated, racists. In a first step, I will analyze the case law leading up to the landmark Grand Chamber judgment of *Nachova*. Here we see the application of the increasingly contested standard of proof 'beyond reasonable doubt' established by the Court itself to show racial motivation. In a second step, I will look at the case law that followed *Nachova*, in which one can observe the Court referring less to the beyond reasonable doubt standard of proof and looking more for the presence or absence of racist verbal abuse. However, this shift has not really made a significant difference. Instead one rather notes a wavering and weak commitment to fighting racial discrimination in this area. Finally, a look at the cases involving Romania and the ECtHR's disturbing trend of accepting unilateral declarations against the applicants will confirm this troublesome aspect of the Court's jurisprudence. I argue that the Court's timidity and case law ultimately contribute to the marginalization of and discrimination against Roma and thereby provide an *ex post* confirmation and protection of the racially motivated actions committed by the national authorities and their agents as well as by private individuals.

II. The ECtHR's Case-law on Anti-Romani Violence

From the late 1990s onwards, the judges in Strasbourg have increasingly been confronted with claims involving racially motivated violence against members of Europe's Romani communities. The fact patterns and procedural histories of these cases resemble each other to an uncanny degree. In fact, the case law before the ECtHR draws a horrifying picture of state-sponsored and state-tolerated violence at the hands of police officers, prosecutors, judges and hospital personnel, coupled with widespread private violence and discrimination.

The first type of cases involves a Romani individual or group apprehended by the police after allegedly stealing something or having become involved in a bar brawl.[2] Often these individuals are young males, at times even minors. Sometimes they are beaten up on the spot, but the pattern usually sees them taken to a police station. The luckier ones get away with bruises, broken ribs or hematomas. The unluckier ones die under mysterious circumstances. These cases therefore concern police/state violence against individuals of Romani origin and hinge on three issues: whether the bruises or deaths were actually inflicted by or attributable to the police; how effective the subsequent investigation into these cases was; and whether the violence and/or the ineffective nature of the investigation were racially motivated.

A second set of cases concern private individuals or groups who burn down Romani settlements or who are responsible for assaulting, battering and/or killing Romani individuals.[3] In these cases the police, and thus the state, are sometimes only indirectly and not actively involved in the violence. The contentious issue here is rather whether the arrests, investigations, prosecutions and convictions related to these crimes were conducted fairly and effectively and without any bias on the side of the authorities.

A separate and disturbing 'byproduct' in many of these two types of cases is the treatment accorded to Romani individuals in hospitals. In a fair number of cases the hospital authorities have colluded with the police and investigative authorities in refusing to provide medical help to Romani victims of violence, in providing untruthful autopsy reports that conceal the real cause of death, in entering false information and/ or diagnoses in medical records, and even in the death of Romani individuals in hospital while under police arrest.[4]

---

2   See e.g. Eur. Court H.R., *Assenov and Others v. Bulgaria*, Judgement of 28 October 1998, Application nos. 90/1997/874/1086; Eur. Court H.R., *Velikova v. Bulgaria*, Judgement of 18 May 2000, Application no. 41488/98; Eur. Court H.R., *Sashov and Others v. Bulgaria*, Judgement of 7 January 2010, Application no. 14383/03; and Eur. Court H.R., *Mižigárová v. Slovakia*, Judgement of 14 December 2010, Application no. 74832/01.

3   See *e.g.* Eur. Court H.R., *Moldovan and Others v. Romania No. 1*, friendly settlement of 5 July 2005, Applications nos. 41138/98 and 64320/01; Eur. Court H.R., *Moldovan and Others v. Romania No. 2*, Judgement of 12 July 2005, Applications nos. 41138/98 and 64320/01; Eur. Court H.R., *Šečić v. Croatia*, Judgement of 31 May 2007, Application no. 40116/02; and Eur. Court H.R., *Dimitrova and Others v. Bulgaria*, Judgement of 27 January 2011, Application no. 44862/04.

4   See *e.g.* Eur. Court H.R., *Ognyanova and Choban v. Bulgaria*, Judgement of 23 February 2006, Application no. 46317/99; Eur. Court H.R., *Šečić v. Croatia*, Judgement of 31 May 2007, Application no. 40116/02, para. 10-11; Eur. Court H.R., *Cobzaru v. Romania*, Judgement of 26 July 2007, Application no. 48254/99, para. 14-16; Eur. Court H.R., *Dzeladinov and Others v. The Former Republic of Macedonia*, Judgement of 10 July 2008, Application no. 13252/02, para. 8-9; Eur. Court H.R., *Carabulea v.*

Hospitals are also where the third type of cases concerning violence against Roma covered before the Strasbourg Court plays out, this time in its gendered variant: forced sterilizations on often very young women. In fact, some very recent cases involving Slovakia and the Czech Republic have denounced this practice.[5]

Without claiming to have unearthed all cases, Table 1 below lists a number of violence against Roma rulings by the ECtHR, broken down by country and by whether a separate claim for racial discrimination was brought or declared inadmissible. Moreover, the table also includes cases in which no discrimination claim was brought and that are currently pending, either awaiting admissibility or a judgment on the merits. The result, as of December 2012, is an aggregate total of 52 cases. Bulgaria, Romania and Greece lead the group, with other former Eastern European countries also heavily represented. One last column contains additional police violence cases of the countries involved where nothing in the files seems to indicate that the victims were of Roma origin. Considering that the Roma population all over Europe is deemed to be between 10-12 million reaching a maximum percentage of 10% of the population in Romania and Bulgaria,[6] the comparison demonstrates the disproportionately high number of Roma amongst the victims before the ECtHR.[7]

Romania, Judgement of 13 July 2010, Application no. 45661/99; and Eur. Court H.R., *Đurđević v. Croatia*, Judgement of 19 July 2011, Application no. 52442/09, para. 7-8.

5   Eur. Court H.R., *K.H. and Others v. Slovakia*, Judgement of 28 April 2009, Application no. 32881/04; Eur. Court H.R., *M.V. v. Slovakia*, Admissibility Decision of 23 November 2010, Application no. 62079/09; Eur. Court H.R., *Ferenčíková v. Czech Republic*, friendly settlement of 30 August 2011, Application no. 21826/10; Eur. Court H.R., *V.C. v. Slovakia*, Judgement of 8 November 2011, Application no. 18968/07; *N.B. v. Slovakia*, Judgement of 12 June 2012, Application no. 29518/10; Eur. Court H.R., *Červeňáková v. Czech Republic*, Admissibility Decision of 23 October 2012, Application no. 26852/09; Eur. Court H.R., *I.G. and Others v. Slovakia*, Judgement of 13 November 2012, Application no. 15966/04; and Eur. Court H.R., *R.K v. Czech Republic*, friendly settlement of 27 November 2012, Application no. 7883/08.

6   See Council of Europe, Parliamentary Assembly, THE SITUATION OF ROMA IN EUROPE AND RELEVANT ACTIVITIES OF THE COUNCIL OF EUROPE, Doc. 12174, 26 February 2010. However, precise data is highly unreliable and difficult to obtain.

7   See on this point in relation to Greece: İbrahim Özden Kaboğlu and Stylianos-Ioannis G. Koutnatzis, The Reception Process in Greece and Turkey, in THE IMPACT OF THE ECHR ON NATIONAL LEGAL SYSTEMS 452, 478 (Helen Keller and Alec Stone Sweet eds., 2008). Part of this disproportion could be caused by pro-Romani NGOs actively pursuing a litigation strategy and thus somehow distorting the picture. The author thanks Morag Goodwin for raising this point.

Table 1: Rulings by the ECtHR on Violence against Roma[8]

---

8   Table 1
Bulgaria:
Column 1: *Velikova v. Bulgaria*, Application no. 41488/98, 18 May 2000; *Anguelova v. Bulgaria*, Application no. 38361/97, 13 June 2002; *Nachova and Others v. Bulgaria*, Applications nos. 43577/98 and 43579/98, 24 February 2004; *Nachova and Others v. Bulgaria* [GC], Applications nos. 43577/98 and 43579/98, 6 July 2005; *Osman v. Bulgaria*, Application no. 43233/98, 16 February 2006; *Ognyanova and Choban v. Bulgaria*, Application no. 46317/99, 23 February 2006; *Angelova and Iliev v. Bulgaria*, Application no. 55523/00, 26 July 2007; *Sashov and Others v. Bulgaria*, Application no. 14383/03, 7 January 2010; *Vasil Sashov Petrov v. Bulgaria*, Application no. 63106/00, 10 June 2010; *Seidova and Others v. Bulgaria*, Application no. 310/04, 18 November 2010; *Dimitrova and Others v. Bulgaria*, Application no. 44862/04, 27 January 2011; and *Yotova v. Bulgaria*, Application no. 43606/04, 23 October 2012.
Column 3: *Assenov and Others v. Bulgaria*, Application nos. 90/1997/874/1086, 28 October 1998 and *Tzekov v. Bulgaria*, Application no. 45500/99, 23 February 2006.
Column 4: *Mihaylova and Malinova v. Bulgaria*, Application no. 36613/08, lodged on 17 July 2008
Column 5: *Toteva v. Bulgaria*, Application no. 42027/98, 19 May 2004; *Krastanov v. Bulgaria*, Application no. 50222/99, 30 September 2004; *Kazakova v. Bulgaria*, Application no. 55061/00, 22 June 2006; *Ivan Vasilev v. Bulgaria*, Application no. 48130/99, 12 April 2007; *Stefan Iliev v. Bulgaria*, Application no. 3121/99, 10 May 2007; *Nikolay Dimitrov v. Bulgaria*, Application no. 72663/01, 27 September 2007; *Nikolova and Velichkova v. Bulgaria*, Application no. 7888/03, 20 December 2007; *Boyko Ivanov v. Bulgaria*, Application no. 69138/01, 22 July 2008; *Vasil Petrov v. Bulgaria*, Application no. 57883/00, 31 July 2008; *Vladimir Georgiev v. Bulgaria*, Application no. 61275/00, 16 October 2008; *Georgi Dimitrov v. Bulgaria*, Application no. 31365/02, 15 January 2009; *Dechko Raykov v. Bulgaria*, Application no. 35256/02, 4 February 2010; *Shishkovi v. Bulgaria*, Application no. 17322/04, 25 March 2010; *Angelov Angel Vaskov v. Bulgaria*, Application no. 34805/02, 25 March 2010; *Bekirski v. Bulgaria*, Application no. 71420/01, 2 September 2010; *Vlaevi v. Bulgaria*, Application nos. 272/05 and 890/05, 2 September 2010; and *Filipovi v. Bulgaria*, Application no. 24867/04, 4 December 2012.
Croatia:
Column 1: *Šečič v. Croatia*, Application no. 40116/02, 31 May 2007; and *Beganović v. Croatia*, Application no. 46423/06, 25 June 2009.
Column 3: *Đurđević v. Croatia*, Application no. 52442/09, 19 July 2011.
Column 5: *Mađer v. Croatia*, Application no. 56185/07, 21 June 2011.
Czech Republic:
Column 3: *Eremiášová and Pechová v. Czech Republic*, Application no. 23944/04, 16 February 2012.
Greece:
Column 1: *Bekos and Koutropoulos v. Greece*, Application no. 15250/02, 13 December 2005; *Karagiannopoulos v. Greece*, Application no. 27850/03, 21 June 2007; *Petropoulou-Tsakiris v. Greece*, Application no. 44803/04, 6 December 2007; and *Stefanou v. Greece*, Application no. 2954/07, 22 April 2010.
Column 5: *Makaratzis v. Greece* [GC], Application no. 50385/99, 20 December 2004; *Alsayed Allaham v. Greece*, Application no. 25771/03, 18 January 2007; *Zelilof v. Greece*, Application no. 17060/03, 24 May 2007; *Celniku v. Greece*, Application no. 21449/04, 5 July 2007; and *Galotskin v. Greece*, Application no. 2945/07, 14 January 2010.

Hungary:
Column 1: *Balogh v. Hungary*, Application no. 47940/99, 20 July 2004.
Column 5: *Kmetty v. Hungary*, Application no. 57967/00, 16 December 2003; and *Barta v. Hungary*, Application no. 26137/04, 10 April 2007.
Macedonia:
Column 2: *Dzeladinov and Others v. The Former Yugoslav Republic of Macedonia*, Application no. 13252/02, 10 April 2008; and *Demir Sulejmanov v. The Former Yugoslav Republic of Macedonia*, Application no. 69875/01, admissibility, 18 September 2006.
Column 3: *Jašar v. The Former Yugoslav Republic of Macedonia*, Application no. 69908/01, 15 February 2007.
Column 5: *Deari and Others v. The Former Yugoslav Republic of Macedonia*, Application no. 54415/09, lodged on 12 October 2009.
Romania:
Column 1: *Moldovan and Others v. Romania (No. 1)*, Applications nos. 41138/98 and 64320/01, friendly settlement, 5 July 2005; *Moldovan and Others v. Romania (No. 2)*, Applications nos. 41138/98 and 64320/01, 12 July 2005; *Gergely v. Romania*, Application no. 57885/00, unilateral declaration - striking out, 26 April 2007; *Kalanyos and Others v. Romania*, Application no. 57884/00, unilateral declaration - striking out, 26 April 2007; *Cobzaru v. Romania*, Application no. 48254/99, 26 July 2007; *Stoica v. Romania*, Application no. 42722/02, 4 March 2008; *Tănase and Others v. Romania*, Application no. 62954/00, unilateral declaration - striking out, 26 May 2009; *Carabulea v. Romania*, Application no. 45661/99, 13 July 2010; and *Soare and Others v. Romania*, Application no. 24329/02, 22 February 2011.
Column 2: *Notar v. Romania*, Application no. 42860/98, friendly settlement, 20 April 2004; *Costică Moldovan and Others v. Romania*, Application no. 8229/04 and other applications, admissibility, 15 February 2011; and *Ciubotaru and Others v. Romania*, Application no. 33242/05, 10 January 2012.
Column 4: *Ciorcan and Others v. Romania*, Application no. 29414/09, lodged on 18 May 2009 analysed together with *Biga v. Romania*, Application no. 44841/09, lodged on 11 August 2009; and *Chirita v. Romania*, Application no. 9443/10, lodged on 25 May 2010.
Column 5: *Barbu Anghelescu v. Romania No.* 1, Application no. 46430/99, 5 October 2004; *Bursuc v. Romania*, Application no. 42066/98, 12 October 2004; *Melinte v. Romania*, Application no. 43247/02, 9 November 2006; *Dumitru Popescu v. Romania No.1*, Application No. 49234/99, 26 April 2007; *Georgescu v. Romania*, Application no. 25230/03, 13 May 2008; *Iambor v. Romania No. 1*, Application no. 64536/01, 24 June 2008; *Lupaşcu v. Romania*, Application no. 14526/03, 4 November 2008; *Niţă v. Romania*, Application no. 10778/02, 4 November 2008; *Rupa v. Romania No.1*, Application no. 58478/00, 16 December 2008; *Olteanu v. Romania*, Application no. 71090/01, 14 April 2009; *Damian Burueana and Damian v. Romania*, Application no. 6773/02, 26 May 2009; *Chiriţă v. Romania*, Application no. 37147/02, 29 September 2009; *Bolovan v. Romania*, Application no. 64541/01, 24 November 2009; *Ghiga Chiujdea v. Romania*, Application no. 4390/03, 5 October 2010; and *Rupa v. Romania No.2*, Application no. 37971/02, 19 July 2011.
Russia:
Column 1: *Kleyn and Aleksandrovich v. Russia*, Application no. 40657/04, 3 May 2012.
Column 4: *Bagdonavichus and Others v. Russia*, Application filed on 2 November 2006, file no. 19841/06; request for priority pursuant to Rule 41 of the rules of the Court filed on 17 February 2011.
Slovakia:
Column 1: *Mižigárová v. Slovakia*, Application no. 74832/01, 14 December 2010; *V.C. v. Slovakia*, Application no. 18968/07, 8 November 2011; *Koky and Others v. Slovakia*,

Country	Violence against Roma cases decided and/or where connected discrimination claim was declared admissible	Violence against Roma cases where discrimination claim was rejected at the admissibility stage	Violence against Roma cases where no discrimination claim was raised	Pending violence against Roma cases awaiting admissibility	Non-Roma police violence cases
Bulgaria	12*	-	2	1	18
Croatia	2	-	1	-	1
Czech Republic	-	-	1		
Greece	4	-	-	-	5
Hungary	1	-	-	-	2
Macedonia	-	2	1	-	1
Romania	9**	3	-	2	15
Russia	1	-	-	1	***
Slovakia	5	1	1		-
Ukraine	1	-	-	1	4
Total	**35**	**6**	**6**	**5**	**46**

* Counts *Nachova* as two separate rulings.

** Includes two cases resulting from one same fact pattern where one was decided by friendly settlement and the other by judgment.

*** Due to the high number of police violence cases against Russia, including numerous applications by Chechens, no separate count of the police violence cases is made here or listed in the endnote.

Application no. 13624/03, 12 June 2012; *N.B. v. Slovakia*, Application no. 29518/10, 12 June 2012; and *I.G. and Others v. Slovakia*, Application no. 15966/04, 13 November 2012.
Column 2: *K.H. and Others v. Slovakia*, Application no. 32881/04, admissibility, 9 October 2007.
Column 4: *Puky v. Slovakia*, Application no. 45383/07, lodged on 17 October 2007.
Ukraine:
Column 1: *Fedorchenko and Lozenko v. Ukraine*, Application no. 387/03, 20 September 2012.
Column 4: *Nikolayenko v. Ukraine*, Application no. 39994/06, lodged on 31 August 2006.
Column 5: *Samardak v. Ukraine*, Application no. 43109/05, 4 November 2010; *Dushka v. Ukraine*, Application no. 29175/04, 3 February 2011; *Bocharov v. Ukraine*, Application no. 21037/05, 17 March 2011; and *Nechiporuk and Yonkalu v. Ukraine*, Application no. 42310/04, 21 April 2011.

Table 1 shows that the ECtHR has had to decide a significant number of similar cases involving allegations of the gravest human rights violations: racially motivated loss of life, torture and/or inhuman and degrading treatment at the hands of the police and/or with official knowledge, as well as forced sterilizations. Given the repeated insistence of the judges on the fundamental nature of the protection of such rights, one would expect a strong stance by the ECtHR in such cases. And indeed in most cases, the Court was willing to find that a violation of either Article 2 or of Article 3 has taken place.

However, when looking at the Court's performance with regard to Article 14 race discrimination claims, the performance is less stellar. Excluding the cases in Column 3 of Table 1, where the applicants themselves did not raise a race discrimination claim, in all other instances the ECtHR has chosen to recognize a racial motivation for the violence concerned in very few cases. That race discrimination has not stood high so far on the Court's schedule has been the subject of earlier critiques.[9] The case law on anti-Roma violence as summarized in Table 2 confirms the basis of such criticism. In fact, the table breaks down the cases which the ECtHR decided to view under their procedural violation aspect – meaning the authorities' investigation into the alleged crime was insufficient and therefore violated the ECHR – and under their substantive violation aspect – meaning the authorities were found responsible for an actual racially-motivated crime (meaning of course that the Court found that a racially-motivated crime had taken place). In a majority of cases, the Strasbourg judges found a violation of Article 2 or Article 3 (procedural, substantive or both) but Table 2 highlights the unwillingness of the Court to find that these violations were racially motivated (Article 14).

---

9   See Marie-Bénédicte Dembour, In the Name of the Rule of Law: The European Court of Human Rights' Silencing of Racism, in SILENCING HUMAN RIGHTS: CRITICAL ENGAGEMENTS WITH A CONTESTED PROJECT, 184, 184-202 (Gurminder K. Bhambra and Robbie Shilliam eds., 2009) and Marie-Bénédicte Dembour, Post-Colonial Denial: Why the European Court of Human Rights Finds It So Difficult to Acknowledge Racism, in MIRRORS OF JUSTICE. LAW AND POWER IN THE POST-COLD WAR ERA 45-66 (Kamari Maxine Clarke and Mark Goodale eds., 2010).

Table 2: Cases of Recognized Article 2, 3 and/or 14 ECHR Violations

Procedural Article 2 violation	Substantive Article 2 violation	Procedural Article 3 violation	Substantive Article 3 violation	Procedural Article 14 violation	Substantive Article 14 violation
15	10	17	15	10	1*

* Does not include *Nachova* Chamber judgment, because the Grand Chamber 'downgraded' the Article 14 violation to a procedural one; nor the *Moldovan No.2* judgment, as the distinction between substantive and procedural Article 14 violations did not yet exist.

A closer and more detailed look at the case law will show why this is the case. One smaller part of the reason is possibly fact driven and due to the general issues and difficulties that arise in connection with the nature of Article 14, which is tied to the other rights in the Convention.[10] However, the suggestion here is that the larger part of the problem is caused by the Court's overly cautious approach to Article 14 claims in general and especially when it is claimed in connection with violence against Roma.

A. *The early case law – establishing and contesting 'beyond reasonable doubt'*

Assenov and Others v. Bulgaria was the first case of police violence against Romani individuals before the ECtHR.[11] A 14-year old boy was arrested while gambling in a market square and allegedly hit by policemen with truncheons and pummelled in the stomach before being released without charge. Having exhausted all domestic remedies, Mr. Assenov's parents claimed, *inter alia*, violations of Article 3 before the ECtHR. No Article 14 violation was brought. Whereas the judges considered the bruises to be 'sufficiently serious to amount to ill-treatment within the scope of Article 3',[12] they found it was 'impossible to establish on the basis of the evidence before it whether or not the applicant's

---

10 This limitation has been addressed by Protocol 12. Note that the first judgment applying Article 14 under the new Protocol No. 12 regime involved a discrimination claim brought by a Roma and a Jewish individual against the constitutional arrangements for Bosnia and Herzegovina. Eur. Court H.R., *Sejdić and Finci v. Bosnia and Herzegovina* [GC], Judgement of 22 December 2009, Applications nos. 27996/06 and 34836/06.

11 *Assenov and Others v. Bulgaria* (note 2).

12 Id., para. 95.

injuries were caused by the police as he alleged.'[13] Nevertheless, while denying a *substantive* violation of Article 3, the Court found a *procedural* violation of the Convention due to the 'lack of a thorough and effective investigation into the applicant's claim that he had been beaten by police officers.'[14] *Assenov* thus extended the distinction between substantive and procedural violations, already used in Article 2 violation cases,[15] to Article 3 violations.

The next case, *Velikova v. Bulgaria*,[16] was brought by the surviving partner of a Romani man who had died after spending 12 hours in police custody following his arrest and detention on charges of cattle theft. She brought an Article 2 claim in conjunction with Article 14. The ECtHR found both procedural and substantive violations of Article 2. However, the Court refused to find a breach of Article 14 despite accepting that a police officer had called the victim a 'Gypsy'[17] and that another investigator had noted that the injuries on the victim's body were not visible due to the 'dark color of the skin'.[18] While remarking that the Article 14 complaint was grounded on serious arguments, the Court nevertheless rejected the claim on the basis that the 'material before it does not enable [it] to conclude beyond reasonable doubt that [the] death and the lack of a meaningful investigation into it were motivated by racial prejudice as claimed by the applicant'.[19]

The Court made a similar finding two years later in its *Anguelova* judgment.[20] In this case, the ECtHR declared Bulgaria had violated Article 2 and Article 3 but was unable to find an Article 14 violation. Referring to *Velikova*, the Court held that the complaint was based on serious arguments but they were unable to reach the conclusion that proof beyond reasonable doubt had been established.[21] Again, the Court's reasoning on Article 14 is brief. However, *Anguelova* saw a single dissent. In what has arguably become the key dissenting opinion in racially motivated police violence cases, Judge Bonello scathingly criticized the majority not only for its decision in the instant case but more in general for its lack of racial discrimination case

---

13   Id., para. 100.

14   Id., para. 106.

15   Eur. Court H.R., *McCann and Others v. United Kingdom*, Judgement of 27 September 1995, Application no. 18984/91.

16   *Velikova v. Bulgaria* (note 2).

17   Id., para. 15, 16 and 18.

18   Id., para. 26.

19   Id., para 94.

20   Eur. Court H.R., *Anguelova v. Bulgaria*, Judgement of 13 June 2002, Application no. 38361/97.

21   Id., para 167-168.

law. He noted that in over fifty years of existence the Court had never once found a violation of Article 2 and 3 in conjunction with Article 14 and argued that this record made Europe look like a 'haven of ethnic fraternity' where 'misfortunes punctually visit disadvantaged minority groups, but only as the result of well-disposed coincidence'.[22] He further criticized the Court's self-created bind of the standard of proof beyond reasonable doubt.[23] Finally, Judge Bonello appealed to the Court's trail blazing tradition and proposed some concrete solutions to change the jurisprudence, such as shifting the burden of proof to the respondent State and/or extending the doctrine of 'procedural violation' that was already operative for Articles 2 and 3 to Article 14.[24]

Judge Bonello's dissent struck a nerve with the majority. The standard of proof 'beyond reasonable doubt' established to assess evidence had been introduced in 1978, in a case brought by Ireland against the United Kingdom.[25] Nothing in the ECHR itself imposes such a standard. Even though cases concerning two state parties raise different and politically more delicate issues than those involving an individual applicant claiming a human rights violation against a respondent State, the ECtHR chose not to adapt the standard of proof accordingly and has automatically applied it in other cases. It is arguably this decision that has led to the rejection of the discrimination claims in the early Roma violence cases.

The effect of Judge Bonello's dissent is visible in the Court's subsequent judgment on the same topic: *Nachova v. Bulgaria*.[26] The case involved the fatal shooting of two Romani conscripts by military police officers that were trying to arrest them. In contrast to previous case law, the Chamber not only recognized Article 2 violations (both procedural and substantive) but also declared a violation of Article 14. What is particularly interesting about this first *Nachova* decision is that the Court followed Bonello's suggestion (who was also part of the panel in this case) by declaring not only a substantive violation of Article 14 but also, for the first time, a procedural breach. According to the Court, state authorities need to take all reasonable steps to unmask racist motives behind crimes in order to distinguish them from regular crimes. Failing to do so constitutes a violation of Article 14 of the

---

22   Id., Bonello Dissenting, para. 2 and 3.
23   Id., Bonello Dissenting, para. 9-11.
24   Id., Bonello Dissenting, para. 13-18.
25   Eur. Court H.R., *Ireland v. United Kingdom*, Judgment of 18 January 1978, series A, no. 25, 65, para. 161.
26   Eur. Court H.R., *Nachova and Others v. Bulgaria*, Judgement of 26 February 2004, Applications nos. 43577/98 and 43579/98.

Convention.[27] As a consequence, the Court found that opening fire in an area crowded with people of Romani origin combined with evidence of racist verbal abuse by the law enforcement agents without any subsequent examination of the facts was sufficient to establish a procedural Article 14 violation in conjunction with Article 2.

Moreover, in conjunction with the substantive violation of Article 14, the ECtHR directly addressed and elaborated on the 'beyond reasonable doubt' standard of proof issue. Whereas in *Anguelova* and *Velikova* it had been sufficient to mention this self-imposed standard and then dismiss the claim, in this case the Court articulated their reasoning. Indeed, the Court stated that 'that standard should not be interpreted as requiring such a high degree of probability as in criminal trials', that 'proof may follow from the co-existence of sufficiently strong, clear and concordant inferences or of similar unrebutted presumptions of fact' and that '[i]t has resisted suggestions to establish rigid evidentiary rules and has adhered to the principle of free assessment of all evidence'.[28] This re-orientation cleared the way for the Court to take into account the inferences of possible discrimination by the authorities, their failure to inquire into the racial motivations of the crime, the general context and the fact that this was not the first case against Bulgaria in which Roma were victims of racial violence at the hands of state agents to shift the burden of proof to Bulgaria. The fact that Bulgaria then did not provide any satisfactory explanation for the events induced the Court to declare a substantive violation of Article 14.[29]

In spite of the *Nachova* judgment's importance, its success was short-lived and limited. In its next decision, *Balogh v. Hungary*,[30] the ECtHR returned to its old approach. Even though the file contained references made by the police to 'Gypsies', the Court found that although ill-treatment by the police had taken place, it had not been racially motivated. The Court distinguished the case from the progressive *Nachova* judgment on the grounds that 'there is no substantiation of the applicant's allegation that he was discriminated against in the enjoyment of any of the Convention rights relied on'.[31] Even more importantly, the Grand Chamber overturned the *Nachova* Chamber

---

27 Id., para. 158.
28 Id., para. 166.
29 Id., para. 175.
30 Eur. Court H.R., *Balogh v. Hungary*, Judgement of 20 July 2004, Application no. 47940/99.
31 Id., para. 79.

judgment precisely on the race discrimination aspect.[32] Ironically, the distinction between procedural and substantive Article 14 violations, for which Judge Bonello had called in a progressive spirit, served as tool to reduce Bulgaria's liability. Indeed, the Grand Chamber separated its assessment into substantive and procedural Article 14 violations.

On the substantive aspect it held that:

> "the possibility that in certain cases of alleged discrimination it may require the respondent Government to disprove an arguable allegation of discrimination. [...] However, where it is alleged [...] that a violent act was motivated by racial prejudice, such an approach would amount to requiring the respondent Government to prove the absence of a particular subjective attitude on the part of the person concerned. While in the legal systems of many countries proof of the discriminatory effect of a policy or decision will dispense with the need to prove intent in respect of alleged discrimination in employment or the provision of services, that approach is difficult to transpose to a case where it is alleged that an act of violence was racially motivated".[33]

In other words, the Grand Chamber decided that it was unacceptable to require a State, with all its financial resources and access to all possible documents and information, to demonstrate proof of intent (or absence of it), and that this burden should rather be placed upon the victim of structural and racial violence instead. It was thus no surprise that the Grand Chamber found the facts referred to by the applicants as insufficient to shift the burden of proof onto the respondent State.[34] Six of the seventeen judges dissented with regard to the Grand Chamber's use of the distinction between substantive and procedural Article 14 violations, claiming that a more holistic approach to Article 14 was needed, that the distinction is artificial and unhelpful, and that Bulgaria had violated Article 14 *tout court*.[35]

---

32 Eur. Court H.R., *Nachova and Others v. Bulgaria* [GC], Judgement of 6 July 2005, Applications nos. 43577/98 and 43579/98.

33 Id., para. 157.

34 Id. para. 144-159.

35 Id., Judges Casadevall, Hedigan, Mularoni, Fura-Sandström, Gyulumyan and Spielmann partly dissenting. In a separate opinion, Judge Casadevall repeated the point in Eur. Court H.R., *Bekos and Koutropoulos v. Greece*, Judgement of 13 December 2005, Application no. 15250/02.

This early phase of Roma violence cases has demonstrated many shadows and some light in the Court's handling of Roma discrimination in violence cases. Certainly some progress has been made from beginnings in which discrimination claims were either not brought or simply discarded.[36]

B. The later cases – looking for racial elements

In the wake of the *Nachova* decisions, one sees an increase in the number of Romani violence cases. However, this increase has not been accompanied by an equally increasing number of substantive Article 14 violations or of admissibility decisions. With the exception of two cases involving Romania (see C. *infra*), the Court keeps finding it difficult to declare racial motivations in violence against Roma.

Only a few months after the *Nachova* Grand Chamber judgment, the Court heard a police violence case involving Romani victims in *Bekos and Koutropoulos v. Greece*.[37] It found a violation of Article 3 and a procedural violation of Article 14, the latter on the basis that the Greek authorities had failed to conduct an investigation into the alleged racist verbal abuse suffered by the applicants. On the question of a substantive violation of Article 14, the Court was more protective of the respondent Government. By using the same formula that had already appeared in the *Nachova* Grand Chamber judgment and by referring again to the standard of proof 'beyond reasonable doubt', the Court found it unacceptable to require of the respondent Government to prove the absence of a particular subjective attitude on the part of the perpetrator.[38] In two concurring opinions concerning precisely this aspect, Judge Bratza noted how such a burden of proof would rarely, if ever, be shifted to any Government simply because of the evidential difficulties with which they would be confronted.[39]

The *Bekos* judgment is only the first in a whole series of later judgments. An overview of the post-*Nachova* case law on the issue of violence against Roma shows a number of trends. Firstly, the consolidation of the initially challenged distinction between substantive and procedural violations;

---

36 For a more positive reading in evolutionary terms see: James A. Goldston, *The Struggle for Roma Rights: Arguments that Have Worked*, 32 HUMAN RIGHTS QUARTERLY 311 (2010).

37 *Bekos and Koutropoulos v. Greece* (note 35).

38 Id., para. 65.

39 *Nachova and Others v. Bulgaria* [GC] (Bratza concurring) (note 32); and *Bekos and Koutropoulos v. Greece* (Bratza concurring) (note 35).

almost all later cases analyze the two aspects separately. Secondly, a decrease in references to the standard of proof 'beyond reasonable doubt', which in the early cases had served as a (quick) way to reject discrimination claims. Thirdly, the ECtHR increasingly looks for racial slurs, racist insults or other racially tainted elements in the facts of the case in order to shift the burden of proof to the State, which then needs to show that such actions were either racially neutral or objectively justified in order to avoid a substantive or procedural Article 14 violation.

However, with the exception of procedural Article 14 violations, these trends have not really produced a radical change in outcome. Declarations of substantive Article 14 violations remain exceptional.[40] In some cases the claim for race discrimination was rejected because it had not been brought at the domestic level,[41] and/or because the ECtHR considered the claim time-barred.[42] Sometimes Article 14 claims are dismissed early on as inadmissible.[43] In most cases, the Court has a hard time in finding evidence of racial elements that justify to the Court a shift in the burden of proof to the respondent State. Moreover, what the ECtHR considers to be 'racist elements' or racial verbal abuse in the facts is also restrictive. For instance, a reference to 'gypsies' by police officers or investigating authorities is not indicative for the Court of racial bias.[44] Similarly, the fact of being mistreated by police officers who erroneously thought the applicants belonged to the Roma minority and addressed them as 'gypsies', when in reality they belonged to the Turkish minority, was held to be insufficient to demonstrate racial bias at any

---

40   Eur. Court H.R., *Stoica v. Romania*, Judgement of 4 March 2008, Application no. 42722/02.

41   See *e.g.* Eur. Court H.R., *Osman v. Bulgaria*, Judgement of 16 February 2006, Application no. 43233/98; Eur. Court H.R., *Ognyanova and Choban v. Bulgaria* (note 4); Eur. Court H.R., *Beganović v. Croatia*, Judgement of 25 June 2009, Application no. 46423/06; Eur. Court H.R., *Sashov and Others v. Bulgaria*, Judgement of 7 January 2010, Application no. 14383/03; Eur. Court H.R., *Stefanou v. Greece*, Judgement of 22 April 2010, Application no. 2954/07; Eur. Court H.R., *Carabulea v. Romania* (note 4); *Mižigárová v. Slovakia* (note 2); Eur. Court H.R., *Dimitrova and Others v. Bulgaria* (note 3); and Eur. Court H.R., *Soare and Others v. Romania*, Judgement of 22 February 2011, Application no. 24329/02.

42   *Stefanou v. Greece*, Id., para. 56-61.

43   See *e.g.* Eur. Court H.R., *Demir Sulejmanov v. The Former Yugoslav Republic of Macedonia*, Admissibility Decision of 18 September 2006, Application no. 69875/01; and Eur. Court H.R., *Dzeladinov and Others v. The Former Yugoslav Republic of Macedonia*, Admissibility Decision of 6 March 2007, Application no. 13252/02.

44   See *e.g.* Eur. Court H.R., *Vasil Sashov Petrov v. Bulgaria*, Judgement of 10 June 2010, Application no. 63106/00; *Dimitrova and Others v. Bulgaria* (note 3); and *Soare and Others v. Romania* (note 41).

level.[45] In contrast, the tendentious remarks made by a deputy police director with regard to the applicant's Romani ethnicity during an administrative investigation was held to be sufficient at least to trigger the obligation upon the authorities to investigate the potential racial motives in the applicant's ill-treatment.[46]

Where private violence and its successive investigation into the facts are concerned, the Court will similarly look for racist elements, such as the fact that the attackers are members of a skinhead group.[47] Absent such racial overtones, the Court will not infer an obligation to investigate or shift the burden of proof to the respondent state. Most importantly, the general racially hostile climate for Roma and the regular occurrence of discriminatory incidents of violence against Roma – whether emerging from its own case law or from the numerous reports of NGOs or international organizations – are not used by the Court as evidence. What the Court instead does is either refer to such reports 'casually' without drawing the pertinent conclusions from them[48] or, whilst noting the concerns raised by NGOs and intergovernmental bodies, assert that its sole concern is to ascertain whether *in the case at hand* the violence or death were the result of racism.[49] In other words, the Court opts for a de-contextualized reading of the cases before them.

Equally problematic in the Court's later case law have been the forced sterilization claims by Romani women against Slovakia and the Czech Republic. Forced sterilizations of Romani women (and other groups deemed social miscreants) are part of a terrifying European tradition, harking back to the Nazi regime[50] and resumed under Communism.[51] From this perspective

---

45   *Osman v. Bulgaria* (note 41).

46   Eur. Court H.R., *Petropoulou-Tsakiris v. Greece*, Judgement of 6 December 2007, Application no. 44803/04.

47   See *e.g. Šečić v. Croatia* (note 3); and Eur. Court H.R., *Angelova and Iliev v. Bulgaria*, Judgement of 26 July 2007, Application no. 55523/00.

48   See *e.g. Mižigárová v. Slovakia* (note 2), para. 122; and Eur. Court H.R., *V.C. v. Slovakia*, Judgement of 8 November 2011, Application no. 18968/07, para. 177-178.

49   See *e.g. Ognyanova and Choban v. Bulgaria* (note 4), para. 147.

50   See *e.g.* Barry A. Fisher, *No Roads Lead to Rom: The Fate of the Romani People under the Nazis and in Post-War Restitution*, 20 WHITTIER LAW REVIEW 513, 525 (1999).

51   See Vera Sokolová, *Planned Parenthood Behind the Curtain: Population Policy and Sterilization of Romani Women in Communist Czechoslovakia, 1972-1989*, 23 THE ANTHROPOLOGY OF EAST EUROPE REVIEW 79 (2005). However, such violence is not limited to countries that had been under Nazi rule or Communism. For instance, Sweden has performed such sterilizations until the 1970s. See Angus Bancroft, ROMA AND GYPSY-TRAVELLERS IN EUROPE. MODERNITY, RACE, SPACE AND EXCLUSION 75 (2005).

one would expect a particularly firm reaction from the ECtHR. However, the first case to make it onto the Court's docket was narrowly and limitedly framed as one involving Article 6 (right to a fair trial) and Article 8 (right to respect of private and family life), mainly because access to their own medical records had been refused to Romani women who suspected that they had been sterilized after giving birth.[52] In this first case, the race discrimination claim was eliminated already at the admissibility stage;[53] moreover, what was completely absent from this case was any recognition of the violence that forced sterilization constitutes.

The first forced sterilization against Romani women case to be heard in the context of racial discrimination was decided recently.[54] Yet, from a race discrimination perspective, the jurisprudence remains weak and timid. *V.C. v. Slovakia* reproduces a similar pattern to that observed in the other Roma violence cases: whereas the Court recognized the violations of the substantive underlying claims – in this case Article 3 and Article 8 – it failed to declare an Article 14 violation in either its gendered or its racial aspect. The Court instead preferred to interpret the material showing how Romani women were particularly likely to be the victim of Slovakia's policies in connection with its Article 8 analysis.[55] As a consequence, it ruled that 'a separate examination of the complaint under Article 14 of the Convention is not called for'.[56] It then confirmed this approach in two even more recent forced sterilization decisions involving Slovakia.[57] However, in justifying the reasoning, a new argument emerged: intent. While finding that 'the sterilisation without [the applicant's] informed consent calls for serious criticism, the objective evidence is not sufficiently strong in itself to convince the Court that it was part of an organized policy or that the hospital staff's conduct was *intentionally* racially motivated'.[58] Thus far in its jurisprudence, the Court had not explicitly addressed the issue of intent in violence against Roma cases but had only addressed 'subjective attitude' and the difficulty of proving its

---

52 *K.H. and Others v. Slovakia* (note 5).

53 Id, Admissibility Decision of 9 October 2007, Application no. 32881/04. The main reason was that the refusal applied equally to everyone due to a generally applicable provision in the Health Care Act and its restrictive interpretation. The applicants had failed to show that they were treated differently from others in the instant case.

54 *V.C. v. Slovakia* (note 48).

55 *V.C. v. Slovakia* (note 48), para. 146-150.

56 Id., holdings by the Court, point 6.

57 *N.B. v. Slovakia* and *I.G. and Others v. Slovakia* (note 5).

58 Id., para. 177 (emphasis added).

absence.[59] As the United States' experience has already demonstrated, the intent requirement – and its demonstration in court – can represent a sort of death knell for such claims, especially those of indirect discrimination.[60] If the Court chooses to travel further down this road, it will contribute to the already strong impression that Article 14 will remain a Cinderella provision,[61] of only secondary importance and relevance.

The Court's reasoning in relation to racial discrimination has not gone uncontested from within its own ranks. In addition to Judge Bonello's dissent in *Anguelova* and the dissents in the *Nachova* Grand Chamber judgment, in a number of other cases in which the majority found no violation or dismissed the claim without consideration, various dissenting judges claimed that at least a procedural violation could or should have been found.[62] Most dissents argue that the fact of the applicants being Romani, combined with widespread reports on police violence against Roma, is sufficient to trigger the obligation to conduct an investigation into the motivation.

The persistent dissents further highlight how weak, narrow and problematic the post-*Nachova* jurisprudence with regard to claims of racial discrimination in conjunction with Article 2 and Article 3 is. This supposition is confirmed by similar cases involving Kurdish people in Turkey,[63] Chechens in Russia[64] and

---

59 See *e.g. Nachova and Others v. Bulgaria* [GC] (note 31), para. 157. But note that intent emerged explicitly in yet another recent ECtHR judgment involving the publication of books containing racially discriminatory language against Roma: Eur. Court H.R., *Aksu v. Turkey* [GC], Judgement of 15 March 2012, Applications nos. 4149/04 and 41029/04.

60 See in particular *Washington v. Davis*, 426 U.S. 229 (1976).

61 See O'Connell, who uses the expression in the opposite sense, claiming that Article 14 is finally being used more frequently and successfully: Rory O'Connell, *Cinderella comes to the Ball: Art. 14 and the right to non-discrimination in the ECHR*, 29 LEGAL STUDIES 211 (2009).

62 *Bekos and Koutropoulos v. Greece* (Casadevall separate opinion) (note 34); *Osman v. Bulgaria* (Vajić and Spielmann dissenting) (note 41); *Carabulea v. Romania* (Gyulumyan, Power and Ziemele partly dissenting) (note 4); *Mižigárová v. Slovakia* (Björgvinsson partly dissenting) (note 2); *Soare and Others v. Romania* (Ziemele, Power and Zupančič partly dissenting) (note 41); and *V.C. v. Slovakia* (Mijovic dissenting) (note 48).

63 See *e.g.* Eur. Court H.R., *Togcu v. Turkey*, Judgement of 31 May 2005, Application no. 27601/95.

64 See *e.g.* Eur. Court H.R., *Musikhanova and Others v. Russia*, Admissibility Decision of 10 July 2007, Application no. 27243/03; Eur. Court H.R., *Azru Akhmadova and Others v. Russia*, Admissibility Decision of 10 January 2008, Application no. 13670/03; Eur. Court H.R., *Luluyev and Others v. Russia*, Judgement of 9 November 2006, Application no. 69480/01, para. 142-145; Eur. Court H.R., *Akhiyadova v.*

other racial(ized) minorities that have been the victims of police violence in different European countries.[65] The Court's jurisprudence on racist violence contrasts starkly with its lofty statements about racial discrimination or racial violence being a particular affront to human dignity which, in view of its perilous consequences, requires special vigilance and a vigorous reaction from the authorities.

C. Case law involving Romania

The ECtHR's track record on racist violence against Roma becomes even more questionable when looking at the cases involving Romania as the defendant state.[66] Besides the judgments in which either no Article 14 violation[67] or only a procedural violation was found,[68] the Romanian cases stand out for two reasons: firstly because on two occasions the Court has held that Romania has violated Article 14 both substantively and procedurally.[69] Secondly, because in spite of such findings, the ECtHR has accepted unilateral (settlement) declarations by the Romanian government against the applicants' will in a surprisingly high number of cases, thus casting an even more shady light on the Court's performance in the area.[70]

Russia, Judgement of 3 July 2008, Application no. 32059/02, para. 100-102; and Eur. Court H.R., *Akhmadov and Others v. Russia*, Judgement of 14 November 2008, Application no. 21586/02, para. 142-145. But see a recent case in which the Court found a substantive Article 14 violation in conjunction with Article 3: Eur. Court H.R., *Makhashevy v. Russia*, Judgment of 31 July 2012, Application no. 20546/07. For an overview of the Chechen cases, see Phillip Leach, *The Chechen Conflict. Analyzing the Oversight of the European Court of Human Rights*, (2008) 6 EUROPEAN HUMAN RIGHTS LAW REVIEW 732.

65 Eur. Court H.R., *Menson and Others v. United Kingdom*, Admissibility Decision on 6 May 2003, Application no. 47916/99; Eur. Court H.R., *Zelilof v. Greece*, Judgement of 24 May 2007, Application no. 17060/03; Eur. Court H.R., *Celniku v. Greece*, Judgement of 5 July 2007, Application no. 21449/04; Eur. Court H.R., *Turan Cakir v. Belgium*, Judgement of 10 March 2009, Application no. 44256/06; and *B.S. v. Spain*, Judgement of 24 July 2012, Application no. 47159/08.

66 See the list of cases in note 8, referring to Romania, Column 1.

67 *Carabulea v. Romania* (note 4); and *Soare and Others v. Romania* (note 40). See also Eur. Court H.R., *Ciubotaru and Others v. Romania*, Judgement of 10 January 2012, Application no. 33242/05, where the judges however rejected all the claims on procedural grounds, *inter alia*, for the applicants' failure to exhaust domestic remedies.

68 *Cobzaru v. Romania* (note 4).

69 *Moldovan and Others v. Romania (No.2)* (note 3); and *Stoica v. Romania* (note 40).

70 The practice of accepting unilateral declarations in racially motivated police violence cases seems not to be limited only to Romania. See Eur. Court H.R., *Šarišská v.*

With regard to the first category of cases, the most relevant case is *Stoica*. Here, for the first time, the ECtHR found both a procedural and a substantive violation of Article 14. Typically for post-*Nachova* judgments, what ultimately determined the outcome was that the police officers involved had openly made racial slurs prior to inflicting a beating on the victim and because the police report described the Romani villagers' allegedly aggressive behavior as 'pure Gypsy'. These events shifted the burden of proof to the Government and, since Romania did not justify the incidents in any racially neutral way, the Court found a substantive Article 14 violation.[71]

The other judgment in this category predates the subdivision into procedural and substantive Article 14 violations. The case of *Moldovan and Others* involved some of the most gruesome fact patterns in terms of physical and structural violence and discrimination against Roma, involving a combination of arson against Romani houses and property, lynching by angry mobs with active police participation and the eventual impunity of the perpetrators. Romania entered into a friendly settlement agreement, admitting that the events posed problems under various Articles of the Convention, including Article 3 and Article 14.[72] However, not all the plaintiffs accepted the friendly settlement and, as a consequence, the Court found that Romania had breached Articles 3, 6 and 8 as well as Article 14 (but only taken in conjunction with Articles 6 and 8).[73]

The *Moldovan* friendly settlement agreement also brings the case under the second category of Romanian cases, described above. In two later cases the Court decided to accept Romania's unilateral declarations in spite of the seriousness of the events (destruction and burning of Romani settlements) and the claimed Article 3, 6, 8, 13 and 14 violations. In both cases the applicants requested a dismissal of Romania's proposal for friendly settlement. However, the ECtHR rejected the requests. While noting that the violations complained of are 'of a very serious and sensitive nature', the Court

---

Slovakia, Unilateral Striking Out Declaration of 30 August 2011, Application no. 36768/09, 30 August 2011; and Eur. Court H.R., *Alder v. United Kingdom*, Unilateral Striking Out Declaration of 22 November 2011, Application no. 42078/02.

71   *Stoica v. Romania* (note 40).

72   *Moldovan and Others v. Romania (No.1)* (note 3).

73   *Moldovan and Others v. Romania (No.2)* (note 3). The fact pattern gave rise to other cases brought by the relatives and descendants of the original applicants: Eur. Court H.R., *Costică Moldovan and Others v. Romania*, Admissibility Decision of 15 February 2011, Application no. 8229/04 and other applications; and Eur. Court H.R., *Lăcătuş and Others v. Romania*, Judgement of 13 November 2012, Application no. 12694/04.

held that they had been exhaustively addressed in the *Moldovan* case and that therefore another judgment on the merits was not useful.[74] The Court later accepted a third unilateral declaration by the Romanian government based on a similar fact pattern involving multiple attacks and burnings of a Romani village at the hands of non-Romani inhabitants, including the priest and the mayor.[75]

While unilateral declarations are allowed pursuant to Article 37 § 1 (c) of the ECHR and the Court has established some guidelines and safeguards for their use, they remain problematic.[76] In fact, they usually occur after failed friendly settlement negotiations between the applicant and the defending government. The suspicion is that the Court increasingly uses unilateral declarations as a means to reduce its case load. Some judges have already cautioned against this practice.[77] Further, there is a strong case for suggesting that unilateral declarations should not be allowed where the most fundamental human rights, such as Article 2 and 3, are at issue.[78] The Court's acceptance of these declarations is even more disturbing given that Romania is the only state party that the Court found – twice – to be in full violation of Article 2 and 3 in conjunction with Article 14. Moreover, the Court's decision to continue with this policy of allowing unilateral declarations in cases of racially motivated violence is also problematic because the Romanian government's implementation of the promises made in the *Moldovan* case has been at best half-hearted.[79] This has prompted the European Roma Rights Centre (ERRC) to submit two separate memoranda to the Committee of Ministers, which is charged with the supervision of the

---

74 Eur. Court H.R., *Kalanyos v. Romania*, Unilateral Striking Out Declaration of 26 April 2007, Application no. 57884/00, para. 27-29 and Eur. Court H.R., *Gergely v. Romania*, Unilateral Striking Out Declaration of 26 April 2007, Application no. 57885/00, para. 24-26.

75 Eur. Court H.R., *Tănase and Others v. Romania*, Unilateral Striking Out Declaration of 26 May 2009, Application no. 62954/00.

76 Eur. Court H.R., *Tahsin Acar v. Turkey* [GC], Preliminary Issue, 6 May 2003, Application no. 26307/95, para. 76-77.

77 See *Toğcu v. Turkey* (Loucaides dissenting and Costa concurring), Unilateral Striking Out Declaration of 9 April 2002, Application no. 27601/95.

78 See in this sense for friendly settlements: Helen Keller, Magdalena Forowicz and Lorenz Engi, FRIENDLY SETTLEMENTS BEFORE THE EUROPEAN COURT OF HUMAN RIGHTS 106-107 (2010). Their reasoning applies all the more to unilateral declarations.

79 See Committee of Ministers, MEMORANDUM, CM/Inf/DH(2011) 37, 16 August 2011, in particular para. 95-106.

implementation of judgments and settlements.[80] In essence both memoranda criticize the Romanian government for lack of or reluctant implementation of the proposed action plans resulting from the judicial settlements and the second one asks for examination under the enhanced supervision procedure.

III. Conclusion

This chapter has provided an overview and a critique of the ECtHR's case law concerning racially-motivated violence against Roma. Whereas in most cases the Court recognized the violation of the right to life or of inhuman and degrading treatment, in only a few cases has it acknowledged the racial motivation of such violence. Part of the problem has been the Court's insistence that applicants must show 'beyond reasonable doubt' that the violence against them (or their relatives) was induced by racial hatred. Why the Court should require such a burden of proof standard of applicants claiming redress for the most serious human rights violations is not clear. In its later case law, the ECtHR's reference to that standard has waned considerably and been substituted by a search for 'racial elements' in the facts of the case. However, this has not necessarily led to a major improvement in its jurisprudence. On the contrary, the cases in which the Court makes a finding of racial discrimination remain rare. Viewed from this angle and in the context of the Court's practice of accepting unilateral declarations in cases involving Romania, the Court's jurisprudence itself is not beyond reasonable doubt when assessing the (in)effectiveness of its fight against race discrimination in contrast to its own lofty statements about the perniciousness of race discrimination. What is worse, through its own case law, the ECtHR contributes to a general toleration of racist behaviour of the worst kind and helps to constructs a legal and social image of a Europe that is free of race discrimination. Instead violence against racial or ethnic minorities in Europe is viewed as an unhappy coincidence or as the isolated act of a lunatic, right-wing individual. The Court's jurisprudence in this area constitutes a failure

---

80   See European Roma Rights Centre, 'Memorandum Concerning the Implementation and State of General Measures in the Judgments of *Moldovan and Others v Romania* (No 1, friendly settlement), *Moldovan and Others v Romania* (No. 2), *Kalanyos and Others v Romania* (friendly settlement), *Gergely v Romania* (friendly settlement) (Applications Nos 41138/98, 64320/01, 57884/00, 57885/00) and Requesting the "enhanced supervision" procedure', 19 July 2011, available at http://www.errc.org/cms/upload/file/second-communication-to-the-committee-of-ministers-on-judgment-implementation-moldovan-kalanyos-gergely.pdf.

to address the broader societal and structural issue that racially-motivated violence against Roma represents.

A practical consequence of that jurisprudence is that at the implementation level of its judgments by the Committee of Ministers, no reference is made to racial discrimination, even when the cases mostly touch upon discriminatory violence. For instance, resolutions and memoranda by the Committee of Ministers discussing the implementation of a number of judgments involving police violence in Bulgaria, of which many concern Romani victims, make no references whatsoever to specific measures in terms of vocational police training or effective investigations concerning racially motivated violence.[81] In other words, without a specific acknowledgement of the racist background by the Court, little or nothing will happen at the implementation level either. Not the best pre-conditions to stop racially-motivated violence against Roma.

---

81 Committee of Ministers, Interim Resolution CM/ResDH(2007) 107, 17 October 2007 and Committee of Ministers, Memorandum CM/Inf/DH(2011) 23, 10 May 2011.

Chapter 3

Proving the Invisible:
Addressing Evidentiary Issues in Cases of
Presumed Discriminatory Abuse against Roma
before the European Court of Human Rights
through *V.C. v. Slovakia*

Jasmina Mačkić*

I. Introduction

23 August 2000, Prešov, East-Slovakia. A 20-year old woman of Roma origin (known as V.C.) was sterilised at the Hospital and Health Care Centre in Prešov during the delivery of her second child. Her delivery record reveals the typed words "Patient requests sterilisation" and below this V.C.'s shaky signature. Her handwriting appears to be unsteady and the maiden name which she used at the time is split into two words. According to V.C., the sterilisation, a term she was not even familiar with, was forced upon her since her consent was sought at a moment at which she was heavily influenced by labour and pain. In addition, she was told by medical staff that sterilisation was necessary as a subsequent pregnancy would lead either to her own death or that of the baby – information that she was unable to verify at that time. V.C. claims that as a consequence of the sterilisation procedure she has suffered serious medical and psychological effects. It has also strongly affected her ability to participate in her family and community life, effects that include her ostracism from the Romani community of which she was a member and divorce from her then-husband, the father of her children.

Before the European Court of Human Rights ('ECtHR' or 'Court'), V.C. claimed that the sterilisation procedure was forced upon her because

* Jasmina Mačkić is a Ph.D. Candidate at the Europa Institute of the Law Faculty in Leiden. Her research focuses on the question how to prove discriminatory violence before the European Court of Human Rights. The research project was financially supported by the 'Netherlands Organisation for Scientific Research' (NWO, Mozaïek-grant) and she would like to express her gratitude for this grant.

of her Romani background and because she is a woman.[1] She relied on the prohibition of discrimination, as laid down in Art. 14 of the European Convention on Human Rights ('ECHR' or 'Convention') taken in conjunction with Art. 3 (the prohibition on torture), Art. 8 (the right to respect for private and family life) and Art. 12 (the right to marry). To substantiate her claim, she submitted a number of documents that both attested to a practice of forced sterilisation of Romani women in Slovakia, as well suggesting a widespread, general intolerance towards Roma. Moreover, V.C. claimed that her case forms part of these patterns through the fact the words "Patient is of Roma origin" appear in her medical file. The Strasbourg Court, although it found that the substantive element of Art. 3 and Art. 8 had been breached, rejected her complaint that the violation of her rights was motivated by her ethnicity, concluding that "the objective evidence is not sufficiently strong in itself to convince the Court that it [V.C.'s sterilisation] was part of an organised policy or that the hospital staff's conduct was intentionally racially motivated".[2] In coming to this conclusion, the Court applied a different set of evidentiary rules than in its earlier cases concerning the placement of Romani children in separate classes or separate buildings during their schooling period (the so-called 'segregation cases').

What the case of V.C. does so nicely is highlight some of the barriers that the Court has constructed in its jurisprudence to applicants who alleged racial motivation in cases of physical abuse. In V.C., the ECtHR applied the rules of evidence that it has developed in cases of presumed discriminatory violence against Roma. Therefore, in order to obtain more understanding on the Court's reasoning under the discrimination complaint in V.C., the ECtHR's case-law on that issue will be explored here. As it will become apparent, stricter rules of evidence, as inspired by Anglo-Saxon criminal law, have been adopted in such cases, requiring the applicants to present concrete proof to substantiate their claims. This in contrast with the segregation cases that have come before the Court, which have generally been viewed as cases of indirect discrimination, and in which the Court has accepted that a

---

1   In this contribution, the focus will be on the discrimination claim as far as it concerns the applicant's consideration that her *ethnic* origin had played a decisive role in the decision by the medical personnel of Prešov Hospital to sterilise her.

2   Eur. Court H.R., *V.C. v. Slovakia*, Judgment of 8 November 2011, Application no. 18968/07, para. 177. In the judgment Eur. Court H.R., *N.B. v. Slovakia*, Judgment of 12 June 2012, Application no. 29518/10, the Court reached similar conclusions. In addition, it should be noted that both in *V.C.* and in *N.B.* the Court examined the discrimination complaint solely in conjunction with Art. 8 ECHR.

discriminatory effect can be established through evidence pointing at a more general situation of discriminatory treatment.

This chapter will argue that the difficulty in proving discriminatory treatment in *V.C.* is linked to two elements. The first concerns the fact that *V.C.*, in terms of rules of evidence, is placed in the same category as racially motivated violence. Secondly, it will be argued that the difficulty in proving that the sterilisation was induced by discriminatory motives may be linked to the type of evidentiary material submitted by the applicant. When discussing the two points, a distinction will be drawn between two categories of cases that are characterised by different rules of evidence: violence cases on the one hand, and segregation cases on the other. Before elaborating on these matters, it may be useful as a first step to recall the Court's relationship with non-discrimination issues and to set out how the Court has dealt with the discrimination claim in *V.C.*

II. Non-discrimination Issues before the ECtHR and More Specifically in the *V.C.* Case

For quite some time, there have been doubts about the significance of the principle of equal treatment to the case-law of the ECtHR. In its early years, the Court rarely applied Art. 14 of the Convention and, where it did, it rarely found it to have been violated.[3] The reluctance to apply the Convention guarantee prohibiting discrimination appears to be connected to the accessory character of the provision, which means that a sufficient connection must be established between the alleged discrimination and one of the rights or freedoms enshrined within the substantive provisions of the ECHR. Gerards has identified certain problematic consequences to the accessory character. Firstly, she claims that in certain cases a rather technical construction may be required to bring alleged discrimination under the scope of both Art. 14 and a substantive provision.[4] Secondly, the accessory character arguably prevented

---

3   Janneke Gerards, *The Application of Article 14 ECHR by the European Court of Human Rights*, in THE DEVELOPMENT OF LEGAL INSTRUMENTS TO COMBAT RACISM IN A DIVERSE EUROPE, 3 (Isabelle Chopin/Jan Niessen eds., 2004).

4   Gerards shows this with a reference to the *Thlimmenos* case, concerning an individual who could not practice the profession of a chartered accountant because of a former conviction for insubordination. The applicant claimed that he was treated differently on the ground of his status as a convicted person, a distinction that could hardly be brought under the scope of one of the substantive provisions of the ECHR. The Court nevertheless found a way to examine the complaint under Art. 14. It ruled

the Court from examining a wide variety of discrimination claims, especially those concerning social or economic rights. Finally, Gerards has suggested that the Court has in many cases not provided for a substantive assessment of the discrimination complaint.[5]

A more specific issue concerns the Court's initial reluctance to recognise the concept of indirect discrimination.[6] In brief, indirect discrimination law says "that discrimination on any of the 'discrimination grounds' may be present in a rule or practice which does not even mention the ground in question, but which has a detrimental effect on persons meant to be protected against discrimination".[7] An important side-note to this is that a detrimental effect in itself does not constitute indirect discrimination. Such an effect may be justified and the rule may be applied provided that "the rule or practice serves a legitimate aim unconnected with prohibited discrimination and does not go over and above what is necessary to achieve that aim".[8] Thus, indirect discrimination focuses on the *effects* of a particular treatment and stands in contrast with direct discrimination which implies a certain underlying *motive* or *cause* for some difference in treatment.[9]

The reluctance from the Court to accept indirect discrimination was visible in *Abdulaziz, Cabales & Balkandali*, a case concerning British immigration rules. Although the rules in question were applicable to all immigrants, they particularly affected individuals from the New Commonwealth or Pakistan. The Court ruled that the detrimental effect was insufficient to establish discrimination on the ground of race.[10] Recognition of the concept of indirect discrimination gradually started to evolve in the Court's case-law from the beginning of the 21st century. In *McShane*, the applicants claimed that a large

---

that the applicant had been convicted because he refused to wear a military uniform for religious reasons. With this in mind, the Court decided that the case resembled a substantive distinction based on religion. *Id.*, 7-8. See also Eur. Court H.R., *Thlimmenos v. Greece*, Judgment of 6 April 2000, Application no. 34369/97, paras. 41-42.

5   Gerards (note 3), 7-9.

6   *Id.*, 12.

7   Dagmar Schiek, *Indirect Discrimination*, in CASES, MATERIALS AND TEXT ON NATIONAL, SUPRANATIONAL AND INTERNATIONAL NON-DISCRIMINATION LAW, 323 (Dagmar Schiek/Lisa Waddington/Mark Bell eds., 2007).

8   *Id*, 323.

9   MARJOLIEN BUSSTRA, THE IMPLICATIONS OF THE RACIAL EQUALITY DIRECTIVE FOR MINORITY PROTECTION WITHIN THE EUROPEAN UNION 137 (2011).

10 Eur. Court H.R., *Abdulaziz, Cabales & Balkandali v. the United Kingdom*, Judgment of 28 May 1985, Application no. 9214/80; 9473/81; 9474/81, paras. 85-86.

number of killings of Catholics and members of republican paramilitary groups by the security forces and police in Northern-Ireland, in comparison to a disproportionately low number of prosecutions and convictions, indicated a discriminatory fashion. The Court ruled that a general policy or measure that reveals disproportionately prejudicial effects on a particular group may be considered discriminatory notwithstanding that it is not specifically aimed or directed at that group. However, at the same time, the Court found the disproportionate effects evidenced by statistics presented were insufficient to disclose any discriminatory treatment.[11]

The turnaround in the Court's attitude towards statistics in the context of proof came in a Dutch admissibility decision, *Hoogendijk*. The applicant claimed that she was discriminated against since the implementation of the income requirement under the scheme formulated in the Dutch General Labour Disablement Benefits Act affected more women than men. The Court stated that when an applicant is able to reveal on the basis of undisputed official statistics a *prima facie* indication of a disproportionate effect of a specific rule on a particular group, the burden of proof will shift to the Government, that must show that the effect is created by objective factors unrelated to any discrimination on grounds of sex.[12]

The most elaborate account of indirect discrimination was provided by the Grand Chamber in the case of *D.H. and Others v. the Czech Republic*, a prominent case on segregation in the educational sphere. Therein, the Court more or less stated that when a provision is brought into existence calling for the placement of children with 'learning disabilities' into separate schools, this may amount into indirect discrimination if the measure affects one specific group. Such a provision, accordingly, which appeared neutral at first sight, affected mainly Romani children.[13] A similar conclusion was reached in *Oršuš*, in which applicants had to attend Roma-only classes on grounds of inadequate language skills.[14] In the case of *Sampanis*, concerning the placement of Romani children in an annexe to the main Aspropyrgos primary school building in Greece, the Court has not explicitly identified

---

11   Eur. Court H.R., *McShane v. the United Kingdom*, Judgment of 28 May 2002, Application no. 43290/98, paras. 135-136.

12   Eur. Court H.R., *Hoogendijk v. the Netherlands*, Decision of 6 January 2005, Application no. 58641/00, p. 21-22.

13   Eur. Court H.R., *D.H. a.o. v. the Czech Republic* Judgment of the Grand Chamber of 13 November 2007, Application no. 57325/00, para. 193.

14   Eur. Court H.R., *Oršuš a.o. v. Croatia*, Judgment of the Grand Chamber of 16 March 2010, Application no. 15766/03, paras. 153-155.

the segregation of Romani children as indirect discrimination. However, it should be noted that the Court has expressed in paragraphs 78 and 79 of the judgement that less strict evidential rules should apply in cases of alleged indirect discrimination. Thus, the latter two paragraphs imply that indirect discrimination was at stake in *Sampanis*.[15]

The Court has thus come a long way in its development of the concept of indirect discrimination in approximately the last ten years, at last bringing its jurisprudence into line with other European norms, notably EU non-discrimination law.[16] However, the Court's reluctance to apply Art. 14 or to find a violation of the impugned provision is still in evidence in the context of cases in which Romani citizens have claimed that their ill-treatment or the killing of a Romani relative was motivated by racial discrimination.[17] These complaints appear to concern direct discrimination, a classification that seems to be suitable when it is alleged that the Roma background was the apparent reason for which the violence was inflicted.

More specifically in *V.C.*, the Court approaches the discrimination claim put forward with a certain restraint. The applicant attempted to argue that her ethnic origin had played a decisive role in her sterilisation. For that matter she relied on general information mainly established by international organisations. The only concrete information that she presented was the statement in her medical record that she was of Romani ethnic origin.

---

15   It is to be noted that there is some discussion about the classification of discrimination in the following two cases: Eur. Court H.R., *Sampanis a.o. v. Greece*, Judgment of 5 June 2008, Application no. 32526/05 and *Oršuš a.o. v. Croatia*. See Sina van den Bogaert, *Roma Segregation in Education: Direct or Indirect Discrimination? An Analysis of the Parallels and Differences between Council Directive 2000/43/ EC and Recent ECtHR Case Law on Roma Educational Matters*, 71 Zeitschrift für ausländisches öffentliches Recht und Völkerrecht (ZaöRV) 719, 738-740 and 749-750 (2011). See also Marija Davidović & Peter Rodrigues, *Roma maken school in Straasburg*, 34 NJCM-BULLETIN 155, 159 and 167 (2009).

16   See the EU Race Discrimination Directive, 2000/43/EC of 29 June 2000 OJ L180/ 22.

17   See for instance Eur. Court H.R., *Carabulea v. Romania*, Judgment of 13 July 2010, Application no. 45661/99, a case in which the Court concluded that it was unnecessary to go into the discrimination complaint. The Court's reluctance to accept the discrimination claim appears from Eur. Court H.R., *Velikova v. Bulgaria*, Judgment of 18 May 2000, Application no. 41488/98 and Eur. Court H.R., *Anguelova v. Bulgaria*, Judgment of 13 June 2002, Application no. 38361/97. As will be discussed below, the Court has found in certain cases concerning presumed discriminatory violence a procedural violation of Art. 14 ECHR taken together with Art. 2 or 3. Yet, in only one case was the Court convinced that discrimination under the substantive limb of Art. 14 ECHR taken in conjunction with Art. 3 had occurred: Eur. Court H.R., *Stoica v. Romania*, Judgment of 4 March 2008, Application no. 42722/02.

Judge Mijović (Bosnia and Herzegovina) was the only member of the Court persuaded that discriminatory treatment was at stake. In her dissenting opinion, she highlighted reports from the European Commission against Racism and Intolerance (ECRI), amongst others, that expressed concern about the current practices on the sterilisation of Romani women in Slovakia. Other persuasive elements according to the judge concerned the fact that there are currently similar cases pending before the Court and that there were no medically relevant reasons for sterilising the applicant. What is particularly relevant in her dissenting opinion for the arguments advanced here, Judge Mijović explicitly draws a parallel between *V.C.* and the earlier segregation cases:

> "Against the background of the principles of the Court's case-law as confirmed in *D.H. and Others v. the Czech Republic* ([GC], no. 57325/00, §§ 175-181, ECHR 2007) and *Oršuš and Others v. Croatia* (no. 15766/03, §§ 147-153, 17 July 2008), I am compelled to disagree totally with the Chamber's finding and regret that the discrimination to which the applicant was clearly subjected is given scant attention in the judgment".[18]

The majority of the Chamber, however, chose a different path. In what is quite a remarkable decision, the Court approached the discrimination issue in *V.C.* in the same way as it approaches discriminatory violence. This is clear from its reference in *V.C.* to an earlier case against Slovakia involving violence against Roma: *Mižigárová v. Slovakia*. This case concerned a Romani individual who was brought into custody on suspicion of having stolen bicycles, yet was shot in the abdomen during interrogation. Claims in *Mižigárová* were brought before the Court by the victim's wife, since the victim himself had died four days after the shooting. According to the applicant, with a view on the fact that her husband was a Romani man and taken into account the legacy of widespread and systematic abuse of Roma in police custody, the Slovak Government was obliged to investigate a possible racist motive to his death. The Court rejected her complaint by ruling that the behaviour of the authorities and the general information about police abuse of Roma in Slovakia were insufficient to establish a racist motive. In addition, the Court decided that there was no sufficient evidence to place an obligation on the authorities to investigate a possible racist motive on the part of the officers.[19]

---

18   *V.C. v. Slovakia* (note 2), *Dissenting Opinion of Judge Mijović*.

19   Eur. Court H.R., *Mižigárová v. Slovakia*, Judgment of 14 December 2010, Application no. 74832/01, paras. 117 and 122-123.

In *V.C.*, the Court decided to examine the discrimination claim solely in conjunction with Art. 8 ECHR for the reason that "the interference at issue affected one of her essential bodily functions and entailed numerous adverse consequences for her private and family life in particular".[20] It thereby dismissed the broader claims to discrimination in relation to Art. 3 and Art. 12. The Court concluded that the material before it was not sufficiently enough convincing as evidence that the sterilisation was part of an organised policy or that the hospital staff's conduct was intentionally racially motivated. The material indicated, according to the Court, that the practice of sterilisation of women affected not only Roma women but also vulnerable individuals from other ethnic groups.[21] At the same time, however, the Court explicitly referred to materials from the Human Rights Commissioner and from ECRI that not only established serious shortcomings in the legislation and practice relating to sterilisations in Slovakia, yet provided views that the shortcomings were liable to particularly affect members of the Roma community. In addition, the Court acknowledged the report from a group of experts established by the Slovak Ministry of Health that accepted the disproportionate correlation between sterilisations and being Roma, and had recommended special measures to prevent this.[22] Yet despite the evidence before it suggesting that the practice of non-consensual sterilisations in Slovakia disproportionally impacted upon members of the Roma community, the Court found that Slovakia had failed "to comply with its positive obligation under Art. 8 of the Convention to secure to the applicant a sufficient measure of protection enabling her, as a member of the vulnerable Roma community, to effectively enjoy her right to respect for her private and family life in the context of her sterilisation",[23] and dismissed the Art. 14 claim.

---

20   *V.C. v. Slovakia* (note 2), para. 176.
21   *Id.*, para. 177.
22   *Id.*, para. 178.
23   *Id.*, para. 179.

III. Underneath the Surface: An Analysis of the Applicable Evidentiary Rules in Cases of Discriminatory Violence and in Segregation Cases

Whether the Court approaches the *V.C.* case similarly to cases of discriminatory violence or the segregation cases is an important issue. In the latter type of cases, the Court has accepted the applicant's claim that the case should be considered from the perspective of indirect discrimination, meaning that it is not necessary to prove any discriminatory intent but merely to reveal the discriminatory effect or impact of a certain rule or measure on a particular group of individuals.[24] While the Court did not explicitly state whether it was considering the Art. 14 claim in *V.C.* as either direct or indirect discrimination, it is clear that what the Court actually did was approach the sterilisation case in the same manner as claims made of racially motivated violence i.e. claims of direct discrimination. This decision by the Court is somewhat peculiar, since *V.C.* does not concern the beatings or killings of a Romani individual, and therefore cannot be regarded as a classic, *Mižigárová*-like case of physical abuse.

What follows in this section is an outline of the evidentiary rules that the Court applies to cases of discriminatory violence against Roma. They will be set out against the rules applied in cases concerning segregation in the educational sphere, with particular attention on the *D.H.* case. Before beginning, one or two words should be said about complaints concerning discriminatory violence against Roma. In general, it may be said that these cases occur in two settings: either the facts concern the death or ill-treatment of one or more Romani citizens in custody, or the violence at issue was inflicted upon the victim(s) in a more public setting. Before the Court, the applicants then mostly rely on Art. 2 (right to life) or Art. 3 ECHR (prohibition of torture), taken alone or in conjunction with Art. 14. The provisions contain both substantive and procedural safeguards.[25] A substantive violation of Art. 14 taken in conjunction with Art. 2 or 3 would entail that a State can be held liable for the deprivation of life or ill-treatment on the basis of the victim's race or origin. If a violation of these provisions under the procedural limb is found, then this means that a State did not comply with its obligation to investigate possible racist motives.[26]

---

24 *D.H. a.o. v. Czech Republic* (GC) (note 13), para. 184.

25 HODGE MALEK *inter alia* (eds.), PHIPSON ON EVIDENCE 32 (2010).

26 Eur. Court H.R., *Nachova a.o. v. Bulgaria* Judgment of the Grand Chamber of 6 July 2005, Applications nos. 43577/98 and 43579/98, paras. 144-168.

A. Proving discriminatory motives in violence cases through the 'beyond reasonable doubt' standard

In cases in which it has been alleged by Romani applicants that violence against them was motivated by racist attitudes, there is a necessity of proving discriminatory motive or cause behind the unlawful treatment.[27] Furthermore, the quantum and quality of evidence are directed by the 'beyond reasonable doubt' standard. This standard was first mentioned in the *Greek* case of 1969, in which the European Commission of Human Rights ('Commission') defined the 'beyond reasonable doubt' as "not a doubt based on a merely theoretical possibility or raised in order to avoid a disagreeable conclusion, but a doubt for which reasons can be given drawn from the facts presented".[28] In *Ireland v. the United Kingdom*, the Court held "that such proof may follow from the coexistence of sufficiently strong, clear and concordant inferences or of similar unrebutted presumptions of fact".[29]

The question of burden of proof in the Court's reasoning obviously differs from the 'beyond reasonable doubt' standard, in that the latter refers to the degree of proof that must be offered and the former to the identity of the actor who must provide it.[30] Where the burden rests on the complaining party, the applicant may hand over a variety of evidence provided that it consists of relevant information.[31] However, the Court does not rely solely upon information submitted to it by either Party. It examines all material put before it, whether originating from the Parties or other sources, and, if necessary, obtains material *proprio motu*. This approach has been described by the Court as a 'free evaluation of evidence'.[32]

The burden and standard of proof seem, at first glance at least, to create a disproportionate disadvantage for an applicant attempting to prove discriminatory violence. In a case simply alleging state responsibility for acts of violence, the applicant can discharge the burden of proof by handing over expert opinion evidence, such as medical records that reveal bruises in cases of

---

27   *Id.*, para. 157.

28   EComHR, *Greek Case*, 5 November 1969 (Application no. 3321/67, *Denmark vs. Greece*; No. 3322/67, *Norway vs. Greece*; No. 3323/67, *Sweden vs. Greece*; No. 3344/67, *Netherlands vs. Greece*), vol. 12a Yearbook of the European Convention on Human Rights, 196 (1972).

29   Eur. Court H.R., *Ireland v. the United Kingdom*, Judgment of 18 January 1978, Application no. 5310/71, para. 161. See also *Nachova a.o. v. Bulgaria* (GC), para. 147.

30   Malek a.o. (note 25), p. 149.

31   *Ireland v. the United Kingdom* (note 29), para. 209.

32   *Id.*, para. 160. See also *Nachova a.o. v. Bulgaria* (GC) (note 26), para. 147.

ill-treatment[33] or autopsy reports where the abuse was fatal.[34] Cases of alleged discriminatory violence are different: in the absence of an explicit confession reflecting bias or a racist attitude, discriminatory motive is extremely difficult to prove. This difficulty is clear in *V.C.*, but also in earlier case-law such as the *Nachova* judgment. The latter case, eventually appearing before the Grand Chamber, concerned two Romani army conscripts who were killed by bullets fired by an officer in the Bulgarian military police, a man called Major G. The victims were trying to escape the major and his companions who were chasing them, after the two men had gone AWOL from a construction site where they had been working. Neither was armed. One of the witnesses to the killings claimed that Major G., immediately following the shootings, said "You damn Gypsies" over the bodies of the conscripts. The family of the victims subsequently complained before the Strasbourg Court that the killings were motivated by racial prejudice. Overturning an earlier Chamber decision, the Grand Chamber ruled that, although Bulgaria had violated Art. 2 in conjunction with Art. 14 on the basis of its failure to investigate the possibility of racial motives for the crimes (a procedural breach), it could not be established that the respondent State was liable for the deprivation of life on the basis of the victim's race or origin (a substantive breach). The difficulty in proving a discriminatory motive stemmed from the fact that reversing the burden of proof and requiring the Government to show that the killings had *not* been racially motivated "would amount to requiring the respondent Government to prove the absence of a particular subjective attitude on the part of the person concerned".[35]

Other issues arise in relation to the applicable standard of proof 'beyond reasonable doubt'. In *Nachova*, the Grand Chamber explained that "it has never been its purpose to borrow the approach of the national legal systems that use that standard" and that "[i]ts role is not to rule on criminal guilt or civil liability".[36] This reasoning is somewhat contradictory, as the Court chooses to apply a rather high evidentiary standard originating from Anglo-Saxon criminal law.[37] In addition, it has noted in its jurisprudence that there

---

33 Eur. Court H.R., *Balogh v. Hungary*, Judgment of 20 July 2004, Application no. 47940/99, paras. 48-54.
34 *Anguelova v. Bulgaria* (note 17), paras. 112-122.
35 *Nachova a.o. v. Bulgaria* (GC) (note 17), para. 157.
36 *Id.*, para. 147.
37 Hans Christian Krüger, *Gathering Evidence*, in THE BIRTH OF EUROPEAN HUMAN RIGHTS LAW (LIBER AMICORUM CARL AAGE NØRGAARD), 249, 253 (Michele de Salvia/Mark Villiger eds., 1998).

are no procedural barriers to the admissibility of evidence or pre-determined formulae for its assessment. The question can be posed as to the added value of this rule. After all, as it will be discussed further below, it is very difficult to collect material revealing the 'invisible' racial discrimination.

An additional question that can be posed concerns the reason behind introducing the 'beyond reasonable doubt' standard. It should be recalled that it was in fact the Commission that first introduced the standard in the *Greek* case. The latter concerned numerous allegations of ill-treatment and torture of prisoners by the Greek military junta. The Commission was charged with the gathering of evidence in order to establish the facts of each case.[38] It is not clear why the Commission chose to apply such a high standard of proof and to establish the facts of the case independently. Perhaps both elements are likely to be related to the political sensitivity of the case and the need to be scrupulously fair. Another reason may be found in the era in which the case took place: in the sixties, the Strasbourg institutions were not overwhelmed by applications and, consequently, the Commission had sufficient time and means at its disposal to conduct independent research into the facts of the case.

B. *The evidentiary rules applied in V.C. – a desirable approach?*

Although the Court did not explicitly mention in *V.C.* that it needs to be persuaded 'beyond reasonable doubt' that the sterilisation was induced by racist motives, it still required from the applicant that she prove discriminatory intent. The question can be posed whether this approach can be justified and whether the evidentiary rules as they have been applied in the Court's earlier case-law concerning the segregation of Romani children in education would not have been more suitable in this case. Could the most prominent case on that matter, the earlier-mentioned *D.H.*, have provided a more appropriate guideline on evidentiary rules in the sterilisation judgment?

D.H. and others concerned the system of so-called 'special schools' in the Czech Republic, the purpose of which was to provide an appropriate curriculum to children with special educational needs. National legislation prescribed that children with mental deficiencies who were unable to attend ordinary or specialised primary schools were to be placed in the special

---

38 Kersten Rogge, *The European Commission on Human Rights*, in THE BIRTH OF EUROPEAN HUMAN RIGHTS LAW (LIBER AMICORUM CARL AAGE NØRGAARD), 5 (Michele de Salvia/Mark Villiger eds., 1998).

schools. The mental capacity of pupils was measured by tests carried out in an educational psychology centre. On the basis of the results of these tests, the head teacher decided whether a child was to be placed in such a school, with the final decision on where to place a child subject to the consent of the child's legal guardian. The applicants in this case – D.H. and seventeen others – were Romani children who had been placed in a special school in the town of Ostrava for all or part of their education and as part of their claim they put forward unofficial statistical evidence that Romani children were overwhelmingly likely to be denied the opportunities of a regular education. The applicants submitted data that was obtained by their attorneys through questionnaires sent in 1999 to the head teachers of the 8 special schools and 69 primary schools in Ostrava. According to that data, 56% of the pupils that were placed in special schools in Ostrava were Romani, while Romani pupils represented only 2,26% of the total of 33,372 primary-school pupils in that town. By way of contrast, only 1,8% of non-Roma pupils were placed in special schools.

The applicants claimed before the Chamber that this amounted to discriminatory treatment on basis of their race, colour, association with a national minority and their ethnic origin and relied on Art. 14 in conjunction with Art. 2 of Protocol No. 1 ('the right to education'). A majority of the Chamber ruled that there was no concrete evidence before the Court to conclude that the placement of D.H. and others in special schools resulted from racial prejudice. The Chamber stated:

> "[T]he rules governing children's placement in special schools do not refer to the pupils' ethnic origin, but pursue the legitimate aim of adapting the education system to the needs and aptitudes or disabilities of the children. Since these are not legal concepts, it is only right that experts in educational psychology should be responsible for identifying them".[39]

Thus, in place of focusing on the discriminatory *impact* of the practice of educational testing, the Chamber chose to focus on whether or not there was discriminatory intent on the part of those conducting the testing, something not alleged by the applicants. On appeal, the Grand Chamber accepted the applicants' arguments concerning discriminatory impact and thus that the national policy on special schooling in education affected mainly Roma.[40]

---

39   ECtHR, *D.H. a.o. v. the Czech Republic*, Judgment of 7 February 2006, Application no. 57325/00, para. 49.
40   *D.H. a.o. v. Czech Republic* (GC) (note 13), para. 193.

The Grand Chamber has set a precedent in *D.H.* for future cases concerning the rules to be applied in cases of indirect discrimination. The applicant alleging such discriminatory treatment needs to show a presumption of a detrimental effect affecting a group in a disproportionate manner. Thus, in that regard, the initial burden of proof rests with the applicant. Once the applicant has established a *prima facie* case, the burden of proof then shifts to the respondent Government to show that the disparate impact is justified.[41] It is thus not necessary for the applicant to prove any discriminatory intent on the part of the relevant authorities in cases in the educational sphere. *D.H.* has also demonstrated that unofficial statistical evidence, albeit that it must be reliable and significant, can be sufficient as *prima facie* evidence of discrimination. Under the specific circumstances of this case, the Court found that the legislation in question produced a discriminatory effect: the statistics revealed a dominant trend of a disproportionate number of Roma children in special schools, something that was confirmed by independent supervisory bodies such as the Advisory Committee on the Framework Convention for the Protection of National Minorities, ECRI, the Committee on the Elimination of Racial Discrimination and the European Monitoring Centre on Racism and Xenophobia.[42]

Given that the Court was willing to show flexibility in applying evidentiary rules in *D.H.*, it is not clear why it chose to apply the tougher evidentiary standard in the *V.C.* case. The Court interpreted V.C.'s complaint as one of direct discrimination rather than seeing her treatment as part of a pattern of deep-seated discrimination against Roma in Slovakia. There was a way, however, for the Court to have taken this latter step. The legislative basis for sterilisations during the contested period can be found in the 1972 Sterilisation Regulation. The annex to the Regulation stated that a woman's sterilisation could be justified, amongst others, where a woman had several children (four children for women under the age of 35 and three children for women over that age). Although it was not brought forward by the applicant or the Court in *V.C.* as such, it is tenable that the latter element might be an additional circumstance through which an indirect causal link could be established between the sterilisation and being of Romani origin. After all, if it appears that Romani women are statistically more likely to give birth to more children than other women in Slovakia and the sterilisation procedure is more frequently applied to them than other female groups as a consequence,

---

41   *Id.*, paras. 196-204.
42   *Id.*, paras. 186-195.

this would have provided concrete evidence of the practices of sterilisation affecting Romani women in a disproportionate manner.[43]

IV. Types of Evidence Romani Citizens Rely upon before the Court

The inevitable question flowing from evidentiary rules is what kind of evidence is sufficient to satisfy a claim that discrimination has occurred. In *V.C.* the applicant argued that her complaint concerning discriminatory treatment should be examined against the background of sterilisation practices during communist times and in a broader context of contemporary intolerance against Roma in Slovakia. The applicant claimed that information substantiating her claims could be found in a number of publications, originating mainly from a range of international organisations and in statistics. Her claim was that this climate of intolerance influenced the medical personnel in their treatment of her. Furthermore, according to V.C., such a climate within Prešov Hospital appeared from the indication in her medical record that she was of Romani ethnic origin and from the manner in which she was treated as a patient in that hospital.[44]

Her claim was not sufficient to persuade the Chamber that her sterilisation was induced by discriminatory motives. Hereunder, attention will be paid to a variety of evidential material submitted before the Court in cases of discriminatory violence and in the segregation cases. An evaluation will follow on three different types of material, namely discriminatory statements or statements of bias, statistics and reports from international organisations, in order to assess whether the significance the Court has contributed to these types of material in *V.C.* has been just.

A. Discriminatory remarks or statements of bias

In the first cases that came before it concerning violence against Roma, the Court did not address the issue of discriminatory remarks or statements resembling some sort of bias at all. The reference made by the authorities to the victim as "the Gypsy", even in official statements,[45] and emphasis on a

---

43   *V.C. v. Slovakia* (note 2), paras. 60-64.
44   *Id.*, paras. 43-47 and 170.
45   *Anguelova v. Bulgaria* (note 17), para. 164.

person's "dark colour of the skin"[46] were not regarded by the Court as signs of discriminatory behaviour. It was in *Nachova* that the Grand Chamber for the first time concluded that the use of racist verbal abuse could amount into a violation of Art. 14. Accordingly:

> "any evidence of racist verbal abuse being uttered by law enforcement agents in connection with an operation involving the use of force against persons from an ethnic or other minority is highly relevant to the question whether or not unlawful, hatred-induced violence has taken place".[47]

In that same case, the Court concluded that the words "You damn Gypsies", alleged to have been uttered by the perpetrator immediately following the shooting of the two victims, required investigation. The failure of the Bulgarian authorities to investigate the possible racist overtones of the events resulted in a violation of Art. 14 read in conjunction with Art. 2 under the procedural limb of the right to life protection.[48]

So, what is the impact of the word 'Gypsy' as such on the Court's evaluation of whether discrimination has taken place? This discussion is all the more interesting since, in 2010, concerns were raised by the European Roma Rights Centre ('ERRC') in relation to a motion that was filed before the Romanian Parliament in 2010 to change the official name of Roma to 'Tigan' (French: 'Tsigane'; English: 'Gypsy').[49] The motivation for this proposal was to preclude any confusion between the terms 'Roma' and 'Romania'. The ERRC objected strongly to the proposal as the word 'Tigan' is a pejorative term associated with deportations of Roma during the Second World War and centuries of slavery. The ERRC further observed that the word 'Tigan' dates back from the Greek language, meaning 'pagan', 'heretic' or 'untouchable'. Rodrigues and Matelski have observed that it has a negative connotation in the Roma and the Sinti community, presumably originating from the German phrase 'ziehender Gauner' which can be translated as travelling rouge.[50]

---

46 *Velikova v. Bulgaria* (note 17), para. 92.
47 *Nachova a.o. v. Bulgaria* (GC) (note 17), para. 164.
48 *Id.*, paras. 162-168.
49 The ERRC wrote a letter to the Romanian Parliament to express its concerns about this development. European Roma Rights Centre, ERRC Urges Romanian Authorities to Reject "Tigan" Terminology, posted on 15 December 2010, available at http://www.errc.org/cikk.php?cikk=3799.
50 Peter Rodrigues & Maaike Matelski, RACISM & EXTREME RIGHT MONITOR. ROMA AND SINTI, 5 (2004).

From the Court's case-law it appears that it is not the word 'Gypsy' as such that amounts to a breach of the Convention; instead it depends on the circumstances in which it is used. The Court found a procedural violation of Art. 14 together with Art. 3 in the case of *Cobzaru v. Romania*. In this case a Romani man was allegedly beaten by police officers during custody. A military prosecutor, who had to decide whether the alleged violence required investigation, referred to the applicant and his father as "antisocial elements prone to violence and theft" in constant conflict with "fellow members of their ethnic group".[51] Moreover, the term 'Gypsy' was used on frequent occasions by the investigating authorities. The Court labelled these remarks as 'tendentious' and stressed that they disclosed "a general discriminatory attitude of the authorities".[52] The use of such remarks, taken together with the refusal of the authorities to verify whether the police officers who had beaten the applicant displayed any anti-Roma sentiments, amounted into a procedural violation of Art. 14 taken together with Art. 3. The Court stated that there was an obligation to investigate *prima facie* discrimination, all the more since there have been numerous anti-Roma incidents in Romania and other documented evidence revealing the repeated failure by the authorities to remedy instances of the violence. The Court pointed out that the incidents, covered regularly by the media, were known to the Romanian public and, as a result, the Government had set up various programs to combat discrimination. Under such circumstances it was to be expected that the investigating authorities in *Cobzaru* were familiar with this general information as well.[53]

In another case, that of *Stoica*, the ECtHR ruled that the remark in the police report describing the villagers' alleged aggressive behaviour as "purely Gypsy" was clearly stereotypical and called for investigation.[54] What is more, the claims by the witnesses that the police officers present asked one of the victims whether he was "Gypsy or Romanian" before beating him, at the deputy mayor's request in order to teach the Roma "a lesson", were regarded as not racially neutral.[55] These remarks implied that the aggressive behaviour had taken place in a racist context. Consequently, *Stoica* is the only case

---

51   Eur. Court H.R., *Cobzaru v. Romania*, Judgment of 26 July 2007, Application no. 48254/99, para. 28.

52   *Id.*, para. 100.

53   *Id.*, paras. 97-101.

54   *Stoica v. Romania* (note 17), para. 122.

55   *Id.*, para. 128.

to-date in which the Court has found a substantive violation of Art. 14 taken together with Art. 3.

No such violation was found in *Soare*, even though the police officer that caused serious injuries to the Romani victim expressly stated on the evening of the incident that he had acted in self-defence when "attacked by a Gypsy". In this case, the Court did not accept that the violence was racially motivated because the racist comments had not been made during the incident but afterwards. Further, the remark of the officer was not sufficient in itself, according to the Court, to require the authorities to conduct an investigation into possible racist motives for the violent attack.[56]

Finally, the case of *Koky* concerned an incident caused by private non-Romani individuals in a Roma settlement in Slovakia. Accordingly, three Romani houses were forcibly entered, damage was caused inside the houses and some of the windows were broken. Three Romani men were physically assaulted by the group. In addition, it was alleged by several witnesses that racist slogans were shouted during the incident by the perpetrators. The Court did not separately examine the discrimination claim, yet it discussed the matter solely under Art. 3. It held that there was a procedural violation of the provision, since the authorities had failed to do everything that could have been expected to investigate the incident, especially given the racial overtones of the attacks.[57]

Another question that may arise is what the consequences are before the Court where biased comments are made by state officials or private persons directed against a Romani individual or the Romani population in general. Further, what impact does mere reference to the victim's ethnic origin have on the examination of a discrimination claim? In *Moldovan (no. 2)*, the Court had to deal with comments made by Romanian judges about the Roma, in which they stated, *inter alia*, that "[d]ue to their lifestyle and their rejection of the moral values accepted by the rest of the population, the Roma community has marginalised itself, shown aggressive behaviour and deliberately denied and violated the legal norms acknowledged by society" and that most of them "have no occupation and earn their living by doing odd jobs, stealing and engaging in all kinds of illicit activities".[58] Remarkably, the Court did not

---

56 Eur. Court H.R., *Soare a.o. v. Romania*, Judgment of 22 February 2011, Application no. 24329/02, paras. 197-209.

57 Eur. Court H.R., *Koky a.o. v. Slovakia*, Judgment of 12 June 2012, Application no. 13624/03, para. 239.

58 Eur. Court H.R, *Moldovan a.o. v. Romania (no. 2)*, Judgment of 12 July 2005, Application nos. 41138/98 and 64320/01, para. 44.

discuss the comments under Art. 14, but considered them as an aggravating factor during the discussion of the substantive case under Art. 3. It found a violation of the latter provision.

In the case of *Petropoulou-Tsakiris v. Greece*, the applicant complained that the police brutality she was subjected to and the subsequent lack of an effective investigation into that matter were caused by her Romani ethnic origin. The authorities commented during investigating procedures that complaints raised by Roma were exaggerated and formed part of their "common tactic to resort to the extreme slandering of police officers with the obvious purpose of weakening any form of police control". The Court viewed the comments as examples of remarks disclosing a general discriminatory attitude and found that the failure of the authorities to investigate possible racist motives for the applicant's ill-treatment, in combination with their attitude during the investigation, amounted into a violation of Art. 14 taken in conjunction with Art. 3 in its procedural limb.[59]

In the subsequent case of *Beganović v. Croatia*, one of the assailants was questioned by the police about the beating of the applicant. During this interview the assailant merely mentioned that the applicant was of Roma origin, but did not further elaborate on this point. According to the Court, there was no violation under Art. 14 read in conjunction with Art. 3. This was due to the absence of evidence that the applicant's ethnic origin was at the roots of the violence inflicted against him. Neither the assailant who was questioned nor the other assailants had indicated that the applicant's ethnic origin was the reason why he was attacked.[60]

What these cases suggest is that where comments are made about a person's ethnic origin (and when it comes to the Romani population these comments are often expressed through the term 'Gypsy') by assailants in an offensive manner in the immediate aftermath of an action of aggressive incident (*Nachova*) or by state officials during an investigation into a violent incident (*Cobzaru, Petropoulou-Tsakiris*), the Court will require the national authorities to have conducted an investigation into possible racist motives. Failure to do so will result in a procedural breach of Art. 14 read in conjunction with either Art. 2 or 3. Further, the case of *Stoica* suggests that racist remarks made by state officials in the execution of violence against the

---

59   Eur. Court H.R., *Petropoulou-Tsakiris v. Greece*, Judgment of 6 December 2007, Application no. 44803/04, paras. 65-66.

60   Eur. Court H.R., *Beganović v. Croatia*, Judgment of 25 June 2009, Application no. 46423/06, paras. 96-97.

victim are likely to result in a substantive violation of Art. 14 ECHR taken together with one of the substantive provisions.

How should the indication that *V.C.* was of Roma ethnic origin in her medical record be interpreted in the light of the case-law set out above? The (written) comment made in *V.C.* shows most resemblance with the *Beganović* case. There was no explicit comment or formulation in any documents that the applicant had been sterilised due to her ethnic origin, merely a remark that she belongs to the Romani ethnic group.

B. Statistics

The applicant in *V.C.* brought forward statistical data drawn from two studies conducted in 1990 and 1989. On the basis of this material, she argued that in the Prešov district in the period 1986-1987, 60% of the sterilisations performed were on Romani women, whereas they represented only 7% of the population of the district. The second study revealed that in 1983 approximately 26% of the sterilised women were Romani, yet this had increased by 1987 to 36,6%.[61]

In cases of presumed discriminatory violence against Roma, statistics have not played a part in uncovering racist motives because they cannot attest to the intent that underlies direct discrimination. This type of evidentiary material has, however, had importance in cases of indirect discrimination. The Court's initial reluctance to accept this type of evidence has been discussed above. In the case of *Kelly*, the Court refused to accept that the circumstance under which the relatives of the applicants had been killed was evidence of discrimination. The applicant alleged that UK soldiers were more likely to use force against young men from the Catholic or nationalist community than from the rival Protestant group and used statistics as evidence. The Court admitted that the statistics suggested a *prima facie* case, yet refused to accept the statistics in themselves in order to establish discriminatory treatment within the meaning of Art. 14.[62] The Court reached an identical conclusion in *Hugh Jordan*, concerning the death of Pearse Jordan by an officer of the Royal

---

61   Ruben Pellar & Zbyněk Andrš, *Statistical Evaluation of the Cases of Sexual Sterilisation of Romani Women in East Slovakia*, in APPENDIX TO THE REPORT ON THE EXAMINATION IN THE PROBLEMATIC SEXUAL STERILISATION OF ROMANIES IN CZECHOSLOVAKIA (1990); Dr med. Posluch & Dr med. Posluchová, *The Problems of Planned Parenthood among Gypsy Fellow-citizens in the Eastern Slovakia Region*, in ZDRAVOTNÍCKA PRACOVNÍČKA 220-223 (No. 39/1989).

62   Eur. Court H.R, *Kelly a.o. v. the United Kingdom*, Judgment of 4 May 2001, Application no. 30054/96, para. 148.

Ulster Constabulary.[63] Having opened the door to the use of statistics in the *Hoogendijk* decision, the Court expressed the following in *D.H.*:

> "188. (...) [T]he Court considers that when it comes to assessing the impact of a measure or practice on an individual or group, statistics which appear on critical examination to be reliable and significant will be sufficient to constitute the prima facie evidence the applicant is required to produce. This does not, however, mean that indirect discrimination cannot be proved without statistical evidence".

The statistical data in *D.H.* was collected by the applicants: questionnaires were sent out to the head teachers of special and primary schools in the town of Ostrava in 1999. Their validity was contested by the Government, which stated that the statistics merely represented the subjective opinions of the head teachers, that no official information on the ethnic origin of the pupils existed and that the Ostrava region had one of the largest Romani populations in the country. The unofficial nature of the statistics was, according to the Court, the reason that it placed weight on supporting evidence as to the discrimination effect of the Czech educational system from reports drawn up by international organisations.[64] Similarly, in *Oršuš*, the Court ruled that the statistics in question were not in themselves sufficient to disclose a general policy to automatically place Roma pupils in separate classes;[65] and therefore, here too, the Court sought and relied upon additional information to establish indirect discrimination.

In *V.C.*, the Court did not go specifically into the value of the statistical data submitted by the applicant. Instead, it chose to elaborate on evidentiary material in general, and drew from it the conclusion that the discriminatory treatment in question has not been demonstrated. The question can be posed, however, whether the statistics submitted in the latter case are relevant at all, since they concern materials collected more than a decade before the treatment at the heart of the case. It is unfortunate, therefore, that the Court did not chose to comment on the evidence provided in this case and how it weighed against the claims made.

---

63   Eur. Court H.R, *Hugh Jordan v. the United Kingdom*, Judgment of 4 May 2001, Application no. 24746/94, para. 154.

64   *D.H. a.o. v. Czech Republic* (GC) (note 13), paras. 190-191.

65   *Oršuš a.o. v. Croatia* (GC) (note 14), para. 152.

C. Reports

At present, a minority of Strasbourg judges are convinced that the existence of reports from international organisations and human rights groups that reveal a high incidence of racially motivated violence against Roma in certain Member States may at the very least trigger a procedural obligation upon a Member State to investigate the existence or not of a causal connection between physical abuse/violence and ethnicity.[66] The Court's starting position on the value of such reports in cases of racially motivated violence has been set out in *Nachova*. Under the substantive part of the complaint, the Court made clear that, even though intergovernmental bodies have expressed strong concerns about the many incidents involving the use of violence against members of the Romani communities, the sole concern of the Court is to ascertain whether in the case before it the violence was motivated by racism.[67] Such reports thus hardly carry any evidentiary weight when the substantive part of the right is at stake.

Under the procedural limb of the complaint, the Court regards authoritative reports as a sort of aggravating factor. If there is an indication that the victim has been subjected to racist verbal abuse and if there are reports of international organisations that document the prevalence of discriminatory violence against a given group, this triggers an obligation to investigate a connection between racist attitudes and the use of force.[68] In the *Mižigárová* case, the Court has even underlined that "[i]n respect of persons of Roma origin, it would not exclude the possibility that in a particular case the existence of independent evidence of a systemic problem could, in the absence of any other evidence, be sufficient to alert the authorities to the possible existence of a racist motive".[69] However, the Court did not specify under what circumstances the evidence is sufficiently strong to suggest the existence of such a motive. Moreover, in neither of the cases that have been ruled upon so far, did the Court establish without any case-specific concrete

---

66 *Anguelova v. Bulgaria, Partly Dissenting Opinion of Judge Bonello*, paras. 5-8; *Carabulea v. Romania, Partly Joint Dissenting Opinion of Judges Gyulumyan and Power* and *Partly Dissenting Opinion of Judge Ziemele*; Eur. Court H.R., *Mižigárová v. Slovakia*, Judgment of 14 December 2010, Application no. 74832/1, *Partly Dissenting Opinion of Judge Davíd Thór Björgvinsson*; *Soare a.o. v. Romania, Partly Joint Dissenting Opinion of Judges Power and Zupančič* and *Partly Concurring, Partly Dissenting Opinion of Judge Ziemele*.

67 *Nachova a.o. v. Bulgaria* (GC) (note 17), para. 155.

68 *Id.*, para. 163. See also Eur. Court H.R., *Bekos and Koutropoulos v. Greece*, Judgment of 13 December 2005, Application no. 15250/02, para. 73.

69 *Mižigárová v. Slovakia* (note 66), para. 122.

evidence that reports by themselves are sufficient to meet the burden of proof of racial prejudice in violence cases, even solely in relation to the procedural part of the complaint.[70]

However, reports from international organisations have played an important role in the finding of a violation of Art. 14 in segregation cases. Following the Court's acceptance of the statistics submitted by the applicants in *D.H.* as not entirely reliable, it continued by looking at more general information provided by independent supervisory bodies on the placement of Romani children in the special schools and not merely in the town of Ostrava. The figures included in the reports, according to the Court, confirmed the dominant trend of the placement of a disproportionate number of Romani children in special schools, something that was already revealed by the statistics that the applicants themselves had provided. In addition, the Court used reports to evaluate whether the tests that the children needed to take were biased.[71] Similarly, in the Grand Chamber judgment in *Oršuš*, statistical evidence was not regarded to be sufficient to establish the discrimination complaint. Here too the Court used reports from ECRI and the Commissioner for Human Rights to support the statistical evidence that the placement of Romani children in separate classes had a discriminatory effect.[72] The lesson that can be drawn from both segregation cases is that statistics are not *per se* necessary to establish a *prima facie* presumption of indirect discrimination. Such a presumption can also be created through more general information included in reports from international organisations. In practice, however, both may be necessary.

The reports submitted by the applicant in *V.C.* were not sufficient to attest that Romani women were particular targets of sterilisation. Instead, the Court held that the materials before it indicated that sterilisation practices without prior consent were applied to vulnerable individuals from various ethnic groups.[73] Yet, as the Court chose to use the *Mižigárová* case as the main lens through which to view the particular claim in *V.C.*, it is questionable whether the presumed discriminatory sterilisation practices could have been proven through reports at all. In a case such as *Mižigárová* – an allegation of racially motivated violence – concrete evidence is required through which the facts of the case and also the motives behind a certain treatment or practice can be

---

70   See, for instance, Eur. Court H.R., *Ognyanova and Choban v. Bulgaria*, Judgment of 23 February 2006, Application no. 46317/99, paras. 146-148.

71   *D.H. a.o. v. Czech Republic* (GC) (note 13), paras. 191-204.

72   *Oršuš a.o. v. Croatia* (GC) (note 14), paras. 152-155.

73   *V.C. v. Slovakia* (note 2), para. 177.

revealed. Such concrete evidence is unlikely to be found in documents that report a more general situation.

V. Conclusion

Almost a decade has passed since Gerards placed question marks over the added value of the principle of equal treatment enshrined within Art. 14. Considering the way in which the Court examined the discrimination claim made in *V.C.*, those same questions can be raised in relation to cases of presumed discriminatory physical abuse. The Court's reluctance in accepting Art 14 claims in these cases may be connected to the accessory nature of Art. 14, as Gerards suggested. Yet, in cases concerning violence against Roma or other cases of physical abuse, such as sterilisation, there appears to be more to it. One explanation for the Court's reluctance to accept the claim of discrimination may have to do with the substantive right at stake. It might well be that in cases in which more fundamental rights are at issue, such as the rights protected in Art. 2 and 3, the Court becomes more cautious in accepting racially motivated conduct.

Another important feature of such cases concerns the rules of evidence. The Court still applies the high 'beyond reasonable doubt' standard, which was introduced for the first time in the sixties by the Commission in the *Greek* case. It would seem that outcome of these early choices linger on in current judgments and questions can be posed as to whether the evidentiary instruments chosen at that time are still the most appropriate for cases in which fundamental rights, more precisely those enshrined in Art. 14 taken in conjunction with Art. 2 and 3, are at stake.

In addition, cases of discriminatory physical violence, and more specifically in *V.C.*, require the applicant to prove a discriminatory motive. However, the motive that the Court is looking for is a well-hidden element: in most cases of violence that have been discussed in this chapter, the authorities often deny any discriminatory intent and there are usually no witnesses to the alleged facts. While blatant hostile (verbal) abuse against Roma is of huge assistance to applicants claiming racially-motivated abuse, because this type of concrete proof is missing in most of the cases before the Court, the racial motivation is more often than not invisible, and therefore remains so. Statistics or reports from NGOs and intergovernmental organisations, which often refer to a more general situation, have not yet been sufficient to persuade the Court of discriminatory intent in cases in which such concrete evidence is missing. Short, therefore, of abusive written statements by the medical staff that they sterilised *V.C.* because she was Romani, the Court was never likely to accept the charge that their actions were motivated, even indirectly, by discriminatory attitudes.

Chapter 4

The Roma and the Framework Convention for the Protection of National Minorities: A Tool to Disentangle the Dichotomy between a Socially Disadvantaged Group and a National Minority

*Roberta Medda-Windischer**

I. Introduction

In 2010 the Parliamentary Assembly of the Council of Europe (PACE) adopted a resolution on Roma,[1] in which Member States were urged to: "treat the Roma issue not only from the perspective of a socially disadvantaged group, but from the perspective of a *national minority* entitled to enjoy the rights enshrined in the Framework Convention for the Protection of National Minorities".[2] In line with the PACE resolution, the present chapter will look at the Roma issue from the perspective of the CoE Framework Convention for the Protection of National Minorities,[3] the first legally binding multilateral

---

* Roberta Medda-Windischer is Senior Researcher/Group Leader at the European Academy of Bolzano/Bozen, Institute for Minority Rights. A longer version of this article first appeared in European Yearbook on Minority Issues, Vol. 10 (2011).

1 The term "Roma", though opposed by some groups that do not recognize themselves under this term, is used in this paper as an umbrella that includes groups of people who have more or less similar cultural characteristics, such as Sinti, Travellers, Kalé, Gens du voyage, etc., whether sedentary or not.

2 CoE, PACE Resolution 1740 (2010), The situation of Roma in Europe and relevant activities of the Council of Europe, 22 June 2010, para. 15.1 (emphasis added). This binary approach is echoed in the recent ECRI General Policy Rec. no. 13 on Combating Anti-Gypsyism and Discrimination against Roma, 24 June 2011, that calls for measures to combat 'Gypsyism' in the field of education, employment, health care but also for measures to aid preservation of the Roma identity as an important instrument for fighting 'anti-Gypsyism'.

3 The CoE Framework Convention for the Protection of National Minorities was adopted on 1 February 1995 and entered into force on 1 February 1998, ETS No. 157 (hereinafter "FCNM" or "Framework Convention"). As many other supra-national legal instruments on human rights, the FCNM provides for a monitoring system

instrument devoted to the protection of minorities:[4] How is the FCNM applied among its Contracting States in relation to the Roma? What is the impact of the FCNM, particularly of the opinions of the Advisory Committee, on the protection of the Roma? Is it possible to identify trends – positive and negative – in the implementation of the FCNM *vis-á-vis* Roma? This chapter will address these questions by examining a selection of relevant documents from the FCNM monitoring mechanism, notably state reports, ACFC's opinions and recommendations of the Committee of Ministers, and analyzing the differences between the first and second, and in some cases, the third state reports as well as the opinions of the ACFC, in order to detect trends and specific country-related issues.

A number of states have been selected as relevant for this study, and although it will not be possible to consider all documents and issues related to the monitoring process of each country, the selection of these countries will provide an overview of the variety among the Member States within the Council of Europe *vis-á-vis* Roma: Spain and Italy as *old* Member States of the Council of Europe from Southern Europe, characterized by the presence of historical Roma communities on their territories and by recent flows of *new* minorities belonging to the Roma communities coming notably from Romania and Bulgaria as a consequence of the enlargement of the European Union; Romania and the Czech Republic as countries emerging from the dissolution of former socialist regimes and, due to the EU accession process, countries that were required to fulfill the Copenhagen criteria, which include, among others, the protection of minorities; finally, the Netherlands and Finland as Northern European countries that have not experienced a large inflow of Roma EU migrants due to the recent enlargement of the

---

based on state reports that are evaluated by a committee of independent experts, the Advisory Committee on the FCNM (hereinafter "AC", "ACFC" or "Advisory Committee"). For further details, see the Official Homepage of the FCNM available at www.coe.int/t/dghl/monitoring/minorities/default_en.asp.

4   Minority rights have been traditionally included in contemporary standards of human rights as rights of individuals rather than collective or group rights. In the context of the FCNM, Alan Phillips, former President of the ACFC, argued: "Most of the Convention's Articles have a collective dimension … and, in practice, can only be enjoyed as a joint exercise by persons belonging to a national minority". See, Alan Phillips, the fcnm: a policy analysis (Minority Rights Group, 2002), available at   <http://www.greekhelsinki.gr/bhr/english/organizations/fcnm_pol_paper_aug. doc>. The Explanatory Report that accompanies the FCNM clarifies, however, that *the joint exercise* of rights and freedoms is distinct from the notion of collective rights (FCNM, Explanatory Report, para.37, available at http://conventions.coe.int/treaty/ en/Reports/Html/157.htm).

European Union, but that have the historical presence of autochthonous Roma communities on their territories.

II. The Implementation of the FCNM *vis-à-vis* Roma

Although the Romani communities living in the Member States of the FCNM are very different from each other and experience diverse problems, this section will provide an overview of the major issues that are common to the countries selected in this study, as well as detail some of the issues that are specific to certain countries only. In this limited space, it will not be possible to provide an exhaustive and comprehensive analysis of all issues experienced by Roma in the selected countries.

A. *Common issues among selected Member States*

The first common issue identified in all FCNM Member States under consideration in this study – from Finland to the Czech Republic, from Italy to the Netherlands – is a generalized socio-economic disparity, though in different degrees, with the mainstream, majority communities; in other words, Romani communities across this diverse group of states experience widespread marginalization and exclusion across the various fields of social life, including school, labour, housing, media and political life.

This marginalization and exclusion from mainstream society is linked to widespread forms of discrimination that most countries acknowledged in their state reports: Roma are generally more likely to be victims of discrimination than any other group.[5] Directly linked to this issue are forms of ill-treatment and other types of misconduct and misbehavior committed by law enforcement agents and police forces, coupled with a generalized lack of effective and serious investigations into these abuses.[6]

A further common area of marginalization is that which takes place in schools and education more broadly, either through *special* schools or *de*

---

5 See, *inter alia*, ACFC, 1st Report, Finland, ACFC/SR(1999)003, 16 February 1999, 10; ACFC, 1st Report, Czech Republic, ACFC/SR(1999)006, 1 April 1999, 8. See, also, EU Fundamental Rights Agency (FRA), Eu-Midis: European Minorities And Discrimination Survey, 22 April 2009.

6 See, COM Resolution, Romania, ResCMN/2002)5, 13 March 2002, para. 1; ACFC, 1st Opinion, Czech Republic, 14 September 2001, ACFC/INF/OP/I(2002)007, 11.

facto special schools,[7] or through disproportionate numbers of Roma pupils placed in special education regimes in ordinary school classes,[8] or in home schooling transfers.[9] Absenteeism, drop-out rates, and a disproportionate number of Romani pupils in vocational schools rather than the upper secondary schools in which the majority enroll their children, are also common issues.[10] In relation to the placement of Romani children in special and adapted education – a common experience among Romani pupils – two peculiar approaches are taken in the state reports under consideration that are worth mentioning for the different views on special education that they illustrate: the approach taken by the Czech authorities, in which they state that "some parents visibly prefer to have their children stay in the same school [elementary schools with curricula for pupils with a light mental handicap], which is why some children end up enrolled in elementary schools for pupils with slight mental handicaps".[11] This approach seems to be motivated mainly by the attempt to share with Roma parents, or even to place completely on their shoulders, the responsibility for the decision to provide sub-standard education to Romani pupils.[12] A different approach to special education is represented by the Finnish authorities, which noted in their report, that: "education arranged in special groups is more expensive than normal school education, and children are not placed in such education unless there are reasonable grounds for doing so. As soon as the child no longer needs special or adapted education, he or she is transferred back to a normal school class".[13] This approach epitomizes a view that considers special educational treatment as a tool that cannot be simply provided upon parents' request without

---

7   ACFC, 2nd Report, Czech Republic, ACFC/SR/II(2004)007, 2 July 2004, 9; ACFC, 2nd Opinion, Czech Republic, ACFC/INF/OP/II(2005)002, 26 October 2005, 31.

8   ACFC, 2nd Report, Finland, ACFC/SR/II(2004)012E, 10 December 2004, 75.

9   ACFC, 3rd Report, Finland, ACFC/SR/III(2010)001, 17 February 2010, 64.

10 ACFC, 1st Opinion, Netherlands, ACFC/OP/I(2009)002, 17 February 2010, 16; ACFC-Finland (note 5), 21.

11 ACFC, 3rd Report, Czech Republic, ACFC/SR/III(2010)008, 3 May 2010, 16 (emphasis added). It is certainly the case that some Romani parents consent to the placement of their children in special schools, primarily because these schools provide a better level of care, such as hot meals and additional activities. See, OSCE-ODIHR, Implementation of the Action Plan on Improving the Situation of Roma and Sinti within the OSCE Area. Status Report 2008, Warsaw, 2008, 41.

12 This burden-sharing approach has been clearly rejected by the Grand Chamber of the European Court of Human Rights in its leading case Eur. Court H.R., *DH. and Others v. the Czech Republic* (GC), Judgement of 13 November 2007, Application No. 57325/00.

13 ACFC, Comments by Finlavnd, GVT/COM/INF/OP/I(2001)002, 3 July 2001, 15.

meticulous test and continuous checks, as it is an extra and expensive didactic instrument that can be justified only in limited, exceptional cases.

In addition to the above common problems, a further issue that emerges from the state reports under consideration is the need to balance respect for the identity and culture of Roma communities with the battle against marginalization from mainstream societies; in other words, the difficult balance that must be drawn between protection of diversity and integration into mainstream societies.[14] In this difficult balancing process, two distinctive approaches surface in the states reports. The first concerns a 'New Right' approach based on the idea that, as a consequence of their cultural way-of-life and socio-economic circumstances, Roma are 'special' and must therefore be treated 'differently' via special measures that are unique or *ad hoc* to this group of communities.[15]

This approach, although not negative *per se*, clearly contains the risk of confining minority groups into ethnic enclaves or self-contained ghettos that are alienated from the mainstream i.e. of reinforcing socio-economic marginalization. Moreover, the labelling of Roma communities as 'special' and 'complex' can, and is, (mis-)used as an excuse to legitimise endless delays in the adoption of measures and policies to facilitate access to basic services, as in the case of Italy, where the authorities argued that the failure to adopt a specific legislation for Roma was due to "the extremely complicated nature of the issue".[16] The second approach that emerges from state reports and government comments is, at best, a paternalistic attitude towards Roma, and, at worst, a prejudiced attitude. In their comments to the AC Opinion, for instance, the Italian authorities stated that "although schools are quite willing to receive nomads, they [the Roma] actually display a low inclination for integration (including in the school community) resulting in the *inborn* tendency to refuse regular attendance to schools in the places where they temporarily stay".[17] Similarly, in discussing education for Romani adults, the Czech authorities noted that: "The students will acquire knowledge and skills that are quite common in the majority society, but quite uncommon in the

---

14   See, for instance, ACFC, 2nd Opinion, Italy, ACFC/INF/OP/II(2005)003, 25 October 2005, 11.

15   See, among those who have commented on this approach, Annabel Tremlett, *Trying to solve a European problem: a comprehensive strategy for Roma minorities* (2011), available at www.opendemocracy.net/annabel-tremlett/trying-to-solve-european-problem-comprehensive-strategy-for-roma-minorities.

16   ACFC, 2nd Report, Italy, ACFC/SR/II(2004)006, 14 May 2004, 20 (emphasis added).

17   ACFC, Comments, Italy, GCT/COM/INF/OP/II(2005)003, 25 October 2005, 11 (emphasis added).

Roma community",[18] with no further details given to explain exactly what these 'uncommon knowledge and skills' are. Likewise, in presenting measures to promote employment among Roma, the Finnish authorities declared that "the completion of comprehensive school and professional education are still *not self-evident* for the Roma".[19]

B. Specific country-related issues

In addition to the issues common to all the reports and opinions of the states under consideration, a number of country-specific problems can be identified.

One issue identified by the AC, particularly in the Italian reports, is the terminology used to refer to Romani communities, namely *Zingari* (Gypsies) and *Nomadi* (Nomads). For the AC, the term *Zingari* has a pejorative connotation, whereas the term *Nomad* is simply misleading since only some Roma retain an itinerant lifestyle.[20] Despite the commitment by the Italian authorities to comply with the recommendation of the AC to use more accurate and sensitive terms, the second state report continued to use terms such as *Gypsies* and *Nomads*.[21] In contrast, the Finnish authorities consistently, and correctly, refer to Roma/Sinti throughout their state reports and governmental replies. The terminological issue is obviously not necessarily symptomatic of substantive problems in minority protection, and thus does not mean that a simple adjustment in the terminology used by the authorities is sufficient to correct a flawed and inefficient policy for Roma. However, it cannot be denied that the terms used as to refer to any minority groups, provide evidence of awareness and sensitivity by the majority to certain issues that may be considered by some as merely symbolic, but that are in fact extremely relevant for the minorities.[22]

A second country-specific problem emerges from the AC Opinion on the report of the Czech Republic, and concerns allegations of the sterilization of

---

18   ACFC, 2nd Report, Czech Republic, ACFC/SR/II(2004)007, 2 July 2004, 10 (emphasis added).

19   ACFC-Finland (note 8), 35. Emphasis added.

20   ACFC, 1st Opinion, Italy, ACFC/INF/OP/I(2002)007, 14 September 2001, 11.

21   ACFC-Italy (note 16), 10.

22   In this regard, note the proposal made in Romania by the Liberal-Democrat, Silviu Prigoana, to change the official name of the Roma to Gypsy, arguing that "the name Roma confuses people, especially foreigners, and thus many tend to take Roma for Romanians". See, Paul Ciocoiu, Gypsy vs Roma dispute in Romania, in *Southeast European Times* (SETimes), 17 December 2010, available at www.setimes.com/ cocoon/setimes/xhtml/en_GB/features/setimes/blogreview/2010 /12/17/blog-02.

Romani women without their prior, free and informed consent.[23] The Czech authorities have acknowledged that dozens of complaints have been submitted to the Ministry of Health, through the Office of the Public Defender of Rights, regarding cases of sterilization without informed consent.[24] In their third report, the authorities gave an account of legislative measures introduced to counteract this hideous practice, including a new model for collecting informed consent for sterilization, compensation for victims and awareness measures among health workers.[25]

A further country-specific issue, consistently criticized by the AC in the strongest terms, is the situation of Roma, in the AC's term, "assembled" in camps in Italy, in which living conditions and standards of hygiene are appalling. As the AC notes: "Far from effectively aiding integration of the Roma, the practice of placing them in camps is liable to aggravate the socio-economic inequalities affecting them, to heighten the risk of discriminatory acts, and to strengthen negative stereotypes concerning them".[26] Consequently, the AC recommended abandoning the "model of separation in camps" and the adoption instead of a comprehensive and coherent strategy at the national level.[27] This lack of a coherent and consistent legislation at the national level has been identified by the AC as a major problem in Italy: in fact, although numerous laws exist at the regional level,[28] and various attempts have been made to adopt national legislation in relation to the Roma – including the

---

23 ACFC-Czech Republic (note 6), 7.

24 ACFC, Comments, Czech Republic, GVT/COM/INF/OP/II(2005)002, 26 October 2005, 14.

25 ACFC-Czech Republic (note 11), 29. Note that a groups of NGOs (*European Roma Rights Center, Life Together,* the *League of Human Rights* and the *Group of Women Harmed by Forced Sterilization*) have publicly denounced the fact that two years since the Czech Government expressed regret for individual sterilizations of Romani women, no effective steps have been taken to provide victims with adequate redress for the irreparable injuries suffered. To facilitate access to the justice system for Roma, the Council of Europe has launched a specific and targeted training to empower lawyers and Romani NGOs to access human rights at the national level. See, CoE, Follow-up to the Strasbourg Declaration on Roma. First Progress Report (Nov. 2010-Apr. 2011) by the Secretary General to the Council of Europe, SG/Inf(2011) 11 rev, 20 April 2011.

26 ACFC, 1st Opinion, Italy, adopted on 14 September 2001, ACFC/INF/OP/I(2002)007, 8.

27 Id. One of the most recent deadly incidents at a Romani camp in Italy occurred on 7 February 2011, when four Roma children aged between 4 and 11 were killed in a fire as they slept at their makeshift camp on the edge of Rome. See, *Corriere della sera,* Rom, I bimbi erano stati identificati, 14 February 2011.

28 See, ACFC, Comments, Italy, GVT/COM/III(2011)004, 30 May 2011, 27.

proposal to extend, with some adaptations, the scope of application of the existing national legislation on the protection of linguistic minorities (Law No. 482/99) to include Roma and Sinti[29] – no legislation on Roma and Sinti has been adopted thus far at the national level. Consequently, the Italian legal framework is extremely fragmented and incoherent; and what does exist focuses too much, according to the AC, "on social and immigration issues at the detriment of the promotion of their [Roma, Sinti and Travellers] identity, including their language and culture".[30] The Committee of Ministers has thus invited the Italian authorities to adopt "a comprehensive strategy of integration at [the] national level".[31] As the example of Spain suggests, a "high degree of decentralization and broad powers exercised by the Autonomous Communities" is seen by the Committee of Ministers as a crucial factor in the promotion of cultural identities and diversity, also *vis-à-vis* the Roma.[32] Thus in order to develop an efficient strategy for the inclusion of Roma, it is not necessary to have a centralized, top-down, set of powers, but, rather, a nation-wide framework coupled with a strong decentralization of competences can be an efficient and valuable strategy of inclusion.

Another country-specific issue, but one that feeds off a problem shared by many countries, concerns data collection in relation to minorities, particularly Roma. Data collection everywhere raises complex issues of ethics and privacy, and is prohibited in many countries of the European

---

29   The Law on the protection of Linguistic and Historic Minorities No. 482 of 15 December 1999, which entered into force in January 2000, aims at promoting the linguistic and cultural heritage of groups other than Italian, according to general principles set by European and international bodies. It recognizes the existence of and guarantees the language and culture of a list of minority groups, among which the Roma and Sinti are *not* included. This protection only applies within the territory of the regions or provinces concerned and under specific requirements. Individuals belonging to these linguistics minorities do not benefit from it outside these zones. The failure of the Italian authorities to adopt specific legislation for Roma is due to the "extremely complicated nature of the issue", ACFC-Italy (note 16), 20. The AC commented in response that "there appears to be no real will amongst main political forces in Italy to carry forward the project of developing a specific piece of legislation to protect the language, culture and identity of these persons", ACFC-Italy (note 14), 10. On a new proposal to extend the scope of application of Law No. 482/1999 on historical-linguistic minorities so as to include Roma and Sinti, see, Italian Parliament, Senato della Repubblica, Commissione straordinaria per la tutela e la promozione dei diritti umani, "Sintesi del rapporto conclusivo dell'indagine sulla condizione di Rom/Sinti e Caminanti in Italia", XVI Legislatura, 9 February 2011.

30   ACFC, 2nd Opinion, Italy, ACFC/INF/OP/II(2005)003, 25 October 2005, 5.

31   CoM, Resolution on the implementation of the FCNM by Italy, 14 June 2006, para.2.

32   COM, Resolution, Spain, ResCMN(2004)11, para 1.

Union.[33] However in Italy in particular, data collection has raised serious human rights concerns. In 2008, in camps located on the outskirts of Rome and Milan, identification procedures, carried out in co-operation with the Italian Red Cross, involved the fingerprinting of all Romani inhabitants of the camps, including children, recalling dreadful memories of the past when databases were created to exterminate minorities, including Roma.[34] These actions were heavily criticized by various international bodies,[35] including the Representative of the Government (*Prefetto*) in Rome, who publicly disagreed with the identification initiative, particularly as regarded the collection of fingerprints from minors.[36]

A further country-specific aspect concerning the protection of Roma as minorities is linked to the personal scope of application of the FCNM. When accepting the FCNM, the Dutch authorities, for example, declared that they would interpret the scope of application of the Convention by using a territorial criterion: as Roma communities are not specifically attached to any specific parts of the Dutch territory, according to this means of interpretation, the FCNM should not apply to them.[37] This approach has been criticized by the AC precisely because it excludes Romani communities – many of whom "have long ties with the Netherlands"[38] – from the protection of the FCNM

---

33   See, OLIVER DE SCHUTTER AND JULIE RINGELHEIM, ETHNIC MONITORING –
      THE PROCESSING OF RACIAL AND ETHNIC DATA IN ANTI-DISCRIMINATION
      POLICIES (2010).

34   See, Decreto del Presidente del Consiglio dei ministri (DPCM), "Dichiarazione dello
      stato di emergenza in relazione agli insediamenti di comunità nomadi nel territorio
      delle regioni Campania, Lazio e Lombardia", 21 May 2008. The decree declaring the
      state of emergency and authorizing the procedures to identify the Roma living in the
      camps was declared illegitimate by the Council of State in a decision of 16 November
      2011.

35   See, EU, European Parliament, Resolution on the Census of the Roma on the Basis of
      Ethnicity in Italy, 10 July 2008; CoE, Commissioner for Human Rights of the Council
      of Europe, Thomas Hammarberg, Memorandum following his visit to Italy on 19-20
      June 2008 (Issues reviewed: Roma and Sinti; Immigration), CommDH(2008)18, 28
      July 2008; For the AC, in particular, it was difficult to accept that this procedure
      could help improving the living conditions of the persons concerned or assist in
      ensuring full and effective equality in their respect (ACFC, 3rd Opinion, Italy, ACFC/
      OP/III(2010)008, 30 May 2011, 13).

36   See, *Corriere della sera* Impronte ai bimbi rom, stop della Ue, 27 June 2008. See, also,
      ACFC, 3rd Report, Italy, ACFC/SRIII (2009)011, 21 December 2009, 24, and ACFC-
      Italy (note 34), paras.54.

37   FCNM, List of Declarations, Status as of 30 June 2008, Declaration by the
      Netherlands, dated 16 February 2005, at http://conventions.coe.int. This approach
      means that for the Netherlands only the Frisians, a minority traditionally living in
      the north of the country, are covered by the scope of the FCNM.

38   ACFC-The Netherlands (note 10), 3.

provisions, which largely "do not imply that the minorities concerned live in their traditional or ancestral settlement areas".[39] The Dutch approach is particularly awkward given that the government accepts that Romani communities are covered by the scope of application of another relevant CoE legal instrument protecting regional and minority languages, namely the European Charter for Regional or Minority Languages, in which context the Dutch authorities have described the Romani languages spoken in the Netherlands as "expressions of the cultural wealth of the Netherlands".[40] It is yet to be seen whether the Netherlands will continue to follow its 'territorial interpretation' in its Second State Report that was due on 1 June 2011 but had not, at the time of writing, yet been submitted.

C. Specific country-related positive trends

In addition to the problems identified in the previous section as specific to some of the countries under consideration, there are also country-specific trends or developments that are positive in relation to the Roma, some of which are described here. For example, Finland has managed to achieve a significant level of involvement of Romani associations and individuals in decision-making processes at the national and local level. In a country where Roma are estimated as being approximately 10,000 individuals, equivalent to 0,1% of the total population,[41] it is remarkable that Finland has set up permanent regional advisory boards for Roma Affairs and, in 2004, has been a driving force behind the creation of the European Roma and Travellers Forum, an NGO founded by Roma and affiliated with the Council of Europe through a cooperation agreement.[42]

Moreover, Finland is setting positive trends in the context of housing: there are no camps or slums for Roma in Finland and instead Roma live in mainstream housing, though mainly dependent on public housing support. As a result of this large dependency on public housing, the Finnish authorities have developed a series of guidelines on *Housing in the Roma Culture* to assist public officers and social workers in better understanding the needs and

---

39   Id., 9.

40   European Charter for Regional or Minority Languages, 3rd Periodical Report by the Netherlands, MIN-LANG/PR(2007)7, 4 September 2007, 60.

41   ACFC, 1st Report, Finland, ACFC/SR(1999)003, 16 February 1999, 7.

42   See, Partnership Agreement between the CoE and the ERTF, 15 December 2004. CoM, Resolution, Finland, CM/ResCMN(2007)1, 31 January 2007, para.1 (a); ACFC, 2nd Report, Finland, ACFC/SR/II(2004) 012 E, received on 10 December 2004, 16.

requests of Roma, for example in relation to the allocation or switching of apartments etc.[43]

Beyond Finland, the Czech and Romanian authorities should also be acknowledged for the number and variety of initiatives for Roma, as illustrated by their state reports. These initiatives range from mediators to the publication of textbooks, from trainings to affirmative action, and all of them in different fields, from education to health, from housing to police force.[44] Clearly, this is not *per se* evidence of the effective protection of Roma. Instead it seems likely that, under pressure from EU accession procedures and the Copenhagen criteria, both countries have multiplied their initiatives on Roma by developing projects, consultative boards, cultural initiatives etc. Indeed, as it emerges from the AC Opinions and CoM Recommendations, these initiatives, though commendable, are generally insufficient for the full realization of human rights for Roma, particularly where the resources allocated for their implementation are limited, the coordination insufficient and a monitoring system to assess the targets achieved and obstacles encountered is inefficient. Despite the generally positive nature of these initiatives, then, it is possible to see this range of initiatives as little more than window dressing.[45]

In Romania, the authorities have introduced positive measures to promote access to university and upper secondary school for Roma.[46] This is part of an attempt to form an educated élite among Romanian Romani communities and it is coupled with various initiatives to protect and promote Roma cultural identity, such as the Romani language and literature studies section at the University of Bucharest, the courses set up to train teachers on Romani history and traditions and to train inspectors to monitor the quality of education given to Romani pupils.[47] These initiatives, while broadly positive, are however somewhat limited in scope. As the AC has noted, while there has been, as a result of the above measures, an increase in the number of Romani pupils studying their mother tongue and heightened interest in

---

43 Id., 35.

44 See, for instance, ACFC, 2nd Report, Romania, ACFC/SR/II(2005)004, 6 June 2005; ACFC, 3rd Report, Czech Republic, ACFC/SR/III(2010)008, 3 May 2010.

45 See, for instance, the Strategy to improve the situation of the Roma adopted by the Romanian Government in 2001 and the comments by the AC. ACFC, 2nd Opinion, Romania, ACFC/OP/II(2005)007, 23 February 2006, p. 12-13.

46 Id., 29. See, also, Analysis of the Impact of the Affirmative Action for Roma in High Schools, Vocational Trainings and Universities, Roma Education Fund/Gallup (2009), at http://www.romadecade.org/files/ftp/Gallup_Romania_english.pdf.

47 Id., ACFC, 2nd Opinion, Romania, 31.

studying the language among the Romani community, the opportunity to benefit from these programmes remains restricted to a limited proportion of the Romani population that might potentially be interested in participating.[48]

In protecting and promoting Romani culture and language, the work of cultural institutes and consultative bodies are crucial. Spain and the Netherlands, among others, have developed positive practices in this regard. Spain has set up an Institute of Roma Culture specifically in charge of protecting and promoting the distinct culture and identity of Roma nationwide,[49] as well as a State Council of the Roma People that is an inter-ministerial consultative and advisory body institutionalizing cooperation between Romani associations and the Spanish General State Administration in relation to the development of social welfare policies based on the full promotion of the Romani population.[50] Likewise, the Netherlands Institute for Sinti and Roma has been working as a centre of expertise for Roma and Sinti since 2009.[51] This initiative, however, has not spared the Dutch authorities from strong criticism from both the AC and the Committee of Ministers for the "overall tone of the public discourse in the Netherlands and the new integration policy, with its particular focus on the preservation of the Dutch identity, [that has] had negative consequences on the preservation of a climate of mutual understanding between the majority population and the ethnic minorities".[52]

Finally, in this short overview of country-specific positive actions, it is worth mentioning a unique action of support for housing created by the Italian Ministry of Labor, Health and Social Policies, and which involves the self-recovery and self-build housing projects involving Roma and Sinti communities.[53] Under the project, the beneficiaries receive specific training in construction and bricklaying and a salary to construct their own dwellings, for which they then pay a monthly rent fixed by the authorities.[54]

---

48   Id., 32.

49   CoM, Resolution, Spain, CM/ResCMN(2008)1, 2 April 2008, para.1(a).

50   ACFC, 3rd Report, Spain ACFC/SR/III(2010)011, 23 August 2010, 24.

51   ACFC, Comments, The Netherlands, GVT/COM/I(2010)001, 17 February 2010, 4

52   ACFC, 1st Opinion, The Netherlands, 25 June 2009 (10), 3. See also, CoM, Resolution, The Netherlands, CM/ResCMN(2010)3,12 January 2011, para.1.

53   See, ACFC, 3rd Report, Italy, ACFC/SR/III(2009)011, 21 December 2009, 22. See, also, ACFC-Italy (note 28), 16.

54   For details, see, Udo C. Enwereuzor/Laura Di Pasquale, Housing conditions of Roma and Travellers in Italy, Thematic Study, COSPE/RAXEN National Focal Point, Italy, paras.100-101 (March 2009).

III. General Comments of the Advisory Committee on the Roma

The most important comment that recurs in the Opinions of the Advisory Committee in relation to the Roma is perhaps the need for state parties to adopt coherent national strategies on different aspects of Romani living conditions complemented by adequate budgets, clear targets and monitoring procedures for evaluating progresses.[55] The central element of these strategies must be a combination of respect for the identity and culture of Romani communities and their integration into mainstream societies without assimilation.[56] The holistic approach advocated by the AC is best summarized in its comment that the "preservation and affirmation of Roma cultural identity will succeed only if the authorities' efforts to effectively improve the social and economic position of Roma, and limit their marginalization and social exclusion, are also successful".[57]

The difficult task of combining in practice these two apparently conflicting principles – respect for identity and integration into mainstream society – is illustrated by the State report of the Czech Republic, in which the authorities noted that as housing is a social problem rather than a minority issue, it does not fall under the office in charge of ethnic minorities – the National Minority Committee – which "should not end up doing the work of the local social services department without proper expertise".[58] Yet, the AC has consistently argued that housing and other forms of social and economic participation for Roma cannot be separated from the protection and promotion of their culture and identity, as minority rights are not only a matter of folkloristic

---

55   See also, EU Framework for National Roma Integration Strategies up to 2020, COM (2011) 173 final, 5 April 2011.

56   Along with other state parties, the Czech Republic has claimed the combination of identity and integration as the ambitious goal of its "Concept of Government Policy towards Members of the Romany Community". ACFC- Czech Republic (note 24), 26. See also, CoE, The Strasbourg Declaration on Roma (CM(2010)133 final, 20 October 2010; EU, The Ten Common Basic Principles for Roma Inclusion (Commission Staff Working Document, Roma in Europe: The Implementation of EU Instruments and Policies for Roma Inclusion: Progress Report 2008-2010, SEC(2010)400 final, 7 April 2010, Annex); CoE, PACE Resolution 1740 (2010), The situation of Roma in Europe and relevant activities of the Council of Europe (note 2), 2; ECRI General Policy Recommendation no. 13 on Combating Anti-Gypsyism and Discrimination against Roma (24 June 2011).

57   See, ACFC, 2nd Opinion, Czech Republic, ACFC/INF/OP/II(2005)002, 26 October 2005, 19.

58   ACFC, 3rd Report, Czech Republic, ACFC/SR/III(2010)008, 3 May 2010, 27.

events, but economic, social and political participation are also substantial and pivotal elements of minority protection.[59] Strong co-operation between the authorities and ministries responsible for the various aspects of Romani protection and integration is thus urgently required.

An extensive range of policies both on and for Roma are a positive factor for the protection of this particular minority but, as suggested in the previous section, the existence of such policies are obviously not sufficient *per se*. Indeed, states that are praised by the FCNM organs for the number and variety of policies are also those that often have significant problems in implementing them. A recurrent problem identified in this respect is that most of these initiatives are conceived at the national level through a top-down process. Such initiatives, however, are always necessarily implemented at the local level where, partly as a result of this top-down approach, there is often a lack of political willingness to implement them effectively. And yet, reforms involving the decentralization of administrative competences to the local level may be detrimental to the protection of the Roma, as the discretion of the local authorities then acquires an even more significant role. The AC has thus suggested that strategies and broad policies should be coordinated and overseen at the national level, but designed and discussed with the local authorities and specifically tailored for communities on the basis of the local context and needs.[60]

Schooling and education is an area in which most countries examined under the FCNM find it particularly difficult to create a balance between identity and integration. The AC consistently refers to the CoM's Recommendations on the education of Romani pupils,[61] in which the Committee underlined the importance of state parties developing comprehensive policies in the field of education "based on the acknowledgment that the issue of schooling for Roma/Gypsy children is linked with a wide range of other factors and pre-conditions, namely the economic, social and cultural aspects, and the fight against racism and discrimination".[62] More precisely, the Committee has indicated that, as guiding principles of an education policy for Roma children, pre-school education schemes, better communication with parents, the use of

---

59 See, Art. 15 FCNM on effective participation in cultural, economic and social life and in public affairs.

60 See, in particular, ACFC-Czech Republic (note 6), 38.

61 CoE, Committee of Ministers, Recommendation No. R(2000)4 on the Education for Roma/Gypsy children in Europe, 3 February 2000.

62 Id., para.7.

mediators where necessary,[63] broader intercultural policies, culturally-specific training for teachers, involvement of Roma at all levels of the design, implementation and monitoring of education policies for Romani pupils.[64]

Indeed, the involvement of minorities, at individual and group level and at various policy-making levels and across all fields of social and economic life, is considered by the Advisory Committee to be a crucial element in achieving positive integration of minorities more generally, and the Roma in particular. It is, however, clear that only authentic forms of involvement in decision-making, policy design, implementation and monitoring, in other words, forms of effective participation and institutionalized dialogue at all levels, can lead to improvements in the integration and inclusion of Roma communities.[65]

IV. The Impact of the FCNM on the Protection of Roma

The FCNM system is the only pan-European supra-national mechanism in which state parties are required to give account of their policies on minorities, including on the Roma. Following the completion of the most recent EU accession period (2004-2007), the only mechanism existing at the European level specifically devoted to minority protection that remains is the monitoring system established under the FCNM. The FCNM therefore represents a useful tool for the protection of minorities, by keeping attention focused on the minority issues at the national and European level, especially through the pressure exerted by NGOs, the media and civil society more generally. The importance placed on the Roma in the work of the FCNM

---

63 On mediators, see, the reference to the European Roma Mediators Training Programme (ROMED), in CoE, Follow-up to the Strasbourg Declaration on Roma (note 25).

64 CoE, Recommendation No. R(2000)4 (note 60), Appendix.

65 See, for instance, ACFC-The Netherlands (note 10), 27. See, ACFC, Thematic Commentary on the Effective Participation of Persons Belonging to National Minorities in Cultural, Social and Economic Life and in Public Affairs, ACFC/31DOC(2008)001, 27 February 2008. The Commentary gives a broad definition of "effectiveness" of participation, essentially based on the "impact on the situation of the persons concerned and on the society as a whole" (para.18). Thus, the participation is effective when it "has a substantial influence on decisions which are taken" and if "there is, as far as possible, a shared ownership of the decision taken" (para.19). See, also, Francesco Palermo, *The Dual Meaning of Participation: The Advisory Committee's Commentary to Article 15 of the FCNM* 7 EUROPEAN YEARBOOK OF MINORITY ISSUES 409-424 (2007/8).

organs – the Advisory Committee and the Council of Ministers – is evident from the number of recommendations and comments elaborated by these organs in the context of the state reports analyzed in this paper.[66]

Moreover, it is possible to identify a number of improvements, albeit that those improvements are limited, as a result of the FCNM mechanism,[67] especially in those countries that have structured their documents for the Framework Convention by providing specific replies to the comments and recommendations of the Advisory Committee and the Council of Ministers.[68] For instance, the decision by the Italian authorities to comply with the invitation of the AC to include Roma and Sinti within the scope of application of the FCNM,[69] the increased awareness of the Czech authorities concerning the problem of sterilization of Romani women without their free consent,[70] or the decision by the Dutch authorities to enter into consultation with the Roma community at least twice a year from 2010 onwards following the specific AC comment in this regard.[71]

More broadly, the impact of the FCNM on the protection of minorities, and notably on the Roma, has resulted in a general increase in the awareness among national authorities of the cultural diversity of the Roma that deserves attention and respect, a pressure to monitor and assess results and progress of projects and initiatives, including clear targets, that carried out by different actors within the public administration; further, the FCNM has been successful in pushing the adoption of comprehensive national strategies for the overall improvement of conditions for the Roma in combination with the protection and promotion of Romani culture and identities. The AC comment

---

66 See, for instance, CoM, Resolution, Italy (note 31), para.2, in which 3 out of 7 recommendations addressed specifically Roma and Sinti; CoM, Resolution, Romania, CM/ResCMN(2007)8, 23 May 2007, para.2, in which 4 out of 9 recommendations specifically refer to the Roma.

67 A complex set of political, legal and judicial indicators to measure the impact of the FCNM has been developed by the European Academy (EURAC) at the request of the Secretariat of the FCNM. See, www.eurac.edu/en/research/ projects/ProjectDetails. aspx?pid=8390.

68 See, for instance, ACFC-Czech Republic (note 24); ACFC, Comments, Finland, GVT/COM/II(2006)004, 22 August 2006.

69 ACFC-Italy (note 16).

70 See, ACFC-Czech Republic (note 24), paras.48-54.

71 See, ACFC-The Netherlands, 25 June 2009 (note 10), 24; ACFC, Comments, The Netherlands, 17 February 2010 (note 50), 4. Note, nevertheless, the recommendation of the CoM, in which it stated that "since Roma policy in the Netherlands is largely delegated to local authorities (…) dialogue between the Roma and Sinti and the national authorities is limited and should be further developed" CoM, Resolution, The Netherlands, CM/ResCMN(2010)3,12 January 2011, para.1.

on the 2004 Italian report is paradigmatic in this regard: "[t]he existing statutory provisions on the Roma, Sinti and Travellers adopted by several regions are clearly inadequate in that they are disparate, lack coherence and focus too much on social questions and immigration issues at the detriment of the promotion of their identity including their language and culture".[72] The approach of the Finnish authorities regarding the teaching of Romanes and Roma culture is exemplary in this respect, even though the authorities acknowledge that the arrangements for teaching Romanes are available in only 5% of Finnish schools with Roma pupils – an unsatisfactory situation that is mainly due to the difficulty in meeting the group size requirement, a lack of teachers and an inadequate supply of textbooks:

> "On account of the social integration of the Roma population (…), issues pertaining to their education and the maintenance of their unique linguistic and cultural heritage shall be paid attention to in basic education too. (…) The instruction must provide Roma pupils a natural medium for expressing their own personal minority identity also at school. Roma education must lead to improved knowledge of the history and language of the Roma people among Roma pupils and contribute to their awareness of the Roma as one of the most important minorities in Europe and in the entire world".[73]

However, despite these achievements, the FCNM system suffers similar flaws to almost all international monitoring treaty-bodies that are based on state reports: firstly, the lack of a specific mechanism to impose implementation; and, secondly, the length of the monitoring process – from the state report until the CoM Recommendation – which often ends with no immediate and concrete results. The FCNM mechanism is in fact characterized by the involvement of two different bodies: the Advisory Committee, composed by experts from state parties that sit in the Committee in a personal capacity, and the Committee of Ministers, a political organ composed by Ministers (or their substitutes) of contracting states, whose decisions are often influenced by geo-political expediency. In lacking a system of sanctions, the FCNM machinery is mainly based on the tenet *pacta sunt servanda* that member states undertake to respect upon ratification of the Framework Convention. It is clear therefore that one of the major factors influencing the implementation of the FCNM is represented by the political pressure exerted on the Member

---

72   ACFC-Italy (note 14), 5.
73   ACFC-Finland (note 8), 79.

States by the Council of Europe, mainly through the Committee of Ministers and other European and Euro-Atlantic institutions, notably the European Union and the OSCE.

In terms of improvements and changes in the minority protection, the impact of the FCNM can thus be measured, as seen earlier, either as long-term and (though limited) short-term, immediate results as well as in the combined pressure exerted by the European system, composed of the Council of Europe,[74] the European Union[75] and the OSCE, as a whole.[76] In this regard, a valuable and constructive part of this combined European system is the interplay between the FCNM and the European Court of Human Rights. The latter refers increasingly in its judgements to the FCNM and, specifically, to the opinions of the Advisory Committee in order to provide evidence of specific obligations or, more generally, of trends particularly in the field of linguistic, cultural and religious diversity which are discernible in the practice of Members States as regards their increasing obligations towards their Romani, Sinti and Traveller communities.[77]

---

74 See, *inter alia*, within the Council of Europe: the adoption of the Strasbourg Declaration on Roma (note 25) that includes guiding principles and priorities; the creation on 16 February 2011 of a new Committee of Experts (CAHROM) that has upgraded the intergovernmental work on Roma Issues to be answerable directly to the Committee of Ministers; the new position, since November 2010, of a Special Representative of the Secretary General for Roma Issues, held currently by Jeroen Schokkenbroek.

75 See, *inter alia*, within the European Union: the setting up of the Platform for Roma Inclusion that is a mechanism of governance in which key actors – EU institutions, national governments, international organizations, NGOs and experts – can interact with a view to exchanging experience and good practice; the adoption of the Ten Common Basic Principles for Roma Inclusion (note 55) and of the Framework for National Roma Integration Strategies up to 2020 (note 54).

76 For the OSCE, see the work of the Office of the High Commissioner on National Minorities and its early warning and early action mechanisms, at www.osce.org/hcnm.

77 On the linkage between the judgments of the European Court of Human Rights and other legal instruments on the protection of minority rights, see Eur. Court H.R., *Sidiropoulos v. Greece*, Judgement of 10 July 1998, Application No. 26695/95. See also the so-called UK Gypsy cases: Eur. Court H.R., *Chapman v. the U.K.*, Judgement of 18 January 2001, Application No. 27238/95; Eur. Court H.R., *Beard v. the U.K.*, Judgement of 18 January 2001, Application No. 24882/94; Eur. Court H.R., *Coster v. the U.K.*, Judgement of 18 January 2001, Application No. 24876/94; Eur. Court H.R., *Lee v. the U.K.*, Judgement of 18 January 2001, Application No. 25289/94; Eur. Court H.R., *Jane Smith v. the U.K.*, Judgement of 18 January 2001, Application No. 25154/94, in which the Strasbourg Court, by referring to the Framework Convention, acknowledged that "there may be said to be an emerging international consensus amongst the contracting states of the Council of Europe recognising the special needs of minorities and an obligation to protect their security, identity and

V. Concluding Remarks: Balancing Diversity and Inclusion

It has been suggested in this chapter that the most significant policy recommendation that has emerged from the FCNM mechanism is that strategies, policies and measures for minority protection should be guided by two general principles, namely respect for diversity and inclusion. Combining these two, apparently conflicting, principles presents major difficulties for European societies in conceptual, practical and policy terms. Where states promote only inclusion, the risk is that they will alienate minorities and provoke resistance at the same time that they damage the cultural diversity that represents the wealth of contemporary societies. If they privilege diversity, however, they risk increasing marginalisation and exclusion.

It has been argued that the logic of policies focusing on diversity encourages the "fragmentation of the national community into a quarrelsome spatter of enclaves, ghettoes, tribes ... encouraging and exalting cultural and linguistic apartheid".[78] Schlesinger, for instance, has claimed that diversity policies rest upon a 'cult of ethnicity' which "exaggerates differences, intensifies resentments and antagonisms, drives even deeper the awful wedges between races and nationalities. The endgame is self-pity and self-ghettoization".[79] In this view, while policies fostering diversity may have noble and sincere intentions – to create a more inclusive and just society – they are likely to have dire consequences in practice, encouraging ethnic separatism and ethnic ghettos, resulting in individual societies becoming increasingly unstable. Yet, the failure to adopt policies that protect and promote identities and diversity may also create the serious risk of marginalisation. For example, without some form of affirmative action, fewer Roma are likely to feel that they have a realistic chance at succeeding within mainstream institutions: only these policies can realistically be seen as helping to fight the potential sources of marginalisation. Moreover, it is perhaps more correct to argue, from the historical experience of discrimination against minorities, that it is not diversity policies as

---

lifestyle, not only for the purpose of safeguarding the interests of the minorities themselves but to preserve a cultural diversity of value to the whole community" (*Chapman v. the U.K.,* para. 92). See also, Eur. Court H.R., *Sejdović and Finci v. BiH,* Judgement of 22 December 2009, Application Nos. 27996/06 and 34836/06, on the ineligibility to stand for election to the House of Peoples and the Presidency of Bosnia and Herzegovina for Roma and Jews.

78 ARTHUR SCHLESINGER, THE DISUNITING OF AMERICA (W.W. Norton, 1992), 137.

79 *Id.*

such that lead to conflict in society but the suppression of the identity of minorities and their social, political and economic exclusion on the basis of belonging to an ethnic, religious, linguistic or religious minority that can spark violence and tensions.[80] People may be fearful of diversity and its consequences, but it is more likely that it is the opposition to diversity polarise societies and fuels social tensions, rather than the adoption of diversity policies.

The impoverishment and marginalisation of the Roma is clearly more complicated than a question of respect for their diversity; not least, because their socio-economic conditions are also deeply entwined with discrimination and the lack of equal opportunity policies. Policies and strategies designed to redress the inequitable position of Roma and to combat formal and substantial forms of discrimination are also just as essential. Obviously, this is not only a matter of just adopting anti-discrimination measures but also implementing them effectively, particularly by respecting both the spirit and letter of the law.

In addition to the long- and short-term impact as well as the pressure exerted by the ACFC through the pan-European system (CoE, EU and OSCE) on all European States *vis-á-vis* the protection of the Roma that has to combine cultural identity and socio-economic dimensions, the role that the FCNM can play in this regard has not yet been fully explored. An important factor in using the Framework Convention to enhance the cultural and socio-economic protection of Roma concerns the increased involvement in the work of the FCNM of Roma themselves, as well as minority associations, researchers, academics, social workers and others, who, at different levels and in different ways, work on and for the Roma.[81] Such involvement is already possible through the so-called Shadow Reports that Third Parties can submit to the Advisory Committee regarding a country and/or specific aspects of minority protection. In this way, it is possible not only to provide additional information to the AC, but also to exert pressure on and increase visibility of Roma issues at the European, national and local level. Strengthening the involvement of civil society, for instance, by encouraging and supporting the submission of Shadow Reports that so far have been rather few and unevenly

---

80 See, UNDP, Cultural Liberty in Today's Diverse World, Human Development Report 2004.

81 Note that for the thematic commentary on participation (ACFC/31DOC(2008)011, 5 May 2008) as well as the forthcoming commentary on language rights, a consultation process was organized by the Secretariat of the FCNM involving civil society and NGOs.

submitted, will assure that this important legal mechanism devoted to the protection of minorities maintains its instrumental role for the emancipation, protection and advocacy of Roma rights in Europe.

Chapter 5

Enforcing Fundamental Rights in the European Union After the Treaty of Lisbon: What Can the Roma Case Tell Us?

Elise Muir and Mark Dawson*

I. Introduction

The extensive row between France and the European Commission over the removal of EU citizens of Roma origin in the summer of 2010 created a wave of media and academic attention in Europe.[1] In September, citizens across Europe were shocked to hear about the mass relocation of individuals identified by direct reference to their ethnic origin (Roma, primarily of Romanian origin[2]) from France.

In a speech on criminality and illegal migration from late July 2010 – following the death of a person in a car pursuit with the police, and riots in Grenoble – the French President, Nicolas Sarkozy, requested the evacuation of illegal Roma campgrounds.[3] By the end of August, an official statement by the immigration minister, Mr Besson, confirmed that 128 illegal settlements

* Associate Professor of EU Law and Marie Curie Fellow, Maastricht Law Faculty; Professor of European Law and Governance, Hertie School of Governance. This chapter was previously published as, 'Individual, Institutional and Collective Vigilance in Protecting Fundamental Rights in the EU: Lessons from the Roma', 48 CMLR 3, 751 (2011). Our thanks to Kluwer Law International for their permission to re-publish the article in this volume, as well as to the participants and organisers of the conference held in Brussels in March 2012, which inspired this collection. This article was last updated in June 2012.

1 To give but two examples: Stanley Pignal, "Brussels condemns France over Roma" (14.9.2010) *The Financial Times* and "France v the world: How the Romani row has dented France's international standing" (23.9.2010) *The Economist*.

2 La Ligue des Droits de l'Homme, "Report to the Committee on the Elimination of Racial Discrimination – Office of the United Nations High Commissioner for Human Rights" (11-12.8.2010, available at: http://www2.ohchr.org/english/bodies/cerd/docs/ngos/LDH_france77.pdf), point 97.

3 French President Nicolas Sarkozy, "Prise de fonction du nouveau préfet" (Grenoble, 30.7.2010).

had been closed down, and that 979 Bulgarian and Romanian citizens had been repatriated since the end of July (151 of them forcibly and 828 through "voluntary" returns, i.e. with financial support).[4] These events were followed, in early September, by the release of a *Circulaire* from the Ministère de l'Intérieur, de l'Outre-Mer et des Collectivités territoriales, dated 5 August 2010, in which the Romani population was directly identified as the target of removal procedures.[5]

While they at first responded to these developments with silence,[6] the Commission[7] and the European Parliament[8] responded to France's activities in September with stern disapproval. Yet after several weeks of intensive political discussions – and even a full blown "war of words" between the Commission and several French ministers – the Commission announced, in early October, that it would not be taking legal action against France "*for the time being*".[9, 10]

Several experts have explored the conformity of the French relocation campaign with European Union law.[11] The main grounds for review identified

---

4   Ministre de l'immigration, de l'intégration, de l'identité nationale et du développement solidaire, Eric Besson, Press conference "A propos de l'évacuation des campements illicites" (Paris, 30.8.2010).

5   Ministère de l'Interieur, de l'Outre-Mer et des Collectivités Territoriales, Circulaire "Evacuation des campements illicites" (IOC/K/1017881/J, 5.8.2010).

6   See e.g. Groupe d'Information et de Soutien des Immigrés (GISTI), "Plainte contre la France pour violation du droit communautaire en matière de libre circulation des personnes du 31 juillet 2008" (20.8.2010, available at: www.gisti.org), in which this very well-established organisation re-calls the urgency of the situation and the existence of early complaints brought to the attention of the European Commission and nevertheless left unanswered.

7   Especially the statement by Viviane Reding, Vice-President of the European Commission, of 14 September 2010 (available at: http://europa.eu/rapid/pressReleasesAction.do?reference=SPEECH/10/428).

8   European Parliament, Resolution on the situation of Roma and on freedom of movement in the European Union (9.9.2010, available at: www.europarl.europa.eu).

9   European Commission press release on recent developments in France (29.9.2010) and Statement by Viviane Reding, Vice-President of the European Commission (19.10.2010).

10 Several accounts of the facts have now been written. E.g.: Zoé Luca, *Roma and France: the Commission's response*, 17 MAASTRICHT JOURNAL OF EUROPEAN AND COMPARATIVE LAW 3 (2011) and Yasha Maccanico, *France: Collective expulsions of Roma people undermines EU's founding principles* 20/2 STATEWATCH JOURNAL (November 2010).

11 E.g. Jean-Philippe Lhernould, *L'éloignement des Roms et la directive 2004/38 relative au droit de séjour des citoyens de l'UE*, 11 DROIT SOCIAL 1024 (Novembre 2010) and for a broader overview of the phenomenon of discrimination against the Roma population in France: Antoine Math, *Roms et autres: la protection sociale des ressortissants communautaires*, 11 DROIT SOCIAL 1037 (Novembre 2010).

by the Commission were breaches of the free movement provisions as laid down in Directive 2004/38 and the prevention of discrimination on grounds of nationality or on account of belonging to an ethnic minority.[12] While a legal analysis of the measures against the Roma people is of great practical relevance for victims and stakeholders, this will not be the primary question addressed in this article.

Instead, this article will use the recent dispute between the Commission and France as a test case to address a broader question: what is the added value of European Union intervention in the field of fundamental rights? The case of the Roma provides new answers to the age-old question of the additional value that EU input into fundamental rights questions can bring in addition to the numerous other protections offered both through national constitutional frameworks and through the system of rights and remedies provided by the ECHR system. In fact, the Roma are perhaps the first *truly European* vulnerable minority justifying (although *a posteriori*) the need for EU anti-discrimination legislation.

Current EU law provides a three-fold approach to the integration of the Roma population in Europe: anti-discrimination law is designed to facilitate integration in both (i) the State of origin and (ii) the host State, while (iii) free movement rules allow EU citizens to freely choose[13] the Member State of the EU in which they wish to reside. Roma citizens should be protected against discrimination in the exercise of such a right to free movement. Since the expiry of the implementation period for the Citizenship[14] and Race Directives,[15] EU law provides for this remarkable three-fold set of rights. This article does not seek to develop a substantive analysis of these provisions but instead uses possible infringements of these rights as an opportunity to test the mechanisms necessary to set such rights in motion.

---

12 European Commission, Assessment of recent developments in France (press release, 29.9.2010) para. 2.

13 This right is subject to the limits and conditions laid down in the Treaties as well as in EU secondary law (see Art. 21(1) TFEU and EC Directive 2004/38 OF 29 April 2004 O.J. 2004, L 158/77)

14 Directive 2004/38, id. Note that citizens from Romania and Bulgaria are still covered by transitory arrangements. See for e.g. Lhernould, (note 2), and Arrêté du 18 janvier 2008 relatif à la délivrance, sans opposition de la situation de l'emploi, des autorisations de travail aux ressortissants des Etats de l'Union Européenne soumis à des dispositions transitoires (NOR: IMID0800327A) that provides for a list of 150 activities for which the existing situation on the labour market cannot be opposed to Bulgarian and Romanian nationals.

15 EC Directive 2000/43 of 29 June 2000, O.J. 2000, L 180/22.

Reflecting on the Roma example asks challenging questions regarding *who is responsible for monitoring and remedying fundamental rights violations in the EU*, and how the system of fundamental rights protection the EU offers *may carry under-realised strengths and weaknesses*. While EU anti-discrimination law has developed a myriad of individual enforcement mechanisms, they may prove to be insufficient to protect vulnerable minorities. In this context, mechanisms like the infringement action of Art. 258 TFEU provide a useful remedy to address rights violations that economically weak and political disenfranchised groups may not be able to enforce themselves. Nevertheless, the Roma crisis also potentially illustrates the ambiguity of that procedure as one that both aims to address *legal* violations yet may also lead to solutions open to political negotiation.

The Roma example therefore illustrates well the need for a *hybrid* system of fundamental rights protection in the EU – a system, as suggested by Grainne De Búrca,[16] that is monitored both through the Courts and by a myriad of networks, NGOs and other monitoring bodies.[17] Drawing inspiration from Bell's approach to the enforcement of fundamental rights[18] and Tomkins' approach to the enforcement of EU law,[19] this essay proposes a three-fold analysis of (I) individual vigilance, (II) institutional vigilance and (III) collective vigilance to enhance the protection of fundamental rights in the EU.

It is argued that in order to ensure adequate protection of non-discrimination rights in the EU, the existing system of dual vigilance based on individual litigation at national level combined with enforcement action initiated by the Commission, needs to be complemented by an intermediate 'collective' level. Such a collective level of vigilance not only uses NGOs and/or equality bodies as intermediaries to enhance individual and institutional enforcement, but also entitles NGOs and/or other organisations representing

---

16 Grainne De Búrca, *EU Race Discrimination Law: a Hybrid Model?* in Law and New Governance in the EU and the US (De Búrca and Scott, 2006) 97.

17 The combination of such techniques is acknowledged by EU institutions. See, for example, European Parliament, Resolution on the situation of Roma and on freedom of movement in the European Union (9.9.2010, available at: www.europarl.europa. eu).

18 Marc Bell, Walking in the Same Direction? *The Contribution of the European Social Charter and the European Union to Combating Discrimination*, in Social Rights in Europe 273 (De Búrca and De Witte eds., 2005).

19 Adam Tompkins, *Of Institutions and Individuals: The Enforcement of EC Law*, in Law and Administration in Europe – Essays in Honour of Carol Harlow 276 (Craig and Rawlings, 2003).

collective interests to ensure collective enforcement of EU fundamental rights.

II. The Strengths and Limits of Individual Vigilance

EU law establishes a legal system that has uniquely relied on individuals to enforce, through litigation, the rights laid down in the founding EU Treaties. It is the very ability of individuals to be the bearer of rights that distinguishes the EU from most international organisations. As the EU has developed free movement principles, and an autonomous anti-discrimination policy, so individuals have made use of these rights to challenge both conflicting national laws, and to hold to account the EU institutions themselves.

In one of the most renowned extracts from EU case-law, the Court of Justice asserted that *"the vigilance of individuals concerned to protect their rights amounts to an effective supervision in addition to the supervision entrusted [...] to the diligence of the Commission and of the Member States"*.[20] This statement gained considerable significance as EU law developed as a legal order regulating increasingly diverse areas of individual lives. EU social and equality law has for many years been a fruitful source of constitutional development.[21] The direct effect of EU law has, for example, recently been pushed to new limits whenever individuals sought to enforce their rights not to be discriminated against before national courts on the basis of EU law.[22]

This development has also been pushed forward legislatively. A set of recent Directives provide for a coherent approach to issues of remedies and enforcement designed to *"put into effect in the Member States the principle of equal treatment"*.[23] Member States of the European Union have been placed under a duty, not only to refrain from violating EU fundamental rights,[24] but also to adopt positive measures, making available the legal remedies necessary to ensure the effectiveness of EU anti-discrimination law through individual litigation. Numerous authors have pointed out the strength of the novel model

---

20 Case 26/62, Van Gend & Loos, ECR English special edition 1.

21 Tamara Hervey, *Thirty years of EU sex equality law: looking backwards, looking forwards*, 14 MJ 2, 319 (2005).

22 Case C-144/04, *Mangold*, [2005] ECR I-9981 and Case 555/07, *Kücükdeveci*, judgement of 19 January 2010, nyr. See Elise Muir, *Of Ages in – and Edges of – EU Law*, 47 CMLR 6 (2010).

23 Race Equality Directive (note 16), Art.1.

24 Case C-260/89, ERT, [1991] ECR I-2925.

of EU anti-discrimination law developed by the Race, Framework[25] and new Sex Equality[26] Directives (hereinafter the Equal Treatment Directives).[27]

It has been observed that the Equality Directives are particularly *"prescriptive"*[28] in so far as they provide detailed rules to ensure the effectiveness of the rights guaranteed. The burden of proof on the claimant ought to be partly shifted.[29] Judicial remedies for the enforcement of these rights must be made available by the Member States.[30] Furthermore, a system of sanctions, which may include compensation to the victim, must also be created so as to ensure that sanctions against violation are effective, proportionate and dissuasive.[31] In addition, the said Directives seek to ensure dissemination of information[32] and to provide protection for individuals against victimization.[33]

The very point of these rights, in particular as set out in the Equal Treatment Directives, is that they may come to the aid of marginalised and victimised groups. Although the Citizenship Directive is less detailed, it also provides for a clear set of procedural safeguards and mechanisms to ensure judicial review and redress procedures in case free movement rights are restrained in contravention to EU free movement rules.[34] Greater difficulties, however, may be presented when one is dealing with a group that has little access to individual legal remedies. What if we are dealing with a group of individuals who are both highly mobile, yet also highly under-resourced? What if these individuals are both severe victims of discrimination, yet also among the group of EU citizens least informed of the rights provided to them under national and European law? In such circumstances, the unique reliance of the EU on systems of individual enforcement may become a weakness rather than an advantage.[35]

---

25 EC Directive 2000/78 f 27 November 2000, O.J. 2000, L 303/16.

26 EC Directive 2004/113 of 13 December 2004, O.J. 2004, L 373/37 and Recast Directive 2006/54 of 5 July 2006 O.J. 2006, L 204/23.

27 De Burca, EU Race Discrimination Law: a Hybrid Model? (note 16) and Lisa Waddington and Marc Bell, *More equal than others: distinguishing European Union equality directives*, 38 CMLR 587, 608 (2001).

28 Takis Tridimas, THE GENERAL PRINCIPLES OF EC LAW 72, 2nd ed., (2006).

29 Race Equality Directive (note 15), Art. 8.

30 Id., Art. 15.

31 Id., Art. 15.

32 Id., Art. 10.

33 Id., Art. 9.

34 Citizens' Directive (note 13), Arts. 30, 31 and 15(1).

35 For an analysis from the perspective of EU judicial remedies and procedural law:

For example, available empirical evidence suggests that the Roma are indeed a group marginalised from childhood. According to the latest pan-European report on the implementation of EU anti-discrimination law in the 27 Member States, segregation against Roma children at school is widespread in the EU. Furthermore, there are only limited instances where the practice of segregating classes has actually been challenged in Court.[36]

Individuals who are marginalised as a consequence of their ethnic origin may lack the resources or abilities to seek remedies against discrimination via national or EU courts. Similarly, the 2010 summer crisis illustrates that procedures designed to remove marginalised groups from the territory may be implemented so quickly that individuals are deprived in practice from the possibility to individually challenge the legality of their removal.[37] It appears that individual enforcement mechanisms may be ill-suited to both the specific needs of vulnerable minorities and to the scale of certain violations of EU law. Hence the need to turn to mechanisms of enforcement provided by the EU institutions and complemented through a multi-dimensional approach to the integration of Roma peoples.

III. The Potential for Institutional Vigilance in the EU

This very 'gap' in fundamental rights protection at the same time points to the added value of EU intervention in the field of fundamental rights in addition to the existence of enforceable legislation. The EU is equipped with mechanisms of *institutional* enforcement.[38] In the case of fundamental rights,

---

see by analogy Tompkins, Of Institutions and Individuals (note 20); for an analysis from the perspective of EU fundamental rights and substantive law: see Sandra Fredman, *Discrimination Law in the EU: Labour Market Regulation or Fundamental Rights?*, in LEGAL REGULATION OF THE EMPLOYMENT RELATION 183 (Collins, Davies, and Rideout, 2000).

36   ISABELLE CHOPIN AND EIRINI-MARIA GOUNARI, DEVELOPING ANTI-DISCRIMINATION LAW IN EUROPE: THE 27 MEMBER STATES COMPARED (November 2009, available at: http://www.non-discrimination.net/en/publications) 42.

37   This has been pointed out by numerous NGOs, e.g. La Ligue des Droits de l'Homme, Report to the Committee on the Elimination of Racial Discrimination – Office of the United Nations High Commissioner for Human Rights (11-12.8.2010, available at: http://www2.ohchr.org/english/bodies/cerd/docs/ngos/LDH_france77.pdf), para. 108.

38   Individual and institutional vigilance mechanisms are complementary. Complaints from individual citizens and businesses for example are an important source of information for the European Commission to become aware of infringements of EU law in the Member States.

the two primary mechanisms in this regard are the procedure for suspension of voting and other rights contained in Art. 7 TEU, and the enforcement action, prosecuted by the Commission or an individual Member State, and elaborated in Art. 258 TFEU. The limited usefulness of the first, and the under-valued nature of the second, are both illustrated by reference to the Roma example.

In the first case, a successful suspension of a Member State for a serious violation of fundamental rights under Art. 7 TEU requires a vote under a specialised qualified majority. Given that the practice of targeting the Roma population is not isolated to France but endemic to a number of Member States, the usefulness of this option seems limited.[39] For the very same reason, the use of enforcement actions on the initiative of a Member State – although in theory possible[40] – also seems unlikely.[41]

In the second case, the widespread practice of Roma targeting in a number of Member States, and the difficulties in restoring compliance with EU law through individual action before national courts,[42] lead to an urgent need for other solutions. The very marginalisation of the Roma by a number of Member States illustrates how the Art. 258 TFEU procedure has an important added value for the protection of European fundamental rights when compared with other mechanisms. The procedure is initiated by an independent body (the European Commission) that is in charge of ensuring that EU law is observed across the EU. The Commission's role in prosecuting enforcement actions is, however, ambiguous. As will be argued below, its dual legal and political functions highlight both the dilemma (A.) and promise (B.) of the Art. 258 TFEU procedure for the enforcement of European fundamental rights.

---

39 Consider here, the support given to the French stance by other EU heads of government such as the Italian and Spanish Prime Ministers: Pop, French expulsions row doing nothing to help the Roma, (20.9.2010) EU Observer.

40 See for example: Case C-145/04, *Spain v. UK (Gibraltar case)*, [2006] ECR I-7917.

41 Consider for example *Romania v. France* but see mitigated feelings in Romania on how to react: compare Parlamentul Romaniei, Declaraţie nr.1 din 21 septembrie 2010 privind situaţia cetăţenilor români de etnie romă, care sunt în proces de expulzare sau repatriere din Republica Franceză şi din alte state europene (published in M.Of. nr. 660/24 Sep. 2010) in which the Romanian Parliament urged the competent authorities to formulate a political reaction with 'Home thoughts: France's expulsion of Romanians arouses mixed feelings in their home countries' (23.9.2010) *The Economist*.

42 See for example the success of two administrative claims brought in Lille: Maccanico, (note 10).

A. *The dilemma of enforcement actions*

The usefulness and innovation of enforcement actions lie in their dual nature. On the one hand, if compared to mechanisms for the enforcement of international law, enforcement actions are remarkably formalised. They allow the Commission to bring a State to Court and to impose lump sums and penalty payments against that State. The mechanism has for example been a formidable tool for the acceleration of the internal market;[43] Member States appear to be genuinely concerned not only with the penalties resulting from an enforcement action but with the threat of naming and shaming.[44] On the other hand, the mechanism retains a strongly informal dimension. The political nature of the procedure both allows it to be a starting point for open-ended dialogue on how violations of EU law, including fundamental rights, can be addressed proactively, *and* leaves it open to political manipulation and 'horse-trading'. In this process, minority groups can be both advantaged and disadvantaged.

One must begin with the stated aim of the procedure. According to Art. 258 TFEU, the primary aim of enforcement is to address violations of the Treaty, and bring them to an end. In that sense, the aim is not to establish a violation per se – and thereby to seek remedies for the parties concerned – but simply to ensure that the original violation ceases. In light of the identities of the addressees of an enforcement procedure i.e. States, this aim of the procedure is best achieved through a combination of informal and formal steps. The mechanism is designed in such a way that solutions are first to be found through political dialogue, and only if no solution can be found, enforced through the Court of Justice. This way, Member States are not 'scolded' but engaged in a *proactive* dialogue about how national procedures and practices can be amended to better reflect EU rules.

Precisely this political dialogue was conducted between the Commission and France between Commissioner Reding's first raising the possibility of enforcement proceedings against France on 15 September and her later statement on 19 October to the effect that the Commission would *"for the*

---

43 Commission, White Paper on Completing the Internal Market (COM(85)310) 217. See e.g. Commission, Internal Market Scoreboard, 2010/21 (available at: http://ec.europa.eu/internal_market/score/docs/score21_en.pdf) 17. For an excellent recent overview of the mechanisms underlying enforcement actions, see Prete and Smulders, *The Coming of Age of Infringement Proceedings*, 47 CMLR 9 (2010).

44 Talberg, *Paths to Compliance: Enforcement, Management, and the European Union*, 56 INTERNATIONAL ORGANIZATION 3, 617 (2002).

time being, not pursue the infringement procedure against France".[45] The practice of blaming and shaming France via the media increased the pressure on France to react quickly. Although this use of informal means of pressure against defaulting Member States thereby enhances the efficiency of the procedure, it also runs the risk of propelling the Commission into a war of words, and into bargaining exercises beyond the scope of the actual legal dispute.[46] In this process, the independence of the body in charge of triggering the Art. 258 TFEU procedure may be threatened. This does not, however, necessarily amount to defeating the purpose of the enforcement procedure. The Commission's initiative to threaten or initiate an Art. 258 TFEU action may serve purposes beyond the termination of a given violation of EU law.

In the example at hand, the consequences of the Commission's efforts are two-fold. The first formal reason for the Commission's decision to put its procedure against France on hold concerns the alleged termination of the violation of EU law. France issued numerous assurances from September onwards that discriminatory practices explicitly targeted at Roma had ceased. This involved both the withdrawal of the original August *circulaire* targeting Roma settlements[47] and documentation submitted to the Commission proposing a detailed calendar and set of draft measures designed to ensure that the procedural safeguards contained in EU secondary legislation on free movement were fully transposed into French law.[48] In the view of the Commission, France had thus brought its legislation into line with EU requirements.

On the other hand, a second, more implicit, reason behind the Commission's decision might also be at play. The statements of both 29 September and 19 October indicate agreements between the Commission and the Member States to take more intensive measures to facilitate the integration and socio-economic improvement of Romani groups. The Commission established in September a Roma taskforce entrusted with monitoring the situation across the EU, which will both present an EU

---

45 European Commission press release on recent developments in France (29.9.2010) and Statement by Viviane Reding, Vice-President of the European Commission (19.10.2010).

46 E.g. "Roms : Viviane Reding retire sa comparaison avec la seconde guerre mondiale ", *Le Monde* (15.9.2010, available at : www.lemonde.fr).

47 Circulaire from the Ministère de l'Intérieur, de l'Outre-Mer et des Collectivités territoriales, "Evacuations des campements illicites" dating back from 13 september 2010 replacing earlier equivalent texts.

48 Statement by Viviane Reding, Vice-President of the European Commission (19.10.2010).

framework for Roma strategies this year, and investigate how EU social and structural funding can better be directed to supporting Roma communities. The Commission also highlighted an invitation to the Member States to submit annual reports on Romani inclusion to be integrated within their National Reform Programmes, as demanded under the framework of the Lisbon 2020 strategy. One may wonder if, under the surface, there may be an implicit compact between the Commission and France (as well as other EU Member States): Legal proceedings may be halted, but only in the context of a concerted effort to create a more effective, and better resourced, pan-European strategy to address the root of the problem, i.e. the social and economic exclusion of the Roma peoples. In this sense, far from being a neutral procedure that ensures the enforcement of European law by an independent enforcer, power games may be played-out within the informal stages of the enforcement procedure itself.

The political outcome of the conflict in France over the free movement of Roma, allowing for an acceleration of pre-existing initiatives to enhance the integration of Roma,[49] is of significant importance. A number of influential Roma scholars – such as Morag Goodwin – have expressed their scepticism of strategies designed to address discrimination against the Roma that focus on legal, rather than political remedies.[50] For a community that is often politically and legally disenfranchised, a strengthening of individual legal remedies may be of limited practical use. Furthermore, seeking damages against the state may create an adversarial climate between Roma and the 'majority' population; a difficult scenario for a community whose future depends on successful integration within the larger community as a whole. The solution offered by the Commission could be an important step towards a holistic effort, in which greater funding and access to housing, health, education and employment is directed towards this vulnerable minority.

A logical consequence of the Commission's dual political and legal roles, however, is that many enforcement actions may be 'traded' for the advancement of a larger political goal or purpose. The dual role of the Commission as both the guardian of the Treaty and a political actor can also often lead to a conflation of legal and political concerns, in which legal

---

49 Earlier initiatives are discussed further below.

50 Morag Goodwin, *Multi-dimensional Exclusion: Viewing Romani exclusion through the nexus of race and poverty*, in EUROPEAN UNION DISCRIMINATION LAW: COMPARATIVE PERSPECTIVES ON MULTI-DIMENSIONAL EQUALITY LAW 39 (Schiek and Chege eds., 2008)

remedies are dropped at precisely the stage where considerations of justice ought to prevail.

A consequence of the Commission's decision to halt proceedings against France may indeed be that there is no judicial enquiry and possible recognition of the unlawful nature of the French campaign. The Art. 258 TFEU procedure is only designed to ensure termination of a breach of EU law. In this sense, as long as the actual breach is brought to an end, the procedure loses an important part of its rationale. The "*dispute settlement*"[51] nature of the Art. 258 TFEU procedure suggests that there is then no *further* need to pursue the action before the Court of Justice of the EU e.g. for a declaration *a posteriori* of a breach of EU law – let alone a need for damages for the specific individuals affected. The dilemma of the enforcement action may be that – while it provides a remedy for vulnerable groups unable to prosecute violations of EU fundamental rights on their own – it also leaves fundamental rights protection in the hands of an uncertain, and in many ways political, process.

B. *The promise of enforcement actions: some recent developments*

Although the section above, and the specific issues relating to the Roma case, demonstrate some existing weaknesses in the EU's system of institutional enforcement *vis-à-vis* fundamental rights, they also bring into relief some interesting features and developments in the mechanics of enforcement actions; features that could be of particular relevance for the protection of fundamental rights in the EU in the years to come.

Firstly, one such feature that has triggered particular attention in the specific dispute over the Roma between the Commission and France is the *speed* of the procedure. Sergio Carrera and Anaïs Faure Atger have argued that the very speed with which EU citizens of Romani origin were deported from France highlights the inability of the enforcement procedure to respond to fast-moving developments.[52] Even by the time the Commission had gotten round to raising the issue of infringement before the French government in September, most of the departures originally envisaged had already taken place. France in this sense could happily comply with the Commission's

---

51 Talberg (note 5), 617.

52 Sergio Carrera and Anaïs Faure Atger, "L'affaire des Roms: A Challenge to the EU's Area of Freedom, Security and Justice", *CEPS Discussion Paper* (29 September 2010, available at: http://www.ceps.eu/book/l%E2%80%99affaire-des-roms-challenge-eu%E2%80%99s-area-freedom-security-and-justice).

complaint, safe in the knowledge that their original objective of dismantling Roma camps had largely been achieved. To counter this threat, these authors suggest the creation of a preventive enforcement action, created on the initiative of the Commission or the European Parliament, and designed to immediately 'freeze' actions which seem to violate EU fundamental rights before their effects can fully be realized.[53]

While it is certainly true that, in this case, EU intervention was too late to aid the many individuals who may have been illegally deported, one wonders whether elements of its practice can already be found within existing procedures. As discussed above, one of the unique features of the enforcement action is the discretion given to the Commission during the informal stages of the procedure. While the Commission must allow Member States a reasonable period to comply with the Commission's initial complaints, the Court has given the Commission a high latitude of discretion to accelerate this part of the procedure.[54] The Court has insisted that *"very short periods may be justified in particular circumstances, especially where there is an urgent need to remedy a breach or where the Member State concerned is fully aware of the Commission's views long before the procedure starts"*.[55] One would imagine that the speedy relocation of large numbers of Roma in the summer of 2010 would be precisely such an example of 'urgency', allowing the Commission to accelerate its enforcement procedure against France if the Commission had closely monitored the situation and informed France of its views on the issue.[56]

The possibility to accelerate enforcement actions goes hand in hand with further features of the mechanism. Just as in other actions of the Court, infringement actions raised before the Court under Art. 258 TFEU are subject to the possibility of interim relief. According to Art. 279 TFEU (emphasis added), *"the Court of Justice of the European Union may in* any *cases before it prescribe* any *necessary interim measures"*.[57] This provision does not de-limit

---

53   *Id.* 17.

54   In cases of urgency, periods of one or two weeks for Member States to respond to reasoned opinions or letters of formal notice have been deemed acceptable – see e.g. Case C-196/07, *Commission v Spain*, [2008] ECR I-41; Case C-328/96, *Commission v Austria*, [1999] ECR I-7479; Case C-85/85 *Commission v Belgium*, [1986] ECR 1149.

55   Case C-293/85, *Commission v Belgium*, [1988] ECR I-305, para. 14

56   GISTI for example had brought a complaint to the attention of the Commission in 2008: GISTI, "Plainte contre la France pour violation du droit communautaire en matière de libre circulation des personnes" (21.7.2008, available at: www.gisti.org).

57   See also Art. 39 of the Statute of the Court of Justice of the European Union (O.J. 2008, C 115/210) and Art. 83 of the Rules of Procedure of the Court of Justice of the European Union (O.J. 2010, C 177/1).

the type of relief which may be offered. It has included 'freezing' measures in the past, such as in the recent *Spring Hunting* case, in which Malta was ordered to temporarily refrain from enacting measures derogating from the wild birds protection directive.[58]

While such relief has been less commonly used in the context of enforcement when compared to other types of actions, why could such measures not be used to temporarily 'freeze' action taken against vulnerable minorities, while a full judicial decision is pending?[59] This approach would have the added value of leaving the decision to 'freeze' in the hands of the EU's proper judicial organ, rather than with political bodies, such as the Commission and Parliament.[60] Moreover, according to Art. 62a of the Rules of Procedure of the Court, the President may exceptionally decide that a case is to be determined pursuant to an expedited procedure where the particular urgency of the case so requires. In this sense, the suggestion of a preventive enforcement mechanism may under-count important features of existing procedures.

A second notable feature of the enforcement action is that its procedure *can* continue even when the initial breach of EU law has stopped. That there is no *need* of such a follow-up to eliminate the breach should not distract from the fact that there may be value in a judicial finding of an infringement of EU law at European level. In this sense, institutional enforcement mechanisms have the purpose of avoiding having to rely on the "*randomness, or at least the arbitrariness, of individual or corporate, private, litigation*"[61] thereby diminishing the uniformity of EU law. Arguably, this dimension of Art. 258 TFEU, in so far as it is the central mechanism for institutional enforcement of EU law, has gained considerable importance in the context of fundamental rights protection. The procedure could be used as a useful complement to the Art. 7 TEU procedure if the European Commission, as the Guardian of the Treaty, shows the political will to make more active use of Art. 258 TFEU.

The Commission itself has acknowledged that infringement procedures can be pursued even when the initial breach of EU law has ceased. It has for example indicated that financial sanctions – in cases where a second enforcement procedure has to be taken against a Member State who has still not complied with a first finding of infringement – will be recommended

---

58   Case C-76/08 R, *Commission v Malta,* [2008] ECR I-64.
59   See Prete and Smulders (note 40).
60   We are grateful to Bruno de Witte for this insight
61   Tompkins, (note 20), 294.

even if the said Member State complies with EU requirements during the course of the second procedure.[62] The Court has also confirmed this reading of Art. 258 TFEU in the early age of enforcement actions: "*The object of an action under article [258] is established by the Commission's reasoned opinion, and even when the default has been remedied subsequently to the time-limit prescribed by paragraph 2 of the same article, pursuit of the action still has an object*".[63] For example, a finding of infringement may be of substantive interest in order to constitute the basis of a claim in damages.[64]

Thirdly, even if the Commission would decide not to initiate an enforcement action against France for the summer removals after France has brought its legislation into line with EU law,[65] enforcement actions may be initiated in the future in cases of administrative practices contravening EU law.[66] Providing evidence of such an infringement of EU law may prove more difficult than having evidence of a formal breach since the Commission will have to show on a case-by-case basis each practical infringement of EU rules.[67] Nevertheless, the Court has in recent years proven very receptive to such claims.

The Court has recently acknowledged that the Commission may seek in parallel "*a finding that provisions of [EU law] have not been complied with by reason of the conduct of a Member State's authorities with regard to particular specifically identified situations and a finding that those provisions have not been complied with because its authorities have adopted a general practice contrary thereto, which the particular situations illustrate where appropriate*".[68] This novel use of infringement actions is designed to target

---

62 Commission Communication, The Application of Article 228 of the EC Treaty (SEC(2005)1658 as last updated by Commission Communication SEC(2010) 923/3).

63 Case 39/72, *Commission v Italy*, [1973] ECR 101, para. 9.

64 Id., para. 11.

65 As such, while one of the great 'success' stories of enforcement actions is the fact that so many are 'resolved' prior to a judicial resolution (European Commission, 27th Annual Report on Monitoring the Application of EU law (COM(2010) 538, 1.10.2010) point 2.2), these statistics tell us little about those infringements of the Treaty that persist, but are not nonetheless pursued. From that perspective, the Commission's announcement that the procedure is only suspended and that it will monitor the implementation of the new French rules shall be welcomed (Statement by Viviane Reding, Vice-President of the European Commission, 19.10.2010).

66 For an early statement by the ECJ in that direction see: Case 167/73, *Commission v France* (Code du Travail Maritime), [1974] ECR 359, paras 40-42.

67 Providing support in that direction see e.g.: GISTI (note 334) and Haute Autorité de Lutte contre les Discriminations et pour l'Egalité (HALDE), Délibération relative à la situation des Roms Roumains ou Bulgares en France (n. 2009-372, 26.10.2009).

68 ECJ, 26 April 2005, *Commission v. Ireland*, C-494/01, ECR I-3331, para. 27.

general and persistent infringements (or GAP).[69] It makes it easier for the European Commission to tackle underlying structural problems of non-compliance with EU law in a Member State.[70] It could be a very powerful tool in the context of endemic violations of fundamental rights.[71] In the context of fundamental rights protection, this approach offers a middle ground between the Art. 7 EU procedure and the classical procedure of Art. 258 TFEU. As Advocate general Geelhoed put it, it could help addressing situations in which "*the remedy [...] lies not merely in taking action to resolve a number of individual cases [...], but where this situation of non-compliance can only be redressed by a revision of the general policy and administrative practice of the Member State*".[72]

Finally, one may wonder whether the Commission's quasi-monopoly and discretion to initiate institutional enforcement actions should be reformed.[73] It shall be recalled that several mechanisms allow Member States either through the Council or individually to trigger mechanisms for a better enforcement of EU fundamental rights.[74] Furthermore, as made clear in the first section of this article, institutional vigilance is complemented by that of entities (such as individuals) at local and national levels to enforce EU law.[75] Should institutional enforcement mechanisms for the protection of fundamental rights in the EU nevertheless be made less dependant on the discretion of the Commission to compensate for its lack of political will to bring the

---

69 Pål Wenneras, *A new dawn for commission enforcement under Articles 226 and 228 EC. General and Persistent (GAP) Infringements, lump sums and penalty payments*, 43/1 CMLR 31 (2006).

70 Opinion of A.G. Geelhoed delivered on 23 September 2004 in *Commission v Ireland*, Case C-494/01, para. 4.

71 By analogy Prete and Smulders (note 40), 23-24.

72 Opinion of A.G. Geelhoed in *Commission v Ireland* (note 71), para. 48.

73 Carrera and Faure Atger, (note 53). On the possibility for Member States to initiate infringement actions see supra. point II.

74 Member States are unlikely to make use of their right in this context, *supra*.

75 Note that the Commission itself stresses the complementarities of individual and institutional enforcement mechanisms. For example, it has in recent years multiplied initiatives to make it easier and more efficient for individuals and businesses to bring complaints related to the implementation of EU law in a Member State to European Commission. Of particular interest is a recent EU Pilot Project to correct infringements of EU law at an early stage thus eliminating the need to trigger an Art. 258 TFEU procedure: see European Commission, A Europe of results – applying Community law, (COM(2007)502) point 2, European Commission, EU pilot evaluation report (COM(2010)70) and European Commission, 27th Annual Report on Monitoring the Application of EU law (COM(2010) 538, 1.10.2010) point 3.4.

action forward? Could such steps be built into the Art. 258 TFEU procedure while respecting its important – and perhaps unalterable – dual nature? It is interesting in that regard to observe that even within the Commission, an increasing weight is given to Directorates General to prioritise infringement proceedings.[76] As a result, the management of such proceedings is more likely to be influenced by political considerations than it would be if left within the hands of the legal service.[77]

A positive answer to either of these two questions would either have to be implemented through a reform of the Treaties or, for example, through an inter-institutional agreement between the European Commission and the Parliament in which the Commission would endeavour to trigger an Art. 258 TFEU in given circumstances if so requested by the European Parliament.[78] A more practical method to ensure better enforcement of EU anti-discrimination rights in the short-term may lie in a third type of enforcement tools: mechanisms of *collective* enforcement.[79]

IV. The Need for Enhanced Collective Vigilance

The two sections above have indicated both the value and the weaknesses of individual and institutional enforcement of EU fundamental rights. These weaknesses suggest both a need to go beyond individual enforcement in circumstances where vulnerable individuals may have limited access to legal remedies, and a need to be cautious of institutional mechanisms vulnerable to power games as illustrated by the weaknesses of enforcement actions.

These two deficits suggest the need for an intermediate level of enforcement in monitoring, establishing, and addressing violations of fundamental rights in the EU. This intermediary – collective enforcement – relies neither on the affected individuals themselves nor on general political institutions,

---

76   This is pointed out by Prete and Smulders, (note 40), 58; e.g. European Commission, A Europe of results – applying Community law, (COM (2007) 502) 10.

77   We are grateful to the CMLR reviewers for their insight on this point.

78   Another possibility here may be allowing requests to be made by the Fundamental Rights Agency. 'Alerting' through this body is considered by Carrera and Faure Atger (note 53). This, however, would involve a rather radical overhaul of the FRA's mandate – as it stands, the institution is even unable to assess the consistency of EU legislation with fundamental rights unless so requested by one of the EU institutions

79   Note that Art. 19(1) TFEU demands unanimity at the Council and consent of the European Parliament for the adoption of harmonisation measures to combat discrimination.

but instead on non-governmental bodies and networks with an interest in protecting vulnerable groups. The crucial role of addressing exclusion of vulnerable minorities through the deployment of NGO and network-based activity is particularly well illustrated by the Roma affair and was actually acknowledged by the Commission in its response to the events.[80] As indicated above, the Commission insisted, in the context of suspending its enforcement action against France, on the need to increase efforts in targeting funding opportunities and monitoring of state practice towards identifying and addressing the root causes of Roma exclusion.

Opening-up access points for vulnerable minorities to European-level remedies and rights may involve more than just a formal strategy of conferring rights but a *hybrid approach*.[81] This response focuses both on non-judicial strategies, such as improving the monitoring of fundamental rights violations and raising awareness over issues of fundamental rights in the EU and judicial strategies, such as empowering bodies able to speak and act on behalf of vulnerable groups. The two strategies are to be used in tandem – while non-judicial approaches are necessary to ensure that violations are recognized and recorded in the first place, judicial approaches are needed to ensure that political strategies aimed at addressing exclusion (such as directing EU structural and social funds towards Roma communities) are pursued in a fair and non-discriminatory manner.

A. Non judicial-processes

The determination to forward the cause of the Roma through non-judicial means was already signalled by the Commission in its April 2010 Communication on the social and economic integration of the Roma in Europe.[82] This document should be understood in the light of two other important institutional interventions on the issue of Roma inclusion – the Conclusions of the Employment, Social Policy and Consumer Affairs Council of June 2010 and the European Parliament's Resolution on the situation

---

80 European Commission (note 13).

81 For two influential examples of a hybrid approach to the relationship between 'new governance' methods and law, see De Búrca (note 17); Trubek, Cottrell and Nance, Soft Law, *Hard Law and EU Integration*, in LAW AND NEW GOVERNANCE IN THE EU AND THE US (De Búrca and Scott eds., 2005).

82 Commission Communication, The Social and Economic Integration of the Roma in Europe (COM (2010) 133 final). See also earlier initiatives such as the Commission Staff Working Document, Community Instruments and Policies for Roma Inclusion (SEC (2008) 2172).

of Roma, issued on 9 September 2010.[83] All three of these documents urge a comprehensive review of how the integration and inclusion of Roma communities is ensured by the EU. Their recommendations for reform are remarkably similar. All three suggest a three-pronged approach to tackling problems of Roma exclusion and discrimination, focusing on i) *monitoring,* ii) *funding* and iii) *the mainstreaming of Roma issues into broader fields of policy.* In all three pillars, EU institutions and Member States are urged to act in concert with non-governmental bodies and networks, as well as members of Roma communities, to fill gaps in the existing system of fundamental rights protection.

The first monitoring approach directly responds to some of the concerns outlined in section I above. If it is true that the Roma are a uniquely marginalised community, there is an even greater need to ensure that violations of fundamental rights relating to Roma are properly recorded and supervised. In the last couple of years, the EU institutions have already taken some steps towards improving the monitoring of fundamental rights relating to Roma communities. Discrimination against Roma was included, for example, in the latest annual work programme of the European Fundamental Rights Agency (FRA),[84] and in the thematic areas to be analysed by the EQUINET equality bodies which were set-up under the EU's equality directives.[85]

Perhaps the most significant development was the creation of the European Platform for Roma Inclusion to exchange good practices and experiences between different national contexts.[86] Finally, the Commission proposes to include reporting on Roma issues in two open coordination processes – the OMC SPSI – set-up to monitor the development of national social inclusion and protection policies – and the 'integrated guidelines' through which Member States report on the implementation of the objectives agreed to under the Lisbon 2020 strategy.[87] In this sense, Member States are urged to

---

83   Council Conclusions, Advancing Roma Inclusion (Luxembourg, 7.6.2010); European Parliament Resolution, The Situation of Roma and on freedom of movement in the European Union (RSP/2010/2842, 9.9.2010) and earlier initiatives listed therein.

84   Fundamental Rights Agency, Annual Work Programme 2010, 15. See also Race Equality Directive, Art. 17(2).

85   In accordance with its 2009 business plan, EQUINET set-up an initiative for Roma equality in 2009. See "Equinet Initiative on Roma Equality" (available at: http://www.equineteurope.org/435.html).

86   A network of NGOs, national representatives, representatives from the EU institutions and legal practitioners set up in April 2009, see the website of the platform, available at: http://ec.europa.eu/social/main.jsp?catId=761&langId=en.

87   Commission Communication (note 3), 7. See also, European Parliament Resolution (note 84), point 22 and Council Conclusions (note 84), point 28.

agree to common goals and objectives in addressing Roma exclusion across various policy areas (employment, health, education, and social assistance), to report on their efforts to achieve them, and (in the context of the Lisbon 2020 strategy) are even subject to recommendations for improvement issued by the Council.

The problem with these monitoring efforts may be less a lack of institutions willing and able to conduct monitoring than a lack of clarity over who is to do what. The activities of the Roma Platform and the FRA must be considered alongside the OSCE's action plan on the inclusion of Roma and Sinti in public life,[88] the Council of Europe's numerous recommendations on Roma inclusion,[89] the national action plans implemented by the 12 states participating in the World Bank 'Decade for Roma inclusion'[90] and the European Network on Social Inclusion and Roma under the structural funds (EURoma), which aims at exchanging good practice in targeting EU funding towards Roma.[91] This plethora of monitoring bodies and networks, many of which have overlapping membership and functions (consider e.g. the dual reporting requirements for Member States under both the OMC processes and the decade for Roma inclusion), risks causing confusion and duplication among these networks.[92]

The second approach is to address Romani exclusion financially. Here, the mutually re-enforcing link between poverty and discrimination is crucial.[93] Under this cycle, discrimination against Roma in housing and in the labour market leads to poverty, which in turn re-enforces negative stereotypes of the Roma as 'dirty', 'idle' or marginalised. The Commission, Parliament and

---

88 OSCE, Action Plan on Improving the Situation of Roma and Sinti within the OSCE Area (Decision no. 3/30, MC.DEC/3/03).

89 See the recommendations of the Committee of Ministers 2006/10 (access to health care); 2005/4 (housing conditions); 2004/14 (movement and encampment of Travellers); 2001/17 (economic and employment situation); 2000/4 (education of Roma/Gypsy children); 1983/1 (stateless nomads and nomads of undetermined nationality); 1975/13 (social situation of nomads).

90 Available at: http://www.romadecade.org/decade_action_plans.

91 See the first EU Roma Report, Roma and the Structural Funds (2010, available at: http://www.euromanet.eu/upload/59/60/EUROMA_REPORT_web.pdf).

92 No surprise then that the Commission asks for better coordination between these bodies: the "challenges ahead", it argues, include "improved cooperation between national, European and international players and representatives of Roma communities". Commission Communication (note 83), 5.

93 See Commission Communication, id., 2.

Council thus call for "*appropriate funding to be mobilised by the EU and the Member States for projects on Roma integration*"[94] i.e. projects which can break the link between poverty and negative perceptions among the public at large.

The Commission suggest three elements as crucial to providing better and more targeted funding.[95] Firstly, bi-lateral meetings for Member States on how to make better use of EU structural and social funding; these meetings are to "*prepare the ground for agreeing targets for a greater use of EU funds for Roma inclusion by setting specific and established milestones*".[96] Secondly, making de-segregation measures a pre-condition for access to structural funding (as urged, for example, by Art. 16 of Regulation 1083/2006/EC).[97] Finally, the Commission has suggested that Member States ensure that Roma communities and stakeholders are themselves involved in designing, allocating and evaluating funding programmes.[98]

The final pillar of this political approach to addressing the problems of Roma exclusion is the use of policy mainstreaming. As the Commission puts it, "*the challenges ahead include mainstreaming Roma inclusion issues into the broad policy areas of education, employment, public health, infrastructure and urban planning, and economic and territorial development rather than treating it as a separate policy*".[99] One would expect the use of the Open Method of Coordination to be a key element of this mainstreaming commitment. The Council is therefore urged to 'mainstream' issues relating to the inclusion and socio-economic situation of the Roma into their existing guidelines for both the OMC SPSI and the 'integrated guidelines' for employment and fiscal policy.[100] The goal of this is to ensure that Member States report on how national employment, health and social policies impact upon the Roma, both developing examples of good practice, and, negatively, allowing themselves to be held accountable for poor policy performance.

This reliance on tried and tested 'new governance' methods, such as the Open Method of Coordination, illustrates some of the promise and pitfalls of non-judicial approaches to tackling Roma exclusion.[101] On the one hand, legal

---

94 European Parliament Resolution (note 84), point 22.
95 Commission Communication (note 83), 6-7.
96 *Id.*
97 See also, Council Conclusion (note 84), point 33.
98 See also Id (note 84), point 31; European Parliament Resolution (note 361), point 21.
99 Commission Communication (note 83), 5.
100 Id, 7. See, also, Council Conclusions (note 84), point 28.
101 For more on the empirical performance of the OMC in the social inclusion domain for

commitments to tackling discrimination are unlikely to be effective if they merely take a passive approach to protecting vulnerable communities. In so far as monitoring developments at the national level, providing funding, and mainstreaming via open coordination involves practical efforts to alleviating the causes of discrimination against the Roma, these are likely to be crucial tools in making anti-discrimination norms more than an empty promise, but a collective commitment across different levels of EU governance.

On the other hand, a commitment to new governance methods ties the EU's Roma strategy to the many familiar critiques that have been advanced in respect of these methods. It is by now common academic currency to point to the limited effectiveness and legitimacy of methods like the OMC as proof that they cannot be trusted – particularly in areas as crucial as that of fundamental rights.[102] The OMC has been repeatedly criticised for developing common norms which have often failed to translate into positive legislative and political achievements at the national level, or for failing to live up to its original billing as a means of improving local and stakeholder participation in EU affairs.[103]

While there is a danger that the same problem could befall the Roma – that non-judicial strategies could be used to evade 'harder' and more enforceable legal and political commitments – this risk could be avoided by following a hybrid approach i.e. considering 'new governance' – and its political potential – *alongside* enforceable commitments provided through legislation, and other forms of 'hard law'. The advantage of a 'hybrid' approach may be that

---

example, see MARK DAWSON, NEW GOVERNANCE AND THE TRANSFORMATION OF EUROPEAN LAW: COORDINATION OF EU SOCIAL LAW AND POLICY (2011).

102 On the application of open coordination methods to fundamental rights issues, see Stijn Smismans, *How to be Fundamental with Soft Procedures? The OMC and Fundamental Social Rights*, in SOCIAL RIGHTS IN EUROPE (De Búrca and De Witte eds., 2005); Grainne De Búrca, *New Modes of Governance and the Protection of Human Rights*, in MONITORING FUNDAMENTAL RIGHTS IN THE EU (Alston and De Schutter eds., 2005); Catherine Bernard, *A New Governance Approach to Economic, Social and Cultural Rights in the EU*, in ECONOMIC AND SOCIAL RIGHTS UNDER THE CHARTER OF FUNDAMENTAL RIGTHS OF THE EUROPEAN UNION (Hervey and Kenner eds., 2003).

103 On the first 'effectiveness' related criticism, see Fritz W. Scharpf, *The European Social Model: Coping with the Challenges of Diversity*, 40 JOURNAL OF COMMON MARKET STUDIES 4 (2002); on the second issue, 'legitimacy', see Milena Büchs, *How Legitimate is the Open Method of Coordination* 46 JOURNAL OF COMMON MARKET STUDIES 4 (2009); Mark Dawson, EU Law Transformed? Evaluating Accountability and Subsidiarity in the Streamlined OMC for Social Inclusion and Social Protection, 13 EUROPEAN INTEGRATION ONLINE PAPERS (2009) 1.

it sees collective vigilance in protecting fundamental rights as a strategy that requires a multi-dimensional legal and political response.

B. *Judicial processes*

The non-judicial mechanisms outlined above may offer an important contribution to addressing the root causes of vulnerable minorities. There are reasons, however, to be sceptical of a purely non-judicial approach; problems which may require us to return to the framework of individual enforcement mechanisms discussed in section I. One problem in particular is the issue of whether monitoring can actually stop the violations of fundamental rights and if funding is actually allocated to its intended recipients. There is some evidence to question this assumption. A notable example comes from Slovakia, where, according to the New York Times, 600,000 euro of EU funding earmarked to help educate Roma communities last year was allegedly given instead to two local football teams.[104] This is just one recent instance of a long suspected problem – that funding allocated to the Member States through regional and cohesion funds is channelled through intermediary projects that may benefit the local population as a whole, but not their intended targets.[105]

The benefits of a 'hybrid' approach may again become apparent as a response to this problem. The point of 'hybridity' is not only to identify how 'soft' strategies, such as supplying funding, can complement 'hard' legal rights, but also the other way around, i.e. how hard law can ensure that soft programmes of incentives and capacity building avoid overtly discriminatory practices. The substantive provisions of the Equal Treatment Directives may be very important in this regard. The prohibitions of the Race Directive, in particular, prohibit direct and indirect forms of discrimination against individuals on the basis of ethnic origin not only in employment, but in education, social security, social advantages and access to housing (all areas of key concern for Roma groups).[106] In this sense, they provide vulnerable

---

104 EU Cash Cow ends in Slovakia, New York Times (9.11.2010, available at: http://www.nytimes.com/2010/11/10/world/europe/10slovakia.html).

105 For a description of some of these challenges regarding the actual use of funds intended for the Roma see the EU Roma Report: the Structural Funds and the Roma of the EU Roma network. (2010, available at: http://ec.europa.eu/employment_social/esf/docs/euroma_report_en.pdf)

106 Directive 2000/43 (note 16), Art. 3. See also: Lila Farkas, *En bonne voie vers l'égalité: la recherche par les Roms d'une protection judiciaire contre la discrimination devant les juridictions européennes*, 3 (2006) European Anti-Discrimination Law Review

groups with enforceable rights that can be used to challenge blatantly discriminatory and corrupt practices in Court. Without such guarantees, there would be a danger of non-judicial remedies acting as a mere 'feelgood' exercise – allowing Member States to spend their way out of awkward social problems, while doing little to improve the socio-economic situation of Roma communities on the ground.

At the same time, while coupling enforcement via the Equal Treatment Directives with non-judicial approaches seems fruitful, it also returns us to an earlier problem – the limited use by Roma communities of the legal remedies available to them. The picture here is not as one-sided as it was depicted in earlier parts of this paper. There has been a steady stream of decisions addressing Roma rights issues before the European "courts". It is notable, however, that much of it has taken place in Strasbourg rather than Luxembourg.[107] Much of this case-law has arisen as a consequence of strategic litigation investigated and funded via organizations representing Roma communities. Perhaps the most notable is the European Roma Rights Centre: an international public advocacy organization founded in Hungary in 1996, which coordinates pan-European litigation strategies.[108] This organization was heavily involved in a number of high profile investigating Roma discrimination before the European Court of Human Rights (ECtHR) or the European Committee of Social Rights (ECSR).[109] A well known example is the *Ostrava* case before the ECtHR, in which the widespread practice in the Czech Republic of placing Romani children in under-funded 'special schools' was deemed by the Court a violation of the applicant's guarantees of non-discrimination and access to education as provided under Art. 14 and Art. 2 of Protocol 1 of the ECHR respectively.[110]

Claims to the ECHR however must be brought by the actual victims of a breach of the Convention or its Protocols.[111] Collective bodies may only

---

21 and illustrations in the 2010 Annual Report of the Romanian Equality Body, "Hotărâri de Constatare Pe Anul 2010 : Clasificare După, criteriul de discriminare" (2010, available at : www.cncd.org.ro).

107 For an overview of the applicable case-law, see James A. Goldstein, *The Struggle for Roma Rights: Arguments that have worked*, 32 HUMAN RIGHTS QUARTERLY (2010) 2; for an overview of the litigation activities coordinated by the ERRC, see Factsheet on the Roma Rights record (available at: http://www.errc.org/cikk.php?cikk=3573).

108 Their website is available at: http://errc.org.

109 See e.g. ECSC, Activity Report 2009 (25.6.2010, available at: http://www.coe.int/t/dghl/monitoring/socialcharter/Presentation/ActivityReport2009_en.pdf).

110 Eur. Court H.R., *DH & Others v the Czech Republic*, Judgement of 7 February 2006, Application No. 57325/00.

111 Art. 34 ECHR.

intervene as a third party or act on behalf of the victim.[112] In other words there is no genuine collective dimension to this legal remedy. The contrast with the mechanisms for the enforcement of the European Social Charter (ESC) is instructive.[113] This Charter also contains extensive anti-discrimination provisions, yet allows a specific route for collective complaints where national breaches are found. The Governmental Committee of the Charter maintains a list of social partner and NGO organizations – which include the ERRC – that may lodge a complaint[114] where their states have ratified the applicable additional protocol.[115] In circumstances in which states may have common reasons to ignore or downplay a particular breach of the Charter, interested and representative collective organisations may step in to fill the monitoring gap.

This mechanism of collective enforcement sheds interesting light on the existing system of remedies in the EU.[116] Scholars have pointed at the weakness of the Equal Treatment Directives in that regard.[117] On the one hand, Member States shall ensure that collective entities with a legitimate interest in ensuring that the provisions of this Directive are complied with *"may engage, either on behalf or in support of the complainant, with his or her approval, in any judicial and/or administrative procedure provided for the enforcement of obligations under [the] Directive"*.[118] On the other hand, the bodies for the promotion of equal treatment created by the Race and new Sex Equality Directives should be entitled to provide *"independent assistance"*[119] to victims of discrimination. These provisions are welcome in so far as they provide support to victims;[120] nevertheless, the enforcement of the rights contained in the Equal Treatment Directives remains in essence based on individual litigation. The Member States are free to go further in granting collective entities the right to bring legal claims, or not.[121]

---

112 Art. 36(2) ECHR and Rule 36 of the Rules of procedure of the ECtHR.

113 Bell (note 19), 274-276.

114 Governmental Committee of the ESC, International Non-Governmental Organisations entitled to submit collective complaints (1.7.2010, available at: http://www.coe.int).

115 Additional Protocol to the European Social Charter, Providing for a System of Collective Complaints (9.11.1995).

116 Bell (note 19).

117 Waddington and Bell (note 28), 607.

118 Directive 2000/43 (note 16), Art. 7(2).

119 Directive 2000/43 (note 16), Art. 13(2).

120 De Búrca (note 17), 97.

121 On the specific situation in France and Romania: Chopin and Gounari (note 314),

The failure of the EU to consider seriously the possibility of collective actions or complaints may hamper anti-discrimination strategies focused on systematic patterns of abuse, or undertaken primarily by interested NGOs. The advantages of such collective mechanisms of enforcement may be significant. They are well explained by Mark Bell in a recent contribution comparing the EU and ESC systems:

> "From the perspective of tackling discrimination, the collective complaints procedure has considerable virtue. Individual litigation depends heavily on the willingness of individuals to bear the financial and emotional costs that are often inherent in pursuing a complaint. Disputes framed around individuals are also less apposite when confronting systematic patterns of inequality. Where certain social groups are subject to disadvantage and exclusion across different aspects of life, individual complaints are unlikely to capture the web of mechanisms through which inequality is perpetuated. In contrast, the possibility for collective complaints allows a focus on the cumulative situation".[122]

For vulnerable groups such as the Roma, these conditions particularly apply. A vigilant attitude towards enforcing fundamental rights for vulnerable minorities may require supplementing individual and institutional mechanisms with the collective ability to monitor and address serious fundamental rights violations.

V. Conclusion

The recent dispute between the Commission and France over the Roma has aroused interest for a number of reasons, not least because it highlights the vulnerability of minority groups in a European Union that prides itself on being at the vanguard of global human rights protection. The practice of France, and possibly other states too,[123] in targeting Roma communities questions the very commitment of the EU Treaties (and of many national constitutions as well) to being a Union founded on, in the words of Art. 2

---

77. See also Opinion of A.G. Maduro in Case C-54/07, *Feryn*, delivered on 12.3.2008, points 12-19 and Case C-54/07, *Feryn*, [2008] ECR I-5187, point 27.

122 Bell (note 19), 275.

123 See reports available at http://www.errc.org/.

TEU, *"respect for human rights, including the rights of persons belonging to minorities"*.

It is also, however, an interesting dispute because of the light it throws on the role and added value of EU intervention in the area of fundamental rights. The Roma dispute illustrates an evolution of the EU's role from a passive enforcer of negative obligations *vis-à-vis* fundamental rights to a more pro-active role, in which anti-discrimination becomes a fully fledged EU policy, enforced through a complex governance architecture. While the set of EU rights to enhance integration of individuals in their home and host countries as well as their free movement rights constitutes a recently developed, and remarkably rich, legal tool box that should prove invaluable for vulnerable minorities such as the Roma, expected societal changes will only result from multi-level vigilance; one that can be exercised at an individual, institutional and collective level.

It has been argued that the key current weaknesses of EU enforcement mechanisms, when faced with the novel challenge of ensuring respect for fundamental rights, are two-fold. Firstly, as regards institutional enforcement of fundamental rights, while a number of developing features in EU-level enforcement mechanisms, such as the possibility for an action based on a general and consistent practice, may allow Art. 258 TFEU to "catch" broader patterns of fundamental rights violations, many of these features remain under-used. A stronger political commitment to make full use of the existing facilities for fundamental protection – particularly those of Art. 258 TFEU – would be welcomed.

Secondly, the job of enforcing and protecting fundamental rights in the EU cannot be left either to individuals or to the EU institutions alone. Legislative intervention to enhance the possibilities for NGOs, Equality bodies and/or other interests groups to bring collective legal action should also be considered in the future. Greater possibilities for *collective* vigilance could enhance the effectiveness of the EU's hybrid model for the protection of individuals against discrimination by giving bodies with a strong interest in minority rights protection the chance to bring claims on their own speed.

The very term 'vigilance' connotes not just enforcement but a collective patience; a willingness, according to the Oxford English dictionary, *"to keep careful watch for possible dangers or difficulties"*.[124] The lessons of the Roma

---

124 Definition of Oxford English Dictionary; available at: http://oxforddictionaries. com/view/entry/m_en_us1304238#m_en_us1304238.

case may be that EU law requires a careful watch at many different levels: from affected individual, to concerned institutions and through the collective eyes of a broader European civil society.

SECTION 2:
COUNTRY PERSPECTIVES

Chapter 6

Great Ideas – Bad Practice: On Implementation of Policies and Programmes for Roma

*Ada Ingrid Engebrigtsen**

I. Introduction

In the last decade we have seen a growing concern in most European states for the inclusion of Roma populations into majority society. This concern stems both from the newly visible poverty among these groups following the incorporation of central and eastern European states into the EU, from media-covered conflicts between Roma populations and majority groups, and from the new EU-internal migration of poor Roma from central and eastern to western parts of the EU and beyond often for unregulated economic activity. This concern to include is important and urgent, but it is not new. Romani populations (including Roma, Sinti, Manush, Kalé and other similar populations) have, in most areas of Europe, experienced several more or less coercive programmes of assimilation, integration and/or inclusion, dependent on the in vogue-concept and ideas of the time. In my experience, working several years with the Roma population in Norway and studying a Roma group in Romania, there is a deeply felt suspicion within Roma groups towards most programmes meant in some way to change their ways of life, social organization and moral and political systems – something that often is a condition for or an expectation of such programmes. In this paper I will present two cases of such programmes: one in Hungary in the late 1890 and one in Norway in 1970-90. The cases are far apart both in time and place, and the Roma groups that were the targets of these reforms differ in socio-economic status and in several features of their ways of life; however, they also share several similarities, both groups are Vlach,[1] romanés-speaking

*   Ada Ingrid Engebrigtsen is Research Professor in Anthropology at NOVA Norwegian Social Research; ada.i.engebrigtsen@nova.no

groups. The cases highlight some important features regarding programmes aimed at the integration and/or inclusion of Romani communities, which are important for the present European-wide ambition of helping the Roma out of poverty and into mainstream society.

This paper is based on my experience working for approximately seven years with Norwegian Roma in the 1970s and 1980s as a leader of a kindergarten and a youth-club for Roma families. These institutions were part of a rehabilitation program directed at Norwegian Roma. The paper is also based on my general knowledge of different Roma groups from fieldwork conducted within the scope of my doctoral research in social anthropology among Roma and non-Roma in Transylvania in the 1990s. In the last five years I have conducted a limited pilot study, talking with, observing and writing about Romanian migrant street-workers in Oslo.

Vlach romanés-speaking Roma constitute the most numerous category of the highly diverse populations that today are generalized as "Roma, Romani etc" for political purposes. Vlach-speaking Roma are, however, also highly diverse when it comes to religion, way of life and their relations to the majority society. The term 'Vlach' is a linguistic term for the Romanés dialect spoken by the populations of Roma that entered Wallachia and Moldova (the western and southern parts of present day Romania) around the 13th century and Transylvania somewhat later; they were incorporated into the economy as slaves in Romania and serfs in Transylvania (then first a part of Hungary and the Austrian/Hungarian empire in the mid-sixteenth century) until around 1860, when feudalism and slavery were banned in both states.[2] All Roma and other Romani groups[3] (all with different ethnonyms) in Wallachia were slaves and only these populations were slaves. They performed most of the manual labor in agriculture, in housework, as miners and as artisans for their owners, owners being the church, the monasteries, the princes and the nobility. In Transylvania, Roma and other Romani groups were "royal serfs", directly dependent on the king.[4] Slaves were not legal subjects, but could be

---

1   *Vlach* from Vallachia, an ancient name for Romania, is the linguist term for the dialect of romanés spoken in Romania and by Roma groups that have emigrated from Wallachia and Moldova after the abolition of serfdom and slavery in 1864.

2   Viorel Achim, The Roma in Romanian History (1998).

3   I am using Roma for the Vlach-speaking groups I am referring to and I will use Romani (instead of the more common "Gypsies" as a general term for Roma and other similar groups with ethnonyms such as Sinti, Kale, Manouche, Kastale etc that are found in most countries of Europe. This is in line with the EU standard, but is new and not well established.

4   Achim, (note 2), 43.

sold, exchanged and handled as movable property. There was throughout this period a prohibition on marriage between slaves and non-slaves (serfs): non-slaves who married slaves became slaves themselves, together with their offspring. The status of the Roma and other Romani groups was quite distinct from the other groups in Wallachia and Transylvania, and they were quite different in the two territories. In both territories, they were created as distinct ethnic groups and set apart from the other populations in several ways, but in most parts of Transylvania Roma were serfs, they were legal subjects and lived under similar conditions as the Romanian-speaking peasants.[5]

This historical background, only very superficially presented here, is indispensible in understanding the cultural norms and ways of life of present-day Vlach Roma and other Romani groups that lived for approximately five centuries in Romania. Descendents of these groups live in all European countries, often forming separate societies in majority society. Other populations of Romani, such as *Sinti, Manush, Kale* etc., have long, but different, histories of persecution, exclusion and discrimination in the countries in which they have lived – histories that should be understood as crucial factors in constituting their present political, economic, social and cultural life.

II. The Roma Settlement in Hungary

In 1995, the Hungarian sociologist, Andras Tapolcai, published an article in the *Journal of the Gypsy Lore Society* with the title 'Assimilative Mechanisms in Late 19th Century Hungary: The History of a Romani Settlement'.[6] The article describes and analyzes an effort by the Hapsburg Archduke Josef to settle and assimilate a group of nomadic Vlach Roma on one of his estates in Fejèr County in Hungary between 1891 and 1893. This project came only 30 years after the abolition of slavery and serfdom in Transylvania and Vallchia (tzara Romaneasca), and groups of nomadic Roma that had arrived in Hungary post-emancipation were now masterless and considered deviant. The new trends in the national division of labor, writes Tapolcai, meant that all forces of production were supposed to have well-defined economic functions. The economic niches of the Roma – small volume handicraft,

---

5 *Id.*, 44.
6 Andras Tapolcai, *Assimilative Mechanisms in Late 19th century Hungary: The History of a Romani Settlement* 5 JOURNAL OF THE GYPSY LORE SOCIETY No. 1 (1995).

smithery, entertainment and fortunetelling – were regarded as uncivilized and unacceptable.[7] The general attitude of government officials towards these groups was punitive, and restrictive measurements, such as imprisonment, confiscation of horses and carriages and sending them back to "their places of origin", were taken.

The Archduke was however a modern liberal; he was a well-known ethnographer and his approach was assimilative and educative rather than punitive. As a member of the reigning royal family, he had large estates throughout the country and, as he was well aware of the failure of the hitherto punitive actions towards the nomadic Roma, his approach was to convince them in their own language of the usefulness and importance of a sedentary life. Based on this idea and on his general knowledge of the Rom culture, he set out to settle around 300 nomadic Roma on one of his estates and include them in his work-force. This estate was one of the most advanced centres of capitalist agricultural at that time, with machinery, irrigation, small industrial plants, roads connecting the plants, saving banks, a post-office and schools for the children of workers. Tapolcai notes that "the main coordinator of production was the head overseer of the latifundio (estate), who's rights, duties and responsibilities transformed the feudal tradition into a capitalistic one".[8]

The first Roma to be settled were families whose horses had been confiscated by the authorities and that were unable to make a living. Later, more families that had received the same treatment were included. The Archduke had huts of straw built for the Roma as their first dwelling places based on his knowledge of their traditional ways of dwelling. His plan was to move them into brick houses after a short period of time once they were accustomed to life in a "village". Many Roma, however, refused to move into these cottages preferring to spend the nights in their traditional tents even in the cold season. When they explained that the houses were full of evil spirits, the Archduke used his ethnographic knowledge about their cultural beliefs to try to convince them to move into the cottages anyway. It did not work and eventually they were allowed to stay in their tents.

Three other assimilation efforts failed, one by one. The Roma were supposed to work on the estate and they seemed to have accepted working for wages. The problem was that the Roma were put to agricultural work that they were not accustomed to and did not like; only those employed as smiths

---

7   *Id.*

8   *Id.*, 3.

performed well, according to the Archduke. None the less they were forced to do agricultural work, but because they resisted so much, the Archduke was obliged to pay them higher wages than the non-Romani workers for the same work. This caused tension with the non-Roma workers. Further, the Archduke expected the Romani children to attend the estate's school. The women, however, resisted school for their children seeing no need for an education as, they argued, the skills they needed were not taught in school. The Archduke was however insistent and the children were eventually, and reluctantly, sent to school. The third mechanism for assimilation was to employ a young Rom as a supervisor for the working Roma. It is not clear whether he was appointed by the Archduke or chosen by the Roma themselves. According to the historical account, he appears to have been appointed by the Archduke as an "agent of assimilation" and was highly unpopular among the Roma. Several conflicts broke out between the Rom supervisor and the settled Roma. After a year and a half, the supervisor was fired and later imprisoned by the Archduke on fraud charges. The settlement began to disintegrate, smaller groups of Roma disappeared and the non-Roma population settled in the area became more hostile towards the Roma. Finally, the church and the authorities withdrew their support and the settlement was closed.

The archduke himself blamed the low level of civilization among the Roma and the lack of support from the government for the failure. Tapolcai, based on his analysis, suggests that the failure was caused by the lack of cultural awareness on the part of the Archduke and by the cultural resistance of the Roma. He also highlights the lack of involvement of the Roma themselves in the decision making processes about their lives.

III. Rehabilitation of the Norwegian Roma

Around a hundred years later a similar effort was made by the Norwegian authorities in relation to a group of approximately 300 Vlach Roma who had settled in Oslo after the Second World War. These families had been travelling in Norway before the war and several had Norwegian birth certificates. Some of them had tried to escape the increasing persecution in 1930s Germany by entering Norway in 1934 but were rejected at the border and sent back to Germany. When those families that had survived the war and the concentration camps reentered the country in the 1950s, they were eventually, after long political and legal processes, granted Norwegian citizenship.

In the 50s and 60s, this group of Roma lived in caravans in a parking lot in the city centre surrounded by high fences. Some human-rights activists contacted the group and, together with one family leader who titled himself as "a gypsy king", they wrote a letter to the Norwegian King asking for help to integrate into Norwegian society. The municipality of Oslo, backed by government authorities, then designed a programme of integration: the so-called "Rehabilitation of Norwegian Gypsies" programme. This programme was designed to settle the Roma in permanent houses, offer appropriate education for children and adults, work-training for men and a kindergarten for the children to enable the women to go to school. These activities were supported by social security funds; all families received allowances for their livelihoods, adults received small wages for school-attendance and the kindergarten was free of charge. The programme was developed in cooperation with the "gypsy king" – the influential but self-appointed Rom-leader – and several other leaders of extended families. After ten years of the programme, most families had been settled in houses (barracks) constructed for extended families in different neighborhoods in Oslo. Literary education was arranged for all adults, who were paid by the hour. Some work-training projects were established and the municipality even started a carpet shop run by one family. Classes for Roma children were established at local schools and school material was developed in *Romanés* and some Roma were appointed as mother-tongue teachers. The municipality started a kindergarten and a youth club for Roma children and a separate social security office for Roma citizens. Roma representatives were involved in the development of all these projects and consented to them.[9]

The program nonetheless ran into several problems from the start. Most families only sporadically sent their children to school and after a while teachers started to collect the children at home and take them to school in taxis or microbuses. The adults attended the adult education programmes only infrequently and very few families paid rents for their houses. Yet fifteen years after it had begun, the programme was expanded to include several activities such as karate-instruction for girls, a youth club for Roma children and youth. The authorities and the public began to question the whole programme: after fifteen years, only one child had completed secondary school, no adult was employed, many of the houses had been abandoned and

---

9   Ada Engebrigtsen and Hilda Lidén, *De norske rom og deres historie*, in Nasjonale Minoriteter I Norge (A. Bonnevie Lund/ B. Bolme Moen eds., Tapir Akademisk Forlag, 2010, 87-99.)

most Roma had kept their caravans and were still travelling in the spring, summer and autumn of each year. After the discovery of a major scam, in which the family of the "Gypsy king" was one of the involved parties, the programme was shut down, and the Roma were left on their own, that is to the general social security system, to ordinary classes in schools and to ordinary kindergartens. The failure of the rehabilitation project was analyzed at the time and the outcome attributed to a lack of cultural awareness by the Municipality authorities, but also to the strong resistance to change among leading Roma.

Today, Norwegian Roma number approx. 500-600.[10] Approximately 50 of the 200-300 Norwegian Roma children attend school more or less regularly, no adults are employed and there are few Roma children in kindergartens. Most families earn their living by a combination of small businesses (for instance, door to door peddling of carpets and other goods) and welfare benefits. Thanks to this combination of the welfare system and their own businesses, the socio-economic condition of most Roma families in Norway is acceptable.[11] In 2006, Norwegian Roma were given the status of national minority (as were the Travellers, the Kvens, the Jews and the Forest Finns), and with this new status the pressure to integrate into mainstream society has increased. In order to obtain the financial support for cultural activities that comes with the status, they are expected to organize in ways that are acceptable to the majority, which includes electing representatives of their community. However, the Roma communities are generally not organized as representative democracies, but rather as family networks with family leaders.[12]

To sum up the two cases: in the first case, the programme was based on ethnographic knowledge of the Roma but they were not involved in the planning and implementation. The Roma resisted, and the Archduke had to use a mixture of compulsion and persuasion to implement his plan. Being forced to perform manual labor was probably viewed as degrading by the artisan Roma (the sort of forced labor that slaves had performed), and paying the Roma higher wages than the non-Roma was a classical divide and rule strategy that increased enmity between Roma and non-Roma workers and heightened the tension among them.

---

10   This number does not include those Roma from the former-Yugoslavia who arrived as asylum-seekers during the war, or Norwegian Travellers.

11   For some Roma, their living standard is over the national level, for others below; however, we do not have any data for this.

12   Engebrigtsen and Lidén, (note 9).

The Norwegian case was slightly different. The authorities had learnt a lesson from the problematic assimilation efforts related to the Travellers and Saami, and were eager not to repeat the same failures. They involved the Roma in their plans; that is they involved some *self-appointed* family heads in the *implementation* of their plans. The outcomes of the programme were, from the very start, given: settlement, education and employment. One of the short-comings of the Norwegian efforts was that the authorities had no knowledge of the history and culture of the actual Roma group concerned; they expected them to want to become Norwegians and to abandon their traditional lifestyle in exchange for better living conditions. But the Roma wanted Norwegian living standards without giving up their way of life – and they partially succeeded. Moreover, in both cases, the persons chosen to represent the Roma in the implementation of the projects had little legitimacy outside their own extended families.

IV. What Are the Lessons to be Learnt from these Examples?

So what can these two cases tell us about official efforts to integrate the Roma in majority society? What are the lessons to be learnt?

These cases illustrate that, being a minority, the Roma live almost constantly under some kind of threat from the majority, both historically and in the present. They are thus dependent upon tolerance from their social environment in order to control their own way of life.[13] One way to gain such tolerance is to incorporate aspects of the majority way of life and traditions into their habits. Religion is an important marker of loyalty and inclusion and Roma populations generally follow the majority religion of the wider community in which they live. They also tend to observe many of the same traditions as the majority population, and leaders generally form alliances with influential majority persons. Another practice is to orally accept suggestions for changes to their culture and way of life, but to at least partly resist such changes in practice. Education, manual labor, wage labor and military service are examples of majority practices, and demands for integration, that cannot be openly opposed but are practically evaded. These techniques are weapons of the powerless, and may be seen as a tactic to oppose the strategies that are "well-controlled weapons of the strong". Tactics

---

13 Tapolcai (note 6).

operate in the dark and in disguise, never showing their real interest and opposing power by avoiding it.[14]

However, we cannot conclude from these cases that the Roma resist change in general. On the contrary, their way of life is dependent on majority populations and thus demands almost continuous change and adaptation to changing social and political environments. The Roma are survivors of generations of persecution, assimilation efforts and discrimination; while they must fight to ensure their survival as a distinct group, this does not imply that the many groups resist in the same way or that resistance to inclusion is their only mode. Large portions of the populations that we call Roma live peaceful lives amongst the majority population, and are well integrated with full-time employment and children in school.

One basic lesson learned is that "cultural awareness" or knowledge of "Gypsy culture" is often too generalized and de-contextualized as the basic knowledge necessary to work for change for or within a specific group or community of Roma. The populations that in today's political discourse are called Roma or Romanies represent a huge variety of people with different histories and practices of adaptation in the societies in which they live. All have relations to the majority population they live among and all have incorporated different elements of that culture and way of life into their own. To understand their preferences and the opportunities genuinely open to them, it is necessary to have a comprehensive understanding of their social history and local knowledge of the present social relations of that actual population or group. In the Norwegian case, the Roma were seen as "a lost tribe", as a population that had been well integrated into mainstream society, but that had "fallen out" because of industrialization of agriculture and of the manufacturing sector. Based on this assumption, it was clear that the task of the welfare-society was to re-include them into society. This interpretation meant that there was no question about how the Roma themselves defined their own interest: they had "fallen out" and therefore necessarily wanted "back in".

Yet the notion of cultural awareness can also be treacherous as it tends to obscure other factors that influence individual's and peoples' behavior, and instead becomes a euphemism for everything different and problematic.[15] For

---

14   MICHEL DE CERTEAU, THE PRACTIVE OF EVERYDAY LIFE (1984).

15   Alexandra Nacu, *The Politics of Roma Migration: Framing Identity Struggles among Romanian and Bulgarian Roma in the Paris region* 37:1 JOURNAL OF ETHNIC AND MIGRATION STUDIES 135-150 (2011).

example, poverty may force people to take actions and form habits that are more instant answers to precarious situations than lasting collective values, norms, habits and practices that we generally understand as cultural aspects of societies. But poverty also influences peoples' cultural repertoires and may form these groups in certain ways. So culture, socioeconomic status and individual choice are only some of the variables that influence people's actions.

In a recent paper, Alexandra Nacu discusses the current migration of Roma from Romania and Bulgaria into the rest of Europe. She describes the role of the NGO's and individuals that act as "volunteers" exercising strong symbolic power when they enter camps with economic resources. Paternalism, often inherent in the role of "helper", may make these activists believe that they know best what is in the interest of "the marginalized other". Nacu describes a case in which a voluntary doctor distributed condoms in a Roma camp without even asking the inhabitants' permission.[16] Material improvement that is the basic offer of welfare society cannot always substitute for strong collective sentiments and a sense of family-based social security that is the strength of most tightly-knit Roma groups.

Shame and pride are important aspects of human life and most Roma groups have developed strategies to avoid the shame inflicted by discrimination and persecution. Marginalization and exclusion from mainstream society is generally understood from a middle-class majority society perspective and as stemming from poverty. However, those that are excluded from mainstream society are often included in other collectives that provide for a sense of belonging and dignity. The poor and discriminated segments of the Roma populations have lived for centuries in difficult conditions, and they have often developed a pride in membership in their specific group, in their way of life and traditions, often accompanied by contempt for the non-Roma lifestyle. Mutual mistrust is thus key to understanding the relationship between Roma and the majority population. Trust must develop over time through the experience of change that does not threaten the sense of pride that has been achieved at such cost.

A further, crucial aspect of the success of any programmes for change concerns the identity of the first person or people to accept the changes. Experience suggests that it is the poorest and most marginal groups of a population that is willing to take the risk of changing norms and practices and thus of losing support from the wider grouping. Self-appointed representatives

---

16 *Id.*, 143.

are often among such outsiders and may have little or no support from the mainstream of the group. Nacu describes the same problem among NGOs in her Paris case.[17] The representatives chosen to approach Roma groups were generally not acknowledged as representatives by group members. Representatives should be regarded critically: who selected them, who do they represent, what is in it for them? Few Roma groups have democratically elected leaders. Most leaders resemble Weber's "charismatic type"; they are self-appointed and approved because of their personality. Among Roma, these leaders are normally male and often only represent their extended family in public. Thus they are "external leaders" not "internal leaders", are therefore better understood as "middlemen" in negotiation with non-Roma, not as legitimate representatives of the wider group.[18]

Another danger highlighted by the two projects described is what we could call the mirage of "holism". Plans for integrating Roma groups are often very comprehensive and require through-going change to all aspects of their lives at the same time. The desire for such a holistic approach is understandable; yet while all aspects of one's life are connected, they do not have the same degree of importance in the "whole". Another lesson, then, is to carefully select – in close consultation and together with the families and groups themselves – one or two aspects of their lives that they want to and are able to change, and that may have knock-on significance for other basic aspects of their life. If these changes do happen and lead to better life-conditions, the chance is much greater that the families will continue the process instead of resisting it.

One final, related lesson is that it is crucial *not* to make successful projects with one group into a model for "working with Roma". Recommendations for "best practice" must always be based on the social history, local and particular interests and opportunities of the actual Roma groups concerned.[19] Only then may projects for inclusion avoid the failure of these two earlier efforts.

---

17   *Id.*

18   Ignacy-Marek Kaminski, *The dilemma of power internal an external leadership. The Gypsy Roma of Poland*, in THE OTHER NOMADS, (A. Rao ed., Bölaug Verlag, 1987), 323-356.

19   Peter Vermeersch, *Reframing the Roma: EU Initiatives and the Politics of Reinterpretation* 38(8) JOURNAL OF ETHNIC AND MIGRATION STUDIES (2012), 1-18.

Chapter 7

Anti-Roma Hate Speech in the Czech Republic, Hungary and Poland

Uladzislau Belavusau[*]

I. Introduction

> *"Even today, we sometimes hear people calling 'Gypsies to the gas chamber'. Even today, we can observe indifference to these calls, quiet support for those who are yelling them, cowardly spectators, the renewal of divisions between people according to their ethnic origin. All of this must be faced up to again and again, because it is the tried-and-true territory of racism."*

(Václav Havel, 1995)

A. Anti-Gypsyism and freedom of expression

Voluminous papers have been written drawing an analogy between anti-Semitism and anti-Gypsyism. While exploring the similarities in xenophobic attitude towards these two – historically largest – "Others" of Europe (the Jews and the Roma), their authors suggest that the roots of hostility date back to Christian obscurantism, medieval segregation, the exclusion from citizenship during modernity and the apogee of European racial supremacism

[*] Assistant Professor, Vrije Universiteit Amsterdam (the Netherlands); u.belavusau@vu.nl. The author is grateful to Morag Goodwin (Tilburg), Michal Bobek (Oxford), Jiří Přibáň (Cardiff), and Wojciech Sadurski (Sydney) for helpful feedback on various drafts. The broader and updated version of this article is forthcoming as a chapter in the monograph, see EUROPEAN ULADZISLAU BELAVUSAU, FREEDOM OF SPEECH: IMPORTING EUROPEAN AND US CONSTITUTIONAL MODELS IN TRANSITIONAL DEMOCRACIES (2013).

in Nazi Germany.[1] Milan Kundera's line about Central European Jews "*Aliens everywhere and everywhere at home*" equally makes a perfect metaphor for the Roma.[2] Approximately 70% of the European Romani population (even on the lowest accounts, this figure amounts to five million people) inhabit Central and Eastern Europe (further CEE).[3] This region's unsavoury past illustrates a similar pattern of degrading treatment and stereotyping of Roma in various CEE states. Albeit with important differences, this pattern mimics the hate speech rhetoric towards the Jewish population. Such rhetorical practices range from burlesquing in folklore to ostracizing or dehumanizing in social discourses, and, one can argue, ultimately, lead to segregation and pogroms.

As captured by Henry Scicluna:

"Anti-Gypsyism is not a form of discrimination based on differences of culture and behaviour, but an attitude of utter contempt. It is not intended to criticise but to humiliate and demean. Anti-Romani speech in the public sphere does not indicate dislike but hate and is intended to hurt. Roma

---

1 *Inter alia*, the "original sin" of the Roma was attributed to their alleged refusal to shelter Mary and the baby Jesus during flight from King Herod into Egypt. Roma have also been accused of forging the nails with which Christ was crucified. The popular medieval obscurantism often blamed Jews for drinking the blood of Christian babies in hidden rituals, while Roma were charged with stealing and even eating babies. Contemporary anti-Gypsy hate speech still draws waters from the archetypical mystification, stereotyping and stigmatization of Medieval Europe. Negative utterances depict the "gypsy propensity" to commit crimes. Neutral narratives refer to Roma as somehow semi-human or childlike. At best, social and media narratives portray them as free-spirited and carefree, similar to animals. For the phenomenon of de-humanisation in anti-Roma discourses, see KLAUS-MICHAEL BOGDAL, EUROPA ERFINDET DIE ZIGEUNER – EINE GESCHICHTE VON FASZINATION UND VERACHTUNG (2011) and Valeriu Nicolae, *Towards a Definition of Anti-Gypsyism*, available at: http://www.ergonetwork.org/media/userfiles/media/egro/Towards%20 a%20Definition%20of%20Anti-Gypsyism.pdf

2 The full quote from MILAN KUNDERA, ÚNOS ZÁPADU ANEB TRAGÉDIE STŘEDNÍ EVROPY (1983) [cited according to – *The Stolen West or the Tragedy of Central Europe*, The New York Review of Books, 26 April 1984]: "*Indeed, no other part of the world has been so deeply marked by the influence of Jewish genius. Aliens everywhere and everywhere at home, lifted above national quarrels, the Jews in the twentieth century were the principal cosmopolitan, integrating element in Central Europe. They were its intellectual cement, a condensed version of its spirit, creators of its spiritual unity*".

3 See the Fact sheet of the World Bank, *Roma inclusion in Central and Eastern Europe*, available at: http://siteresources.worldbank.org/INTROMA/Resources/Policy_Note_ Fact_Sheet.pdf Some authors estimate the number of CEE Roma as six million, approximately eight million in Europe, and ten million worldwide. E.g., see Zoltan Barany, *Orphans of Transition: Gypsies in Eastern Europe*, 9 Journal of Democracy 142 (1998).

are not disliked for some characteristics which are perceived as negative – they are hated because they are Roma. It is not even aimed at assimilating Roma by force – which would also be unacceptable – it is merely aimed at excluding them."[4]

Yet there is a striking difference between anti-Semitism and anti-Gypsyism in the way in which the right to freedom of expression has been constructed in Europe. The often-discussed European exception to freedom of expression – the exclusion of hate speech from the scope of the right's protection – stems from the trauma of the Holocaust (*Shoah* in Hebrew tradition). On the contrary, the Romani Holocaust (*Porajmos* in Romani dialects) has been almost entirely neglected in European discourse until relatively recently. Similarly, post-war international law has determined that Shoah denial can be regarded as a crime,[5] while overlooking the history of persecution of Roma and homosexuals in the Third Reich and occupied territories.[6]

---

4   Henry Scicluna, *Anti-Romani Speech in Europe's Public Space – The Mechanism of Hate Speech*, available at European Roma Rights Center: http://www.errc.org/article/ anti-romani-speech-in-europes-public-space--the-mechanism-of-hate-speech/2912

5   Trapped between the political dissents of the world's superpowers and particular cultural memory of the Holocaust and racist atrocities, the post-war construction of the right to free speech has echoed decolonisation as well as anti-imperial discourses. Article 20 of the UN International Covenant o Civil and Political Rights maintains, *"any advocacy of national, racial or religious hatred that constitutes incitement to discrimination, hostility or violence shall be prohibited by law"*. Projecting this article on Holocaust denial in the case of *Faurisson* [1996], the UN Human Rights Committee upheld the decision of a French court to punish a professor of literature at the Sorbonne and Lyon for manifestation of Holocaust denial viewpoints (Communication No. 550/1993, 8 November 1996). A Jewish lawyer, Rapael Lemkin, introduced the very term genocide. In his post-Holocaust essay *"Crime of Barbarity"* [1944], he formulated a proposal for a ban on crimes against humanity. This proposal suffered serious rebuffs at the Paris Peace Conference in 1945 but was finally taken into consideration by the General Assembly and framed into the Convention on the Prevention and Punishment of the Crime of Genocide.

6   This fallacy in the vision of the World War II genocides persists. David Fraser, *inter alia*, suggests that *"the members of no other group [apart from Jews] were targeted for complete and instant annihilation simply because they were racially identified as belonging to the enemy race"*. Thus, the author considers that Gypsies were persecuted as asocial and criminal elements rather than for their nomadic lifestyle and racial identity. See David Fraser, *On the Internet, Nobody Knows You're a Nazi: Some Comparative Legal Aspects of Holocaust Denial on the www*, in EXTREME SPEECH AND DEMOCRACY 511, 571 (Ivan Hare & James Weinstein eds., 2009). I radically disagree with this position. The segregation of Roma and Sinti people (along with the histories of the genocide against homosexuals, disabled people and adherents of the Jehovah's Witness sect) is a truly shameful part of post-war historiography and is due to a deliberate avoidance of the oral-history evidence from survivors of

B. Freedom of Expression and Non-Discrimination in Central & Eastern Europe

It would be impossible to provide details of all the notorious instances of anti-Roma hate speech occurring in the three countries of CEE selected for consideration in this paper: the Czech Republic, Hungary, and Poland. The goal of this article is somewhat different. I shall identify the legal recourses available to combat the phenomenon of hate speech. Hence, the ambition is to illuminate the legal and judicial framework that has emerged for social movements of Czech, Hungarian and Polish Roma during the last twenty years since the fall of Communism. A discussion on anti-Gypsyism stems from the Western debate about the scope of the hate speech exception to the right to freedom of expression, with its radical split between European (restrictive) and American (libertarian) approaches.[7]

What unites CEE perspectives on freedom of expression and non-discrimination are certain experiences of the relatively late nation-building, the communist legacies, the ethos of the "return to the Western cradle", as well as a series of law reforms before and after the EU's "eastward" enlargement that these countries have all undergone. The post-communist application of similar constitutional models that borrow from "American" and ("Western") "European" samples of judicial design make them an important object for generalisations and comparison in relation to the hate speech phenomenon.[8]

A certain historical and socio-legal proximity in the roots and aspects of the anti-Gypsyism in the region also present a similar pattern for my

---

the *Porajmos*. In 1942 and 1943 Heinrich Himmler issued several decrees ordering the deportation of all German Roma to Auschwitz. See MICHAEL BURLEIGH & WOLFWANG WIPPERMANN, THE RACIAL STATE: GERMANY 1933-1945 (1991).

7   The contrasts and similarities between free speech concepts in the USA and Europe are well documented. In particular, I provide a detailed analysis of the semiotic differences between European and American approaches to hate speech, in Uladzislau Belavusau, *Judicial Epistemology of Free Speech through the Lenses of Ancient Rhetoric*, 23 INTERNATIONAL JOURNAL FOR THE SEMIOTICS OF LAW 165 (2010). Unlike in continental Europe, the approach of the U.S. Supreme Court has enfolded hate speech into the protective scope of the First Amendment. This is perhaps the most striking discrepancy between the two principal Western free speech models.

8   For a broader perspective on the transitional CEE constitutionalism, see WOJCIECH SADURSKI, RIGHTS BEFORE COURTS. A STUDY OF CONSTITUTIONAL COURTS IN POST-COMMUNIST STATES OF CENTRAL AND EASTERN EUROPE XI (2005). Jiří Přibáň, *Happy Returns to Europe? The Union's Identity, Constitution-Making, and Its Impact on the Central Accession States*, in SPREADING DEMOCRACY AND THE RULE OF LAW? THE IMPACT OF EU ENLARGEMENT ON THE RULE OF LAW, DEMOCRACY AND CONSTITUTIONALISM IN POST-COMMUNIST LEGAL ORDERS 193, 203 (Wojciech Sadurski, Adam Czarnota & Martin Krygier eds., 2006).

analysis. Scrutiny of each country will begin with the appraisal of the socio-historical context of hate (in particular, anti-Roma) speech production, as well as with an overview of the legal instruments that structure the debate about the problem. I will then proceed with examining the adjudication of the constitutional and other relevant courts. In my conclusions, I will scrutinise the transnational framework available for the protection of Roma against hate speech in the region.

II. Czech Republic

A. *The Social and historical context*

The Czech Republic (comprising the historic lands of Bohemia, Moravia, and Silesia) is an offspring of the Austro-Hungarian Empire, and remained for centuries strongly Germanised under Habsburg rule. Peacefully dissolved from Slovakia, the country under the present borders has existed *de jure* since 1993. Further historical factors also explain the contemporary national composition of the Czech Republic and the specificities of nationalist discourse. The historically large Roma and Jewish minority were tragically wiped out during the Nazi occupation, while a significant German minority was either deported or escaped the country after World War II. In the contemporary Czech Republic, among the ten million-strong population, Roma and Germans constitute the biggest minority groups. Other ethnic minorities include Poles, Ruthenians (Rusyns), and Hungarians.

Historical references to Roma settlements date back to the 14th century.[9] Similarly to other medieval lands in Europe, in Bohemia the gypsies (*cikáni*) were confused with either Turks (Saracens) or Arabs from Egypt.[10] The greatest pre-Porajmos persecution of Roma in the Czech Lands came after 1697, when an Imperial decree placed Roma outside the law. Most notoriously, killing of Roma was not considered a crime. In the middle of the 18th century, Maria Theresa attempted to assimilate the Romani populations within the Austrian empire (comprising Bohemia, Moravia, and Hungary). Her decree prohibited the nomadic lifestyle and the use of the Romani language. In this period

---

9 For a detailed historical account, see ANGUS FRASER, THE GYPSIES (1995).

10 As in many other European languages, the exonym most probably originates from the *Atsinganoi* in the Byzantine Empire. Compare Czech *Cikán*, Polish *Cygan*, Hungarian *Cigányok*, Rumanian *Tsigan*, Belarusian & Ukrainian *Cyhán*, German & Dutch *Zigeuner*, French *Tsigane*, Italian *Zingaro*, etc.

of "enlightened absolutism" under Maria Theresa and Joseph II, a sizable number of Roma settled in the Czech lands (mostly, but also in Slovakia) or passed through in a semi-migratory way of life. The settlers included bricklayers, tinkers, blacksmiths, trough-makers, road-menders, musicians, and other itinerant trades. The results of the imperial efforts were evident in the Czech lands, where the Bohemian-Moravian Roma were to a large extent assimilated into the majority population. However, in the course of the 19th century, Roma again became outsiders as a consequence of their lack of adaptation towards the new economic realities of industrialisation. In the years preceding World War I, most Czech Roma were illiterate and exposed to ostracisation by the '*gadje*' (in Romani dialects, non-Roma) population. As elsewhere in CEE, the Czech Roma experienced the genocide of the Nazi and axis regimes. After liberation, only 583 Romani men and women returned to their homes from a pre-war population of circa 8000.[11] The original Romani population of the Czech lands was thus almost annihilated during the period of the Nazi occupation. A similar fate befell the Sinti and Roma of the detached Sudetenland.

During the Communist period, Roma continued to suffer the unwanted attentions of the authorities. The Czechoslovak Roma did not enjoy a status of ethnic minority, but were considered instead as a "socially degraded stratum".[12] Significant portions of Roma migrated to Czechoslovakia from Romania and Hungary. The authorities made an effort at the forceful settlement and dispersion of the Romani population. In return, the Czechoslovak government offered financial benefits for dispersal, which increased the conspiracy phobias and stereotypes about "lazy gypsies" amongst the ethnic Czechs and Slovaks. Most shamefully, in the late 1970s and early 1980s, government social workers in Czechoslovakia encouraged Romani women to undergo sterilisation by offering financial inducements at a time of economic hardship. In addition, many women were sterilised without their consent, and without the financial compensation, as they underwent caesarean sections or abortions.[13]

---

11 Fraser, (Note 9), 267.
12 For an account of Czech Roma history, see Ctibor Nečas, Romové v Čr Včera a Dnes (1999). See also an NGO report, *The History of Roma in the Czech Republic* (2000), available at: http://romove.radio.cz/en/article/18913
13 See Morag Goodwin, *Holding up a Mirror to the Process of Transition? The Coercive Sterilization of Romani Women in the Post-1991 period*, in Law in Transition. Human Rights, Development and Transitional Justice (P. Zumbansen & R. Buchanan eds. forthcoming Hart Publishing 2013).

B. *The legal framework*

The European Commission against Racism and Intolerance in its 2009 report noted that there is still no comprehensive anti-discrimination legislation in force in the Czech Republic.[14] At the same time, the Commission suggested that the Czech Charter of Fundamental Rights and Freedoms[15] does not appear to provide effective protection against racial discrimination. Moreover, the report draws attention to a disturbing intensification in the activities of the extreme right-wing milieu, including the setting up of uniformed paramilitary groups.[16] This information has become outdated, as on 17 June 2009 the Czech Republic adopted anti-discrimination legislation which guarantees the right to equal treatment and bans discrimination in areas including access to employment, business, education, healthcare and social security on the grounds of sex, age, disability, race, ethnic origin, nationality, sexual orientation, religious affiliation and faith or worldview. The last-minute passing of the Anti-Discrimination Act by the Czech Chamber of Deputies was a necessary step to avoid legal proceedings by the European Commission for failing to implement the obligations contained in the EU Race Equality Directive (Council Directive 2000/43/EC) and the Employment Equality Directive (Council Directive 2000/78/EC).

The Czech Republic has signed but has not ratified Protocol No. 12 of the European Convention on Human Rights, an important anti-discrimination instrument of the Council of Europe (as of January 2012, it has 19 ratifications and 18 signatories) that makes the non-discrimination provision of the Convention free-standing. Similarly, it has neither signed nor ratified the Additional Protocol to the Convention on Cybercrime, concerning the criminalisation of acts of a racist or xenophobic nature committed through computer systems. The non-recognition of corporate criminal liability in domestic law prevents ratification of this Convention, without which the Additional Protocol cannot be ratified.

In 2010, a new Criminal Code (*Trestní zákoník*, enacted in 2009) came into force. The adjudication further described in this paper was based upon the provisions of the previous 1961 Code, which are essentially similar on the issues of hate speech. §42 (b) of the new Code explicitly details hate

---

14   ECRI (European Commission Against Racism and Intolerance) Report on the Czech Republic (fourth monitoring cycle), CRI, 30, 2009. 8.

15   The Czech Constitution does not include a catalogue of human rights. Therefore, the Charter forms part of the constitutional legal order.

16   ECRI (European Commission Against Racism and Intolerance) Report on the Czech Republic (fourth monitoring cycle), CRI, 30, 2009. 8.

crimes, i.e. hate-aggravated offences of murder, grievous bodily harm, bodily harm, torture and other inhuman and cruel treatment, false imprisonment, unlawful restraint, kidnapping, blackmail, breach of secrecy of documents held in private, damage to private property, abuse of the authority of an official, violence against a group of persons and against an individual, as well as some military offences. Racist motivations remain a specific aggravating circumstance that judges are required to take into account when sentencing offenders. The additional aggravating circumstances have been added for a number of offences where the commission of an offence is motivated by the real or perceived race, ethnicity, nationality, political convictions, religion or real or perceived lack of religious belief. §352 prohibits violence against a group of inhabitants and individuals.

The clauses on pure hate speech are provided by §355 and §366. The former prohibits the defamation of a nation, race, ethnic or other group of persons, *inter alia*, on grounds of an individual or group's real or perceived race, membership of an ethnic group, nationality or political or religious convictions or lack thereof. Under the terms of this provision, racist motivations can only be considered as an aggravating circumstance in relation to the media, i.e. when the offence was committed *via* the press, film, radio, TV, a publicly accessible computer network or other similarly effective means.[17] In contrast, §366 does not link "hateful" utterances to a particular forum, and prohibits incitement to racial, national, ethnic, class or religious hatred and the promotion of restrictions on human rights and freedoms.[18]

---

17 § 355 (Hanobení národa, rasy, etnické nebo jiné skupiny osob):
(1) Kdo veřejně hanobí
a) některý národ, jeho jazyk, některou rasu nebo etnickou skupinu, nebo
b) skupinu osob pro jejich skutečnou nebo domnělou rasu, příslušnost k etnické skupině, národnost, politické přesvědčení, vyznání nebo proto, že jsou skutečně nebo domněle bez vyznání,
bude potrestán odnětím svobody až na dvě léta.
(2) Odnětím svobody až na tři léta bude pachatel potrestán, spáchá-li čin uvedený v odstavci 1
a) nejméně se dvěma osobami, nebo
b) tiskem, filmem, rozhlasem, televizí, ve řejně přístupnou počítačovou sítí nebo jiným obdobně účinným způsobem.

18 § 356 (Podněcování k nenávisti vůči skupině osob nebo k omezování jejich práv a svobod):
(1) Kdo veřejně podněcuje k nenávisti k některému národu, rase, etnické skupině, náboženství, třídě nebo jiné skupině osob nebo k omezování práv a svobod jejich příslušníků, bude potrestán odnětím svobody až na dvě léta.
(2) Stejně bude potrestán, kdo se spolčí nebo srotí k spáchání činu uvedeného v odstavci 1.
(3) Odnětím svobody na šest měsíců až tři léta bude pachatel potrestán,

The Code provides for a two-year prison term upon conviction. Thus, §366 of the Czech criminal code sets an explicit content-based restriction to freedom of expression.

Moreover, under §403 the establishment, support, promotion or publicisation of a movement aiming to suppress the rights and freedoms of human beings is prohibited. The commission of this offence *via* a publicly accessible computer network has been added as an aggravating circumstance (*přitěžující okolnost*). In addition, §404 prohibits manifestations of sympathy with such movements.

C. Constitutional court

Interestingly, the first and only decision on freedom of speech in the short practice of the Czechoslovak constitutional court (which had existed for less than a year in 1992) addressed the problem of hate speech, stemming from §260 and §261 of the Criminal Code 1961.[19] In the recent Criminal Code 2009, these clauses correspond to somewhat modified formulations in §355 and §366, described previously. The former criminal code embraced those clauses under the reference of "support and promotion aimed at suppressing human rights and freedoms" (*podpora a propagace hnutí směřujících k potlačení práv a svobod člověka*).

The 1992 case commenced as a petition by a group of 52 MPs challenging the conformity of §260 and §261 of the Criminal Code (amended in 1991) with constitutional texts and international instruments. The amendment brought communist propaganda under the scope of hate speech.[20] The Court did not support the petitioners' claim that, by adopting §260 and §261, the state had bound itself to an exclusive ideology. By no means, according to the Court, was it the case that only a certain ideology was permitted merely due to the fact that the law criminalised fascist and communist movements that were explicitly directed at the suppression of civil rights or at the declaration of hatred designated by the concept of malicious intent. Support for those ideologies that fall within the material elements of §260 was declared

---

a) spáchá-li čin uvedený v odstavci 1 tiskem, filmem, rozhlasem, televizí, veřejně přístupnou počítačovou sítí nebo jiným obdobně účinným způsobem, nebo
b) účastní-li se aktivně takovým činem činnosti skupiny, organizace nebo sdružení, které hlásá diskriminaci, násilí nebo rasovou, etnickou, třídní, náboženskou nebo jinou nenávist.

19   *Ústavní soud* 5/92, 4 September 1992.
20   Act No. 557/1991.

both impermissible and criminal, while all other ideologies were allowed unrestricted dissemination.

Within a few years after the dissolution of Czechoslovakia, the Czech Constitutional Court was snowed under with a review of substantially similar hate speech cases.[21] These numerous judgements of the 1990s concerned the ordinances of the local authorities from different cities and small towns (Ústí nad Labem, Brno, Jičín, Hořice v Podkrkonoší, Nová Paka, Pardubice, Vysoké nad Jizerou, Náchod, Červený Kostelec). The ordinances outlawed the promotion of non-parties and movements that spread national, racial, religious, or class hatred. In all of those judgements, the Court indicated the incompatibility of the local specification of the hate speech provisions stemming from the Criminal Code (§260 and §261) with Article 39 of the Charter of Fundamental Rights and Freedoms, annulling the ordinances. The local acts were struck down because they could not define the substance of the crime, even though they were simply paraphrasing the existing clause in the Criminal Code.

Finally, the most recent hate speech judgment of the Constitutional Court (2009) dealt with anti-Romani expression.[22] In 2001, the applicant František Kroščena brought a claim before an ordinary court against a restaurant owner. For a long time, the restaurant premises had displayed a statue of a Greek goddess of antiquity holding a baseball bat in her hand with a visible inscription "*Na cikány*" (a rough translation being "Get the gypsies!"). During the 1990s, members of the skinhead subculture often used baseball bats as a symbol to represent the intimidation of Romani communities. Both a regional and a High (*vrchni*) Court rejected this claim. Despite the fact that both found the defendant's act "inappropriate", they refused to hold the defendant liable for infringement of personality protection rights. According to established case law, the scope of the provision on the personality protection did not cover harassment. The claimant appealed repeatedly against the decisions of lower courts until he reached the Supreme Court.[23] The Court needed to reverse the appeal judgments of the lower courts twice, ordering them to decide on

---

21 *Ústavní soud* 29/95, 19 December 1995; *Ústavní soud* 41/95, 24 April 1996; *Ústavní soud* 42/95, 12 June 1996; *Ústavní soud* 43/95, 3 June 1996; *Ústavní soud* 44/95, 26 March 1996; *Ústavní soud* 45/95, 11 June 1996; *Ústavní soud* 1/96, 19 November 1996; *Ústavní soud* 4/96, 10 June 1996; *Ústavní soud* 68/04, 6 June 2006; *Ústavní soud* 38/03, 13 January 2004.

22 *Ústavní soud* 2943/08, 28 January 2009.

23 The Supreme Court (*Nejvyšší soud*) is the highest appeal court, except for administrative and constitutional cases, with jurisdiction over criminal and civil cases.

the merits again. After the third unsuccessful appeal to the Supreme Court against the decision of the lower courts, the applicant submitted a complaint to the Constitutional Court. Of crucial significance in coming to its decision was that the Constitutional Court referred to the EU "Race" Directive 2000/43/EC. Based on the Race Directive, the Court cancelled the judgment of the Supreme and High courts and referred the case back to the High Court for a new decision. In this regard, it is important to mention that, in 2008, the Court of Justice of the European Union (CJEU) used the Race Directive to frame hate speech into EU non-discrimination law.[24]

D. Supreme court

One of the most important judgements on hate speech in the Czech Republic was given by the Supreme Court (*Nejvyšší soud*).[25] The Court considered the appeal of a publisher Michal Zitko, who had been convicted of releasing a Czech translation of Adolf Hitler's *Mein Kampf*. The book combines elements of autobiography with an exposition of Hitler's political ideology, and remains banned in a number of European countries. The Czech translation (*Můj boj*) was released by the publishing house *Otakar* in March 2000 without any additional comments or annotation. It did, however, contain an explicit anti-racist disclaimer.

The Supreme Court annulled Mr. Zitko's conviction and returned the matter to the police for further investigation. The lower courts had viewed the distribution of the Czech version of the book under provisions prohibiting support for fascism or anti-Semitism. Zitko was originally given a three-year suspended prison sentence and fined CZK 2,000,000 ($ 56,500). Failure to pay the fine would have resulted in a one-year prison term. The Supreme Court found this interpretation of §260 of the Criminal Code to be overbroad, and held that it was necessary within the meaning of the crime that the promotion of a real movement as well as an action at the time of the crime be demonstrated. There should be a specific movement that is to some extent organised and structured (*organizovana a strukturovana skupina osob*) with an explicit common position and malicious purposes as listed in

---

24   See Case C-54/07, *Centrum voor gelijkheid van kansen en voor racismebestnijding v. Firma Feryn NV*, 2008 ECR I-5187. For a detailed scrutiny of the judgement and developments on hate speech in EU non-discrimination law, see Uladzislau Belavusau, *Fighting Hate Speech through EU Law*, 4 AMSTERDAM LAW FORUM 20 (2012).

25   5 *Tdo* 337/2002, 24 July 2002.

§260. Anti-Semitism is not a movement but an ideology promoting hatred of Jews, which may serve as an intellectual resource for various movements. Moreover, it was necessary, according to the Supreme Court, to demonstrate that the conduct of the accused (in this case, the release of *Mein Kampf*) was designed to encourage and promote this movement.

E. An overview of the current hate speech issues

The reconstruction of the *Mein Kampf* case by the Supreme Court appears incomplete without an insight into some sensitive aspects of the neo-Nazi movement in the Czech Republic. The latest ECRI Report on the Czech Republic, from 2009, focuses particular attention on the disturbing evidence of intensification in the activities of extreme right-wing groups, whose repeated demonstrations have led to escalating tensions and, at times, violent acts, especially towards the Roma community.[26] In 2008, the *Národní strana* ("National Party", existing since 2002) published sweeping attacks on Muslims on its website following the death of the Czech ambassador to Pakistan in a terrorist bombing. However, the legal proceedings against the party were dismissed by the relevant court, which did not find that any law had been violated. Similarly to the analogous Polish and Hungarian organisations, the National Party strongly opposes Czech membership in the EU. In 2007, the party established a paramilitary group *Národní garda* ("National Guard"). Racism and homophobia have been central to the populism advanced by the organisation. *Inter alia*, the experts noted that the group drew attention by organising patrols outside a school in mid-2008, ostensibly to protect local schoolchildren from assaults by Roma children as well as by attacking the participants of Gay Pride in Brno, in June 2008.[27] In the course of recent years, marches with hate speech slogans have been organized by the Workers' Party and well-known neo-Nazi groups such as the National Resistance and the Autonomous Nationalists with increasing frequency and publicity. In addition, Nazi groups have tried to organise patrol groups to "monitor" the situation between the majority and the so-called "inadaptable" (*nepřizpůsobivý*) minority (a derogatory term referring to the Roma).

Another judgement from a lower local court is illustrative of the application of the hate speech provisions in the Criminal Code. In July 2009, a Czech

---

26 ECRI (European Commission Against Racism and Intolerance) Report on the Czech Republic (fourth monitoring cycle), CRI, 30, 2009, 20.

27 *Id.*, 20 (para. 48).

singer, Michal Moravec from the neo-Nazi band *Imperium*, was sentenced to a 3-year prison term for the promotion of fascism in his song lyrics by a court in the southern city of České Budějovice. An appeal court upheld the conviction. The subject of the case was Imperium's album '*Triumf vůle*' (Triumph of the Will), the title of which echoed the Nazi propaganda film (*Triumph des Willens*) shot in the 1930s by Leni Riefestahl. The infamous film chronicled the 1934 Nazi Party Congress in Nuremberg. The Court found evidence of hateful propaganda in the lyrics of this album. For example, one of the songs contained the phrase "*chceš odplatu, chceš řešení, chceš bílou revoluci*" ("you want revenge, want a solution, you want a white revolution"). The defendant's advocate argued that, taken abstractly, such wording does not contain any explicit promotion of hatred. Following the American test of content-based restriction with no clear present danger or hate crime,[28] the case would have failed. However, the Czech court followed the Strasbourg model of contextualised reading, under which a speech act is not complete without a contextual affirmation (historical references, evidence of a group persecution or racial tensions, (non-)presence of a disclaimer, audience and the nature of the source of expression, visual background, etc.). Michal Moravec was a member of the militant neo-Nazi movement "*Národní odpor*" (National Resistance), and was invited to perform his songs during its meetings. In addition, a court expert on extremism from a public university, *Univerzita obrany* (the University of Defence), Ivo Svoboda, confirmed that the cover design of the album contained the traditional symbolic elements of racist propaganda.[29]

Despite the fact that in accordance with the Broadcasting Act and the Czech Television Act, the broadcast media are subject to a duty to strike the right balance, and in particular not to promote intolerance, civil society actors report that, while some journalists are sympathetic to minority issues and willing to cover positive stories, feedback on such stories is generally negative. The tabloid press frequently typecasts members of the Romani

---

28 The First Amendment jurisprudence of the US Supreme Court relies on the presumption of the inadmissibility of the "content-based restrictions", i.e. a restriction on the exercise of free speech based on the subject matter or type of speech. Such a restraint is permissible only if it is based on a compelling state interest and is so narrowly worded that it achieves only that purpose.

29 See Miroslava Nezvalová, *Zpívání o „bílé revoluci" vyneslo hudebníkovi tři roky vězení*, available at:
http://zpravy.idnes.cz/zpivani-o-bile-revoluci-vyneslo-hudebnikovi-tri-roky-vezeni-pr9-/krimi.asp?c=A090729_145348_krimi_pei

community as people that steal by definition, fail to pay their rent, are violent and refuse to work.[30]

Under this atmosphere of constant ostracising and burlesquing, many Czech Roma prefer to conceal their identity. For example in the 2001 census, only 11,716 people identified themselves as Romani, while informal estimates suggest that the actual number is between 15 to 30 times as high. In the course of the "Velvet divorce" from Slovakia, a new law on citizenship was enacted which was explicitly designed to prevent Roma from obtaining the new Czech citizenship. The respective law was eventually amended in 1999.[31] The historic prejudices, caricaturing of the Roma minority in media as well as the climate of radical racist slurs create an atmosphere of constant intimidation of Czech Romani communities. An exemplary episode of this hateful climate is the decision by the local authority of Ústí nad Labem to construct a wall in order to divide houses inhabited by Roma from the rest of the settlement.[32] The decision was ruled as unlawful under anti-racist provisions before the regional and High courts.

In another case, the Supreme Court was asked to grant compensation to Romani individuals for refusal of service at a restaurant.[33] In a similar case from 2005, the Regional court in Ostrava decided in favour of Romani plaintiffs who had been refused service in a restaurant. The claimants conducted an experiment on the restaurant premises. While the ethnic Czech customers were properly served, the Romani would-be customers were told that the restaurant was a private club and that thus they could not access any services. The Ostrava regional court awarded compensation of 50,000 CZK (approximately EUR 2000) to each of the plaintiffs. However, the High Court in Olomouc reduced the amount of compensation, after which the claimants appealed to the Supreme Court. The Supreme Court annulled the decision of the High Court in Olomouc, holding that it was irrelevant that the plaintiffs were conducting situation testing while experiencing the discriminatory

---

30   ECRI (European Commission Against Racism and Intolerance) Report on the Czech Republic (fourth monitoring cycle), CRI, 30, 2009, 21.

31   Clemens Wiedermann, Czech Republic, in COMPLIANCE IN THE ENLARGED EUROPEAN UNION. LIVING RIGHTS OR DEAD LETTERS? 27, 35 (Gerda Falkner, Oliver Treib & Elisabeth Holzleithner eds., 2008).

32   Somewhat symbolically, the first case on hate speech before the Czech Constitutional Court (in a series of similar cases, described earlier in the context of the Constitutional Court decisions) also originated from Ústí nad Labem. In the former case from the early 1990s, local authorities were rather overactive in their willingness to translate the hate speech clause from the Criminal Code into a local act.

33   30 *Cdo* 4431/2007.

treatment.[34] The reluctance of the lower courts to frame anti-Roma utterances into the criminal construction of hate speech is further vividly illustrated by the case before the Constitutional Court involving the restaurant statue with the baseball bat (discussed briefly above). The inscription "Get the gypsies" was regarded as incitement to hatred or aggression by neither the regional nor the High courts.

The ECRI report highlights another case, brought under the hate speech provision by the deputy chair of the Government Council for Roma Community Affairs against an extreme right-wing party, followed by two judicial decisions of lower courts in 2008 concerning neo-Nazi websites. The first decision upheld a three-year suspended sentence against X for supporting a skinhead convicted of launching and running neo-Nazi web pages. In the second decision, two men were sentenced to prison for two and three years respectively for running a neo-Nazi website supporting and promoting hateful movements.[35]

In synthesis, the Czech legislative and judicial approaches to hate speech fit with the dominant continental constitutionalism based on the presumptions of so-called *militant democracy*, i.e. the idea that certain freedoms (first of all, freedom of expression and freedom of association) should be limited to prevent the growth of authoritarianism via the unrestricted exercise of civil liberties. However, the case of anti-Roma hate speech reveals the unwillingness of the lower courts to frame anti-Gypsyism within the core of the protective mechanism. The slow changes that are visible in this regard are heavily influenced by the incentives from Strasbourg and Brussels. The reconstruction of the Roma hate speech sagas demonstrate that the outcome often depends on the persistence of social movements in pushing the case up to the Supreme and Constitutional courts.

---

34   See the case note by Pavla Boučková, *Supreme Court Decides on Amounts of Compensation Awarded in Racial Discrimination Cases*, European Network of Legal Experts in the Non-Discrimination Field (4 January 2010).

35   ECRI (European Commission Against Racism and Intolerance) Report on the Czech Republic (fourth monitoring cycle), CRI, 30, 2009, 21-22 (point 56).

III. Hungary

A. *The social and historical context*

Like the Czech Republic, Hungary is an offspring of the Austro-Hungarian dual monarchy. Unlike Poland and the Czech Republic, it underwent Ottoman occupation in the 16th and 17th centuries. Until 1918, Hungary remained under Austrian Habsburg rule, experiencing only a relatively short period of independence before the installation of the communist regime in 1948. Within the communist bloc, the Hungarian state was more liberal throughout the 1980s than the majority of Soviet satellites. Since the collapse of the communist system, Hungary has undergone a series of political and economic reforms and became one of the economic frontrunners in the CEE region.

The historical context explains the predispositions of contemporary nationalism in Hungary, as well the structure in ethnic composition. Towards the end of the 19th century, non-Hungarian nationalities living within the borders of the country constituted more than 50% of the population. Following the revision of the borders after World War I, this proportion changed significantly. Some 33% of Hungarians populating the Carpathian Basin (around 3 million people) found themselves outside the new country's borders, while the number of minorities living within the borders declined. Similarly to the Czech Republic and Poland, a very significant part of the Jewish (often comprising half of the city dwellers) and Romani populations were tragically reduced during World War II. Under the post-war arrangements in CEE, Hungary was accused of acting as a Nazi satellite and lost a large part of its territory. Those arrangements contributed to an enormous sense of nationalist victimhood among Hungarians, partly as a result of the large portions of Magyar population left outside the country borders, especially in Romanian Transylvania and the Slovak Republic. This peculiar victimhood has become a strong element of the Hungarian nationalist ethos, with explicit implications for the problems of hate speech and historical revisionism.[36]

Act LXXVII of 1993 on the Rights of National and Ethnic Minorities recognises 13 national minorities (ethnic groups). It proclaims the protection of their educational and linguistic rights as well as safeguards a system of

---

36 For an appraisal of the Hungarian national tradition in legal settings, see Zoltán Péteri, *National Tradition and Outside Influence in the History of Human Rights in Hungary*, 2 JOURNAL OF CONSTITUTIONAL LAW IN EASTERN AND CENTRAL EUROPE 145 (1996).

local self-government. Among the ten million population of Hungary, Roma constitute the biggest minority (around 400,000-600,000). Other recognized minorities groups include Armenians, Bulgarians, Croats (around 90,000-100,000), Germans (around 200,000), Greeks, Poles, Romanians, Ruthenians (Rusyns), Serbians, Slovaks (around 100,000), Slovenians, and Ukrainians.[37] Unlike Poland, predominantly Catholic Hungary is a significantly less religious country, with a long tradition of religious tolerance and strong secularisation left over from the Communist period. Religion is regarded as a private matter and Hungarians keep their religious belief and practice confidential. "Religiosity" is also lower than in most countries of Western Europe.[38]

The first reference to Roma in Hungarian lands (at that time confused with Egyptians, "gypsy", as in many other parts of medieval Europe) dates back to the 14th century. From the 16th century and especially in the 17th century, the Roma population (*cigányok*) grew steadily in Hungary, in particular, in Transylvania. As was mentioned above in the Czech context, the Habsburg rulers attempted to assimilate the Romani population. In particular, the Decree of 1761 prescribed that Roma (commonly referred to as *zigani* at the epoch) were in future to be called "new citizens" (*ujpolgár*), "new Hungarians" (*ujmagyar*) or "new peasants" (*ujparasztok*). The decree of 1772 prohibited Roma from speaking Romani and even marrying among themselves. Most notoriously, it ordered that Romani children should be removed from their families and placed into the families of peasants. However, those decrees were never fully implemented due to both the Roma resistance to assimilation and the lack of the resources by the imperial machinery of the epoch to control the implementation. In the *interbellum* period of the 20th century, the police were authorized to undertake raids on Roma settlements. During the World War II, the deportation of Transdanubia's Roma population began in November and December 1944 and continued throughout the first three months of 1945. Moreover, some Roma were murdered close to their homes by Hungarian military police and Arrow Cross party officials. In the 1970s, the Victims of Nazism Commission estimated the number of Romani victims

---

37 For a more detailed account of the Hungarian minorities in the context of human rights protection, see Péter Paczolay, *Human Rights and Minorities in Hungary*, 3 Journal of Constitutional Law in Eastern and Central Europe 111 (1996).

38 Emmanuelle Causse, Hungary, in Compliance in the Enlarged European Union 61, 63 (2008).

of the wartime authorities to have been 28,000. In the 1950s-1960s, the Roma became subject of forceful "proletarisation" and settlement.[39]

B. The legal context

Article 68 of the Hungarian Constitution grants protection to national and ethnic minorities; it ensures opportunities for their collective participation in public life and enables such groups to foster their own culture, and to use and receive school instruction in their mother tongue. Moreover, it protects their freedom to use their names as spelled and pronounced in their own language. Section 32/B Subsection 2 of the Constitution and Act LIX of 1993 provide for the institution of a parliamentary commissioner to protect the rights of national and ethnic minorities. The Office for National and Ethnic Minorities established in 1990 is responsible for co-ordinating the implementation of the government's objectives. Furthermore, the Minorities Ombudsman is responsible for investigating any kinds of abuse of rights that comes to her (or his) attention and for initiating general and individual measures in order to remedy it. According to Hungarian constitutional scholar Renáta Uitz, the minority ombudsman was successful in prompting the Constitutional Court to remind parliament about missing guarantees (i.e. rules) for the adequate political representation of ethnic and national minorities both on the national governmental and local levels.[40]

Overall the institutional structure of minorities' protection in Hungary appears to be more developed than in Poland and the Czech Republic, especially with regard to the current transposition of the EU equal treatment clauses. The enactment of the Equal Treatment and Promotion of Equal Opportunities Act in December 2003 introduced into Hungarian law a prohibition on discrimination in a variety of public and private law relationships, including racial origin, nationality or ethnicity, mother tongue and religious convictions, and the subsequent establishment of the Equal Treatment Authority in 2005. It provided individuals with a direct avenue of redress for violations of non-discrimination norms and generated considerable interest in Hungarian society, with nearly 500 complaints being

---

39   For an account of the history of Hungarian Roma, see István Kemény, *History of Roma in Hungary*, available at: http://www.mtaki.hu/docs/kemeny_istvan_ed_ roma_of_hungary/istvan_kemeny_history_of_roma_in_hungary.pdf

40   Renáta Uitz, Hungary. *High Hopes Revisited*, in Democratization and the European Union. Comparing Central and Eastern Post-Communist Countries 45, 64 (Leonardo Morlino & Wojciech Sadurski eds., 2010).

lodged in the first year alone, a number that has risen steadily ever since.[41] In this respect, Hungary is several steps ahead of the Czech Republic and Poland. In order to improve accessibility for individuals and NGOs outside Budapest, the Equal Treatment Authority signed a formal cooperation agreement with the Houses of Equal Opportunities that now operate in each of Hungary's 19 counties.

Most importantly, the Act also enables NGOs to act as plaintiffs (*actio popularis*) in cases where they consider a provision to be discriminatory, even though no individual has yet suffered any harm. The possibility of turning to the Equal Treatment Authority has empowered plaintiffs to request fines be applied to offending parties as well as to publish the names of bodies that have breached the requirement of equal treatment.

Similarly to both the Czech Republic and Poland, (at the time of writing) Hungary has not ratified Protocol No. 12 to the European Convention of Human Rights, nor the Additional Protocol to the Convention on Cybercrime, concerning the criminalisation of acts of a racist or xenophobic nature committed through computer systems. Both of these instruments are highly relevant to hate speech within the Council of Europe. The latest 2009-ECRI report on Hungary notes that the Hungarian authorities envisaged serious incompatibilities of the Protocol with the Hungarian vision of freedom of speech:

> "[...] despite their legislative efforts in this direction, the present constitutional position with respect to the balance to be found between freedom of expression and the prohibition of hate speech make it impossible to predict when the Protocol may be ratified".[42]

Similarly to the analogous provisions in the Czech Code, Article 174B of the Criminal Code defines specific offences as hate crimes on the grounds of national, ethnic, racial or religious groups. These offences are subject to more severe penalties than analogous offences (acts of violence, cruelty, or coercion by threats) committed against persons not belonging to such groups. Article 269 of the Criminal Code contains a hate speech provision, several formulations of which have been consistently challenged before the Constitutional Court. At the present moment, it prohibits incitement against

---

41   ECRI (European Commission Against Racism and Intolerance) Report on Hungary (fourth monitoring cycle), CRI, 3, 2009, 7.

42   *Id.*, 12 (point 8).

a community as well as the use of symbols of despotism (Article 269/B). In addition, several other provisions (on defamation, libel and desecration) provide a certain scope for hate speech-like claims before courts.

In concluding this account of the socio-legal context of free speech legislation in Hungary, it is necessary to mention a symptomatic recent shift towards censorship. Following the victory of the conservative right under the leadership of the current Prime Minister Viktor Orbán in April 2010, the Hungarian parliament passed a new media law already by the autumn of 2010. The law establishes a government-controlled media council with the authority to supervise independent media, issue decrees and fines. This new law has attracted serious criticism from various organisations and constitutional scholars as threatening the democratic gains of the past 20 years. The editorial board of the leading Hungarian newspaper has promised to challenge the law before the Constitutional Court.[43]

C. The hate speech saga before the constitutional court

Describing post-communist reform of Hungarian criminal law, Gábor Halmai has noted that, in 1989, in parallel with the comprehensive amendment of the Constitution, a modification of the 1978 Criminal Code 1978 lifted incitement to hatred from the category of *crimes against the State* and, with its criminal liability greatly reduced, placed it among the *offences against public peace*.[44] The new clause was attributed to the taxonomy of *"incitement against the community"*. Initially under this title (Article 269), the Code detailed two crimes: (1) incitement to hatred, and (2) offence against

---

43 The law has been widely criticised by the Hungarian and European press. Moreover, the text of the new Hungarian Constitution developed by the Fidesz ("Hungarian Civic Union") government has been condemned as authoritarian. Amongst others, see "Hungary Begins First EU Presidency with Warnings over Press Freedom", available at:
http://www.guardian.co.uk/world/2011/jan/03/hungary-press-crackdown-eu-presidency

44 Gábor Halmai, *Criminal Law as Means Against Racist Speech? The Hungarian Legal Approach*, 4 JOURNAL OF CONSTITUTIONAL LAW IN EASTERN AND CENTRAL EUROPE 41, 42 (1997). Similarly, Petér Molnár makes an important observation that during the Communist years the primary use of the incitement provision was to protect the ruling totalitarian ideology from dissent. The ideological character of the Criminal Code is well captured in its provision of "insult against a community" that included "socialist conviction" among the listed targets, instead of including political conviction in general. See Petér Molnár, *Towards Improved Law and Policy on 'Hate Speech' – The 'Clear and Present Danger' Test in Hungary'*, in EXTREME SPEECH AND DEMOCRACY 237, 243 (Ivan Hare & James Weinstein eds., 2009).

a community in public or in media. This two-fold construction by Hungarian legislators has given rise to a long judicial saga in several parts before the Constitutional Court.

Wojciech Sadurski quotes the words of Chief Justice László Sólyom (later a president of Hungary, from 2005 to 2010) who declared that the first decision [30/1992] concerning hate speech in 1992 "opened the 'Hungarian First Amendment' [sic] of the Constitutional Court, laying down at the start a liberal, extensive interpretation of the right to the freedom of expression".[45] The parallels with First Amendment adjudication do not end with this quote. Similarly, Hungarian scholar Petér Molnár has suggested that the prevailing argument behind the hate speech decisions of the Constitutional Court was the adoption of the American approach, which he characterises as "risky, but still the most prudent".[46] In decision 30 of 1992, the Constitutional Court rejected a petition that sought a determination of unconstitutionality of the first part of Article 269 (incitement to hatred). Instead, it took a substantially different position with regard to the second part (offence of community), essentially echoing the wording of American judicial practice.[47]

The case was referred to the Constitutional Court by a judge of a lower court sitting in a hate speech case against a right-wing newspaper, which had published humiliating statements relating to a particular nationality. The petitioners sought an *ex post facto* review of the constitutionality of Article 269 of the Criminal Code. The restriction of freedom of expression under Article 269(1) was justified by the historically proven harmful effect on certain groups of incitement to hatred, the protection of fundamental constitutional values and compliance with international law by Hungary. The Constitutional Court found that the first part of Article 269 was sufficiently precise and did not define over-broadly the scope of behaviour subject to criminal sanction. Thus, the criteria of specificity, clear definition and demarcation (and, by their virtue, proportionality) were met.

However, the Court held that Article 269(2), criminalising pure offensive speech, was unconstitutional. In rhetorical terms, the judges constructed freedom of expression in that case through the metaphorical lenses of the "mother right to communication".[48] The Constitution guaranteed free

---

45 Sadurski, Rights Before Courts 161 (2005).
46 Molnár, Towards Improved Law and Policy on 'Hate Speech' – The 'Clear and Present Danger' Test in Hungary', 237, 238 (2009).
47 Here and further, Decision 30 (1992).
48 Gábor Halmai deduces an original vision of the Hungarian Court stemming from the metaphor of "*mother right of communicative rights*" that the Court uses for

communication as a manifestation of individual behaviour and as a social process. At this point, the Hungarian Constitutional Court launched two traditions of free speech constructions, marrying the American test of content neutrality with Strasbourg adherence to the ideals of militant democracy.[49] Article 269(2) tackled merely the opinion on the basis of content. The message conveyed by certain utterances was so clearly linked to a given situation and cultural context (which was subject to change) that the abstract, hypothetical definition of an offensive or denigrating expression (in the absence of an actual breach of peace) was just an assumption that did not sufficiently justify the restriction of the external boundary. Consequently, although upholding the first part of Article 262(1), the second part of Article 262(2) was declared null and void.

Explaining the difference, András Sajó draws parallels with the Hungarian doctrine of "inciting words" and the American "fighting words" (as in cases such as *Chaplinsky*[50] and *Beauharnais*[51]).[52] Yet Hungarian balancing is far from the American approach taken in *Skokie*[53] and *R.A.V.*,[54] not to mention case law concerning totalitarian insignia, described below. According to chief justice László Sólyom, in its 1992 hate speech decision the Constitutional Court "established a hierarchy of basic rights in which the freedom of expression ranks second to the right to life and human dignity".[55]

---

freedom of expression. Following Jürgen Habermas, he describes communicative rights as those that enable the citizen to form and express opinions or voluntarily refrain from communicating. In more usual parlance, these are the rights to free speech, freedom of information, freedom of the press, freedom of association and privacy. See Gábor Halmai, *'Communicative Rights' in the Hungarian Constitutional Practice*, 3 Journal of Constitutional Law in Eastern and Central Europe 181 (1996).

49 So-called "militant democracy" (*Streitbare Demokratie*) is a popular Germanic concept, designed as a remedy to prevent a repeat of the Weimar Republic's failure to react effectively to an authoritarian threat to a free democratic order (*freiheitlich-demokratische Grundordung*). In line with this approach, hate speech should be excluded from the scope of the freedom of speech protection as it threatens the very foundations of democracy.

50 *Chaplinsky v. New Hampshire*, 315 U.S. 568, 572 (1942).

51 *Beauharnais v. Illinois*, 343 U.S. 250 (1952).

52 András Sajó, *Hate Speech for Hostile Hungarians*, 78 EAST EUROPEAN CONSTITUTIONAL REVIEW 82, 86 (1994). See also Kim Lane Scheppele, *Limitations on Fundamental Rights: Comparing Hungarian and American Constitutional Jurisprudence*, 8 JOURNAL FOR CONSTITUTIONAL LAW IN EASTERN AND CENTRAL EUROPE 53 (2001).

53 *Collin v. Smith*, 439 U.S. 916 (1978).

54 *R.A.V. v. City St. Paul*, 505 U.S. 377 (1992).

55 László Sólyom, *The Interaction Between the Case-Law of the ECHR and the Protection of Freedom of Speech in Hungary*, in PROTECTION DES DROITS DE L'HOMME: LA

Interestingly, in its decision, written in Hungarian, the Court quoted the *clear and present danger* test in English.

The battle over Article 262 of the Criminal Code has continued since this case both in Parliament and within the government. Attempts to rebut the approach of the Hungarian Court have been impressively numerous. The rather neutral formulation of Article 262(1) permitted by the Court was criticised as toothless in terms of providing an actual criminal basis for prosecution. Several redefinitions of Article 262, widening the scope of penalised hate speech beyond a *clear and present danger* test, have been suggested. However, in a subsequent series of judgements, the Constitutional Court of Hungary has declined the opportunity to broaden the scope of the prohibited "incitement" to "arousal of hatred" (decision 12/1999), "inflaming hatred" (decision 18/2004), "gestures reminiscent of a totalitarian regime and denigrating a member of a given group" (decision 95/2008), as well as an attempt to prescribe hate speech prohibition in the Civil Code (decision 96/2008).

D. "Hungarian" hate speech

The latest monitoring report on Hungary by the European Commission against Racism and Intolerance maintains that the very high level of constitutional protection afforded to freedom of expression has made it impossible for the authorities to legislate effectively against racist expression:

> "[...] under Hungarian law, only the most extreme forms of racist expression, i.e. incitement liable to provoke immediate violent acts, appear to be prohibited, a standard so high that it is almost never invoked in the first place. While it is true that legislation alone cannot turn racist attitudes around, the almost total absence of limits on free speech in Hungary complicates the task of promoting a society that is more open and tolerant towards its own members".[56]

This observation of the ECRI appears somewhat simplistic, in particular, for explaining the available avenues of legal redress for Romani social movements. As has been previously demonstrated, the approach of the

---

PERSPECTIVE EUROPÉENE. MÉLANGES À LA MÉMOIRE DE ROLV RYSSDAL 1317, 1320 (2010).

56   CRI, 3, 2009, (Note 42) 8.

Hungarian Constitutional Court has actually been much more sophisticated and the general non-acceptance of the incitement to hatred remains in line with dominant "Strasbourg" visions of militant democracy: the prohibition of the incitement to hatred of certain groups is still prescribed by criminal statute. That "incitement" clause has been invoked in criminal proceedings by national courts. Nonetheless, there is some substance to the ECRI's "invisibility" argument. The hate speech decisions of the Hungarian Constitutional Court have made ordinary courts extremely reluctant to apply Article 269 of the Criminal Code. Both anti-Roma and anti-Semitic hate speech remain particularly pertinent in the Hungarian context.

After a rally by several hundred skinheads in Budapest in 1996, the police questioned a neo-Nazi leader Albert Szabó about his anti-Semite speech under the allegation of an incitement against a community. A year earlier, the attorney general initiated a lawsuit against Szabó and charged him with racial incitement against Roma and Jews. At his trial in March 1996, despite general public expectations and to the consternation of many, Szabó was acquitted. The court concluded that there had been no incitement to racial hatred and that the defendant had merely availed himself of freedom of speech.

A similar story to the Czech legal saga concerning the publication of *Mein Kampf* arose in Hungary. In the 1990s, the book also appeared in a Hungarian translation. Unlike the Czech (*Michal Zitko*) case, in which the publisher provided a genuine disclaimer in the book denying any allegations of hate speech *ab initio*, the Hungarian publisher, Áron Monús, was openly anti-Semitic and even had a previous conviction for his book *Conspiracy: the Nietzschean Empire*. The latter publication (which echoes the sentiments expressed in *The Protocols of the Elders of Zion* and *Mein Kampf*) was confiscated by the authorities. A Hungarian émigré, Monús claimed that *Mein Kampf* belonged to a universal cultural heritage and should be made available in Hungarian "to set things straight". A court overturned the ban, granting Monús's appeal on the basis of freedom of speech.[57]

The intensification of anti-Roma hate speech is a troublesome sign in the public discourse of Hungary. As in the case of the similarly titled Czech organization (*Národní garda*), this trend can be illustrated with the rise of the radical right-wing Hungarian Guard (*Magyar Gárda*). Since its creation in 2007, the Guard has organized numerous public rallies throughout the country, including those in villages with large Roma populations. Despite

---

57 David Singer, *East-Central Europe*, in AMERICAN JEWISH YEARBOOK 342, 348 (1998).

apparently innocuous articles of association, amongst the group's chief messages is the defence of ethnic Hungarians against so-called *cigánybűnözés* ("Gypsy crime"). Members of the Hungarian Guard parade in matching, paramilitary-style black boots and uniforms, with Nazi insignia and flags.[58]

In 2008, the Prosecutor General initiated court proceedings to ban the *Gárda*, alleging that its activity differs from its memorandum of association. The case was delayed several times. On the first day of litigation members of the Guard physically blocked journalists from entering the court, leading to a change in court rules and creating an intimidating atmosphere. On 16 December 2008, the Metropolitan Court of Budapest, (*Fővárosi Bíróság*) as the court of first instance, disbanded the organisation. It held that the activities of the organisation were discriminatory towards minorities. The Gárda appealed against the judgment. But on 2 July 2009, the Metropolitan Court of Appeal (*Fővárosi Ítélőtábla*) upheld the judgment of the first instance court. Following the judgment, the Guard's representatives announced that they would apply for review by the Supreme Court and ultimately challenge the judgment before the ECtHR in Strasbourg.[59]

To sum up, Hungary is an excellent example of a transitional democracy importing free speech transplants from both Western Europe and the United States. The Hungarian case demonstrates an unusual attempt to marry the continental *Volksverhetzung* (incitement to popular hatred) and American fighting words and content-neutrality. This contradiction brought about an exceptionally rich jurisprudence of the Constitutional Court, which in numerous judgements had to restrict the attempts of the Parliament to add flesh to the core of the criminal provision. In the climate of constant challenges to the provision by the Constitutional Court, the lower courts became unwilling to prosecute virulent haters. Anti-Roma hate speech has become one of the principal rhetorical casualties of the ever-strong radical right in the landscape of Hungarian politics, media and social life.

---

58 http://www.coe.int/t/dghl/monitoring/ecri/activities/22-freedom_of_expression_
    seminar_2006/NSBR2006_proceedings_en.pdf
    ECRI Report on Hungary (fourth monitoring cycle), CRI, 3, 2009, 24, Point 61.
    In January 2008, the Prosecutor General initiated court proceedings to ban the
    Hungarian Guard.

59 For the description of the intimidating blockage of the court proceedings, see ECRI
    Report on Hungary (fourth monitoring cycle), CRI, 3, 2009, 24, Point 62.

IV. Poland

A. *The social and historical context*

Paradoxically for a country that is itself a splinter of a multinational empire, Poland is often said not to shelter any significant national minority exceeding 0,5% of the population. However, the characterisation of Poland as a mono-national state is simplistic. It is impossible to adequately comprehend the hate speech issues in this country without consideration of the historical specificities that nourish Polish political and religious populism.

Until the 18th century, Poland existed as a multinational commonwealth (the first *Rzeczpospolita*) in association with the Grand Duchy of Lithuania, comprising a grouping together of pre-modern ethnicities for Poles, Lithuanians, Belarusians, Ukrainians, on the one hand, and Jews, Roma, Tatars, etc., on the other had.[60] After three partitions of the Commonwealth in the 18th century, the country ceased to exist for almost two centuries and found its lands divided between Austria, Prussia, and Russia. The intellectual tradition of Poland is intimately connected with the memory of the deprivation and regaining of national statehood.[61] In 1918, Poland restored its sovereignty as a multinational state. The interwar period of Polish independence is celebrated in national history, with the increasingly authoritarian state practices (including those affecting freedom of expression), especially with regard to national minorities, often neglected in populist constructions. World War II led to another partition of Poland between Nazi Germany and Soviet Russia, as well as to a loss of approximately six million Polish citizens. Half of those who died were Jewish, whose population was decimated from 3,000,000 pre-war to 300,000 at the war's end. A significant portion of Germans from Silesia were forced to leave the country after the post-war division of the map of Europe. Furthermore, Poland was forced to exchange with the Soviet Union the population of the so-called *"Kresy Wschodnie"* (eastern part of the first *Rzeczpospolita*, comprising the then Soviet Republics of Lithuania, Belarus, and Ukraine). Both of these factors, together with the annihilation of the Polish Jewry and Roma, are what have led to the remarkable homogeneity in the ethnic composition of the country.

---

60   For an English-language account of complicated Polish identity embracing several pre-modern ethnicities, see TIMOTHY SNYDER, THE RECONSTRUCTION OF NATIONS: POLAND, UKRAINE, LITHUANIA, BELARUS 1569-1999 (2004).

61   For an account of Polish history and the role of *zabory* (partitions), see JERZY ZDRADA, HISTORIA POLSKI 1795-1914 (2005).

According to the 2002 census, 96,74% of the citizens consider themselves Poles. The biggest minorities include Germans and Silesians who live relatively compactly in the western parts,[62] and Belarusians densely inhabiting the eastern region of Poland. Other minorities include the autochthonous Koshubians (in the north of the country), Ukrainians, Lithuanians, Russians, Roma, Jews, Slovaks and Tatars. Yet, much bigger Polish communities live in the neighbouring Belarus, Ukraine, and Lithuania, where they constitute significant minority groups.[63]

This apparent ethnical homogeneity of the country is, however, no barrier to xenophobic hate speech. The traditional nationalist populism in Poland has been nourished by a Catholic messianism, strong anti-Semitic rhetoric, anti-Roma ostracism, anti-Germanic narratives, and the victimhood of the lost '*Kresy*' (eastern borderlands). As demonstrated in a remarkable sociological survey by Sergiusz Kowalski, the main addressees of hate speech in Polish media are Jews, Roma, socialists, the LGBT community, Germans, and eastern neighbours (foremost Russians and Ukrainians), as well as liberal politicians, feminists, atheists, and advocates of European integration.[64] The Polish hate speech narratives have been fostered by peculiar narratives that allege various collaborative practices between those groups. Exemplary in this regard is the alleged linkage of the so-called "*Żydokomuna*" (Judeo-communism), a pejorative anti-Semitic stereotype, which came into use between the two world wars, and which blamed Jews for the rise of communism in Poland.[65]

Olga Wysocka gives an interesting explanation of Polish political populism, nourished by xenophobic discourses. She links it to the 19th century Russian movement of "*narodnichestvo*" (*народничество*),[66] based on the

---

62　On the complicated national identity of Polish Germans, see JAMES E. BJORK, NEITHER GERMAN NOR POLE. CATHOLICISM AND NATIONAL INDIFFERENCE IN A CENTRAL EUROPEAN BORDERLAND (2008).

63　For a socio-logical account of Polish minorities, see Wanda Dressler (ed.), E SECOND PRINTEMPS DES NATIONS. SUR LES RUINES D'UN EMPIRE, QUESTIONS NATIONALES ET MINORITAIRES EN POLOGNE (HAUTE SILÉSIE, BIÉLORUSSIE POLONAISE), ESTONIE, MOLDAVIE, KAZAKHSTAN (1999).

64　Sergiusz Kowalski & Magdalena Tulli, ZAMIAST PROCESU. RAPORT O MOWIE NIENAWIŚCI (2003).

65　See JAN T. GROSS, FEAR. ANTI-SEMITISM IN POLAND AFTER AUSCHWITZ: AN ESSAY IN HISTORICAL INTERPRETATION (2006) (Chapter 6, *The Myth of "Judeo-Communism" or Żydokomuna*, 261-331); MAREK JAN CHODAKIEWICZ, AFTER THE HOLOCAUST. POLISH-JEWISH CONFLICT IN THE WAKE OF WORLD WAR II (2003).

66　Olga Wysocka, *Populism. The Polish Case*, European University Institute, unpublished doctoral thesis, 2010, 10.

strong binary opposition of the peasant people-hood (the concept excluding Jews and Roma) *vis-à-vis* the nobility in the Russian empire. Likewise, the never fulfilled (unlike in the Czech Republic) Polish lustration after the fall of Communism has been a powerful fostering factor for hateful discourses. Wysocka concludes that a specific element in Polish nationalist populism is the anti-establishment emphasis that derives from dissatisfaction with the settlement of accounts with Communism. This dissatisfaction is rhetorically materialised in the concept of a "network" that links post-Communist bureaucrats and compromised opposition forces.[67] Adam Bodnar suggests that the return of right-wing politicians to government after EU accession (in the ultra-conservative government of Lech Kaczyński) coupled with a still-vulnerable civil society and media were particularly fruitful for Polish hate speech. He concludes that due to the crisis after the failure of the Constitutional Treaty, the EU failed to address the situation in Poland and showed "a lack of capability in dealing with [the] 'step-by-step' road towards liberal democracy in Poland".[68]

Most of the Polish Roma (with the biggest ethnic group amongst them referred to as *Polska Roma*) migrated to Polish lands in the 16th century, escaping the persecutions in the Holy Roman Empire. Since the migration was caused by pogroms and anti-Romani rights, "Polska Roma" have been more suspicious of outsiders (*gadjo*) than other Polish Roma and are thus less assimilated. In particular, the so-called *Bergitka Roma* (from German *berg*, for mountain), populating the Carpathian part, migrated to those lands earlier in the 15th century from Hungary and Transylvania. Unlike Polska Roma, Bergitka Roma are predominantly non-nomadic, and have lived in settlements since approximately the 18th century.

Throughout the 18th and 19th centuries, the Roma were given permission for a degree of self-organisation and institutional hierarchy, including the election of the so-called "gypsy kings". In the first Polish Constitution of 3 May 1791, together with other non-nobility classes, Roma were given citizenship status. However, the relatively peaceful attitude towards Roma ended with the partition of the first Rzeczpospolita by Austria, Prussia, and Russia. Each of them spread their discriminatory anti-Roma decrees onto the Polish territories. During the *Porajmos*, Polish Roma were explicitly targeted and killed by the German SS in mass executions. In contrast, Roma in other

---

67   *Id.*

68   Adam Bodnar, Poland: EU Driven Democracy? in DEMOCRATIZATION AND THE EUROPEAN UNION 19, 24 (2010).

countries of the CEE that perished in the Great Devouring were first placed in ghettos and sent to concentration camps.

Under Communism, similarly to the Czechoslovak and Hungarian authorities, the Communist Polish governments pursued the politics of assimilation of Roma populations: first via financial benefits and, subsequently, using forceful means.[69] Unlike in Hungary and the Czech Republic, the Roma are a relatively small minority at less than 1% (approximately 30,000) of the population. Nonetheless, the climate of anti-Gypsyism is similar to its CEE neighbours.

B. *The legal context*

After the fall of Communism, Poland made considerable advances in instituting European standards of the right to freedom of speech and the liberal vision of media space. Public TV and radio are regulated by the governmental agency, called *Krajowa Rada Radiofonii i Telewizji* (the National Radio & TV Committee). A number of private and public TV and radio channels, along with diverse published editions and electronic sources make Poland one of the most versatile media markets in the EU. Along with freedom of speech, Polish Constitution guarantees non-discrimination, based on the very wide clause of Article 32:

1. All persons shall be equal before the law. All persons shall have the right to equal treatment by public authorities.
2. No one shall be discriminated against in political, social or economic life for any reason whatsoever.

Article 256 of the Polish Criminal Code makes anyone found guilty of promoting a fascist or other totalitarian system of state or of inciting hatred based on national, ethnic, racial, or religious differences, or for reason of the lack of any religious denomination, liable to a fine, a restriction of liberty, or to imprisonment for a maximum of two years. Article 257 makes anyone found guilty of publicly insulting a group or a particular person because of national, ethnic, racial, or religious affiliation or because of the lack of any religious

---

69 For a detailed history of Roma in Poland, see MARIAN G. GERLICH, HAUTE ROMOWIE: PRZEKRACZANIE GRANIC WŁASNEGO ŚWIATA (2001). For an account of Romani activism via ethnographic representation in Poland, see Peter Vermeersch, 22 *Exhibiting Multiculturalism, Politicised Representations of the Roma in Poland*, THIRD TEXT 359 (2008).

denomination liable to a fine, a restriction of liberty, or to imprisonment for a maximum of three years. The construction of a hate speech clause beyond incitement, which failed in Hungary, has not been challenged before the Constitutional Tribunal in Poland and covers insults.

Similarly to the other scrutinized countries, Poland has not ratified the Protocol to the Cybercrime Convention. Recently a Government Plenipotentiary for Equal Treatment has been appointed and the National Program for Counteracting Racial Discrimination, Xenophobia and Related Intolerance, which she coordinates, has been extended until 2013. A draft bill has been prepared to transpose the EU equality directives, including the Council Directive 2000/43/EC of 29 June 2000, incorporating the principle of equal treatment between persons irrespective of racial or ethnic origin.[70]

C. Amendments to the criminal code

Considering the particular problem of hate speech in Poland, several NGOs and governmental agencies have drafted amendments to the Criminal Code. For instance, LGBT organisations, drawing on Swedish and Canadian experiences, suggested adding sexual orientation to the bases protected against hate speech.[71] Thus, the inclusion of sex, gender identity, age, disability and sexual orientation into Article 119 (1) was proposed, defining a hate crime, along with "traditional" grounds of nation, ethnicity, race, as well as political and religious beliefs. It was also proposed that sexual orientation should enter the scope of Articles 256 and 257.[72] In drafting the proposals,

---

70 On 4 May 2010 the European Commission referred Poland to the Court of Justice of the EU for incorrectly implementing Directive 2000/43/EC. The Commission pointed out that Poland has not transposed the Directive outside the field of employment. There are no specific provisions in Polish legislation that would prohibit discrimination on grounds of racial or ethnic origin with regard to social protection and social advantages, access to goods and services, including housing, membership in trade unions, employers' bodies and professional organisations and access to education. Similarly, the Polish provisions on protection against victimisation cover only the field of employment and not the other areas within the scope of the Directive.

71 For accounts of homophobic hate speech in Poland, see Jerzy Szczęsny, *Retoryka antyhomoseksualna w Trzeciej Rzeszy*, in Przekonania Moralne Władzy Publicznej a Wolność Jednostki 55 (Mirosław Wyrzykowski & Adam Bodnar eds., 2007); Robert Biedroń, *Wprowadzenie do raportu*, in Raport o Homofobicznej Mowie Nienawiści w Polsce 75 (Greg Czarnecki ed., 2009).

72 See Eleonora Zielińska, *Opinia w sprawie projektu zmian kodeksu karnego*, in Raport o Homofobicznej Mowie Nienawiści w Polsce 75 (Greg Czarnecki ed., 2009).

NGOs and scholars noted the need for amendments to bring the Code into line with the EU anti-discrimination directives.

Similarly to the Hungarian discussion around the criminal clause on hate speech, the very wording of "incitement" (*nawoływanie do nienawiści*) in Article 256 of the Criminal Code was questioned as "enigmatic". For example, a scholar of criminal law Lech Gardocki, suggested that it is unclear as to why the legislator does not punish the very fact of calling for hatred (*wywoływanie nienawiści*).[73]

In 2008, the Polish parliament discussed a project to amend hate speech legislation, based on a clause structured into four parts. On 26 November 2009, the conservative President of Poland Lech Kaczyński signed the bill, which came into force on 8 June 2010. A new version of Article 256 in the Criminal Code contains a clause, constructed in an essentially different mode than in Hungary and the Czech Republic, linking hate propaganda and totalitarian symbols:

§ 1. Whoever publicly promotes a fascist or other totalitarian system of state or incites hatred against the background of differences in nationality, ethnic, racial, or religious affiliation or because of the lack of religious beliefs shall be subject to a fine, restriction of liberty or imprisonment up to 2 years.

§ 2. The same penalty shall be applied to a person who in order to disseminate produces, records or brings, acquires, holds, owns, shows, transports or transmits a printed, recorded or other item, with a content described in § 1 or containing the symbols of fascist, communist or other totalitarian regimes.

§ 3. An offence specified in § 2 should be considered as non-committed if the described actions were performed in the view of artistic, educational, scientific, or collecting purpose.

§ 4. In the event of a conviction for an offence referred to in § 2, the court shall order the seizure of objects referred to in § 2, even when the objects were not in the property of a perpetrator.

Thus, § 1 of the amended Article 256 of the Criminal Code actually constitutes the incorporation of the previous variant of the article. It was perhaps to be expected, but is nonetheless unfortunate, that a conservative Polish legislator did not follow the proposals of the NGOs and omitted to include the grounds

---

73   LECH GARDOCKI, PRAWO KARNE 297 (2006).

of age, gender, sexual orientation, and disability from protection against hate speech. Considering the enormous scope of homophobia in Polish political populism and the aggressive role of a number of Catholic organisations and priests on the issue, the response of the legislator leaves much to be desired.

§ 2 of the Article is drafted in a characteristically clumsy and populist manner. What the Polish legislator performed is essentially a copy pasting of an analogous clause of Article 202 in the Criminal Code, dedicated to pornography. This approach illustrates nicely the misunderstanding among the political authorities of the problem of hate speech. It is unclear how the possession (especially taken in its classical civil law meaning) of "hateful items" contributes to the incitement of hatred.[74] In addition, the insertion of the clause on fascist and Communist (as well as unclear and overbroad "other totalitarian") symbols in the scope of the article on hate speech is in itself disputable. It appears even more disputable in light of the recent Strasbourg judgement on Hungarian Communist symbols, referred to above. It is unclear, for example, if wearing a T-shirt with an image of Che Guevara or a symbol of the North Korean Republic becomes a criminally punishable offence under the clause.

Moreover, rather oddly, the reference to the *collecting* activity in § 3 as a legitimate mode of possession and purchase of totalitarian attributes gives a green light to what is officially prohibited in France and several other EU states, namely the trade in Nazi memorabilia. Further, the safe harbour of artistic usage of hateful utterances or symbols in § 3 remains ultimately vague. Would it for instance mean that in the Polish context a Czech case involving criminal prosecution of the leader of a neo-Nazi music band would fail due to the hateful utterances also constituting artistic activity?

The history of the criminal clause on incitement sets an indispensable background for the further discussion of the adjudication of hate speech in Poland. Unlike in Hungary and the Czech Republic, it is important to underline that the Polish legislator developed the statutory clause on hate speech (essentially a constitutional issue bordering, as it does, the right to freedom of speech) without any involvement of the Constitutional Tribunal.

---

74   For a detailed analysis of the amendment, see Mateusz Woiński, *Projekty nowelizacji art. 256 k.k.*, in Mowa Nienawiści a Wolność Słowa. Aspekty Prawne i Społeczne 21 (Roman Wieruszewski, Mirosław Wyrzykowski, Adam Bodnar, Aleksandra Gliszczyńska-Grabias eds., 2010).

D. Hate fpeech before the courts

Following the analysis of the amendments in the Criminal Code, it is important to underline that the main problem with the country's response to hate propaganda lies not in inadequate legal drafting but rather in its indecisive implementation by Polish courts and prosecutors. It is arguably scandalous that the country's most aggressive, enormously influential and highly visible hate propagandist, an ultra-Catholic radio station and media group *Radio Maryja*, has not only not been shut-down, but has to date avoided criminal prosecution.[75]

Founded in 1991 in Toruń, Radio Maryja has been run by Tadeusz Rydzyk, a highly controversial individual whose statements have been met with concern even by the Vatican. This radio station, with an audience of millions, has become known for the expression of nationalist, anti-Semitic, anti-Roma, anti-socialist, anti-German, anti-EU, anti-feminist, and homophobic prejudices. A report of the Council of Europe stated that Radio Maryja has been "openly inciting anti-Semitism for several years" and that there is a "lack of effective implementation of measures intended to prohibit anti-Semitic acts and statements" in Poland.[76] Yet the National Broadcasting Council's investigation into Radio Maria and related media found no case to answer. The CoE report noted that although the Council operates a complaints mechanism, it has dealt with only one racial-discrimination case involving a pun on the name of a football club and the word "Jew".[77] The Council took action on this matter. Nonetheless, the dearth of complaints concerning matters related to racism and intolerance reflects a lack of confidence in the complaints mechanism or a lack of awareness of its existence.

One of the most striking features of the Polish hate speech situation in general is the unwillingness on the part of the authorities (mainly prosecutors) and a resistance by the courts to proceeding with cases involving Catholic priests or organisations. The Catholic Church in Poland is effectively a sacred cow and benefits from a disproportionate level of protection under freedom of speech. The level of obscurantism of many priests and religious public figures, as well as the degree of popularity of political movements appealing to religious morality in Poland, is truly remarkable for a 21st century secular state in the EU.[78] In a 2008 interview with one of the Polish channels (TV

---

75   For the monitoring of hate speech utterances on Radio Maryja, see http://www. radiomaryja.pl.eu.org.

76   ECRI Report on Poland (fourth monitoring cycle), CRI, 18, 2010, 26, Point 95.

77   *Id*, point 96.

78   On the peculiarities of the Polish attachment to the church and the role of religion in

Polsat) during a meeting organised against the demonstration of LGBT organisations in Kraków, a priest, Rafał Trytek, announced that he "hopes that Poland will return to the bright days when faggots were burnt in the market-place". Somewhat typically, he has not been prosecuted under the criminal clause on incitement to hatred, despite the fact that the video with his interview is still easily downloadable on the Internet.[79]

Similarly, Polish nationalist organisations (*All Polish Youth, League of Polish Families, Polish National Rebirth*, etc) often appeal to ultra-Catholic rhetoric, exploiting the stereotypes of xenophobia, anti-Semitism, anti-Gypsism, and homophobia. The cases of prosecution under the criminal incitement to hatred clause have been rare. In one such case an anti-Semitic campaigner, Kazimierz Świtoń (also known as an opposition activist during the communist epoch) was found guilty by the Regional Oświęcym Court of inciting hatred (of Jews and Germans). In January 2000, he received a six-month jail sentence, suspended for two years, for distributing anti-Semitic leaflets at Auschwitz two years earlier. The case had been brought not by the prosecutor but by a local NGO. In June 2000, his punishment was reduced to a mere month-long suspended sentence. In December 2000, the Court acquitted Mr. Świtoń of earlier charges. On leaving the court he pledged to continue his struggle against 'Jewish chauvinists'.[80]

The 2010 ECRI report criticises a different judgement of February 2007, in which the Supreme Court (*Sąd Najwyższy*) decided that holding a placard reading "We shall liberate Poland from [*inter alia*] Jews"[81] did not amount to an offence under Article 256 of the Criminal Code. To reach this conclusion

---

the national identity of Poles, see Mira Marody & Sławomir Mandes, *On Functions of Religion in Molding the National Identity of Poles*, 35 International Journal of Sociology 49 (2005-6). The authors analyse historical relations between religion and the formation of nationhood. They argue that the formation of nationhood in Europe was related to the growth of secular rituals that could not develop in Poland because of its prolonged lack of political sovereignty. Religion was (and still is) the main source of collective rituals through which the national identity was formed and is sustained in Polish society.

79 Available electronically at: http://www.youtube.com/watch?v=6DTeIhwkrIk&feat ure=related (statements in Polish: "*Policja powinna chronić rynek przed marszem pedałów i innych zboczeńców [...] jeszcze w średniowieczu ludzi o takich skłonnościach palono na stosach, [...] może powrócimy do tych wspaniałych czasów jeszcze i tych ludzi będzie się palić na stosach. Miejmy nadzieję!*").

80 For details see Marcin Kornak, *Brunasta księga – Katalog wypadków*, 12 Nigdy Więcej (2000-2001). See also an article in a Polish newspaper Rzeczpospolita, *Świtoń jest winny* // available electronically at: http://new-arch.rp.pl/artykul/258926_Switon_jest_winny.html

81 "*Wyzwolimy Polskę od euro-zdrajców, Żydów, masonów i rządowej mafii*".

the Court referred to Article 54(1) of the Constitution, i.e. to the constitutional protection of freedom of speech. The ordinary meaning of the word "liberate" and the use of the indicative, as opposed to the imperative, showed no intention to incite national hatred according to the Court.[82] In its ruling, the Supreme Court clarified the wording of Article 256 of the Criminal Code, in particular the term "*nawoływanie*" (incitement), constructed in all three scrutinised countries in a way similar to the German term "*Volksverhetzung*" (literally, "incitement to popular hatred"):

> "Incitement to hatred on grounds listed in Article 256 of the Penal Code – including on the grounds of national differences – leads to the type of statements, which arouses strong feelings of dislike, anger, lack of acceptance or outright hostility to individuals or social groups or religious groups, including also due to the form of expression exacerbate, and which indoctrinate these negative attitudes and by their virtue underline the privileged status, the superiority of a specific nation, ethnic group, race or creed."[83]

Thus, the Court placed the emphasis in the definition of incitement on concrete intention (*dolus directus coloratus*).

In March 2002, the Supreme Court had clarified the notion of "propagate", or "promote" (*propaguje*) in Article 256 of the Criminal Code. A regional court referred to the Supreme Court for an opinion, inquiring whether the lexical change in the wording brought legal consequences. Former Article 270 (2) of the Criminal Code 1969 referred to the verb "*pochwala*" (literally, "appraise") instead of "*propaguje*". The case before the regional court arose against neo-fascists organising a meeting in a local club, during which Nazi symbols were used and the dissemination of totalitarian propaganda took place. The participants used symbolic greetings with the right hand accompanied by salutes of "*Sieg Heil*" and "*Heil Hitler*". The court inquired if the notion of "promotes" covers the approval (*pochwalanie*) of fascist or other totalitarian orders, apparent in the demonstration of the swastika, gestures

---

82 ECRI Report on Poland (fourth monitoring cycle), CRI, 18, 2010, Point 21, 14.

83 "*Nawoływanie do nienawiści z powodów wymienionych w art. 256 k.k. – w tym na tle różnic narodowościowych – sprowadza się do tego typu wypowiedzi, ktore wzbudzają uczucia silnej niechęci, złości, braku akceptacji, wręcz wrogości do poszczególnych osób lub całych grup społecznych czy wyznaniowych bądz też z uwagi na formę wypowiedzi podtrzymują i nasilają takie negatywne nastawienia i podkreślają tym samym uprzywilejowanie, wyższość określonego narodu, grupy etnicznej, rasy lub wyznania*". Postanowienie, Sąd Najwyższy IV KK 406/06 (5 February 2007).

of fascist greetings, and so on, only when it is accompanied by the public popularisation of the knowledge about such an order, i.e. propaganda. In its Resolution, the Supreme Court noted that everything depends on the unique circumstances of a specific event, which, as in this case, will determine whether a given conduct constitutes a public presentation of this order and if it is done with the intention of the explicit popularization for this system.[84] The crime can be committed only with an intention to publicize approval of such a system. As a result, the Court held as follows:

> "To 'promote', within the meaning of Article 256 of the Penal Code, means any conduct consisting of a public presentation of a fascist or other totalitarian system of the state, with intent of persuasion of the public."[85]

The Court also mentioned that it is indisputable that hate speech should be regarded as an exception to the constitutional protection of freedom of expression, with regards to *inter alia* the practice of the European Court of Human Rights. Thus, "Strasbourg law" was positioned as a mandatory free speech model for Poland.

Unlike in the Czech Republic and Hungary, the Constitutional Tribunal of Poland has not become involved in clarifying the hate speech clauses. Although in 2008 it held another clause in the Criminal Code to be unconstitutional, the so-called "slander of the Polish Nation" (*pomówienie Narodu Polskiego*) clause, the judgement does not directly deal with hate speech.[86] However, Polish case-law has involved a number of attempts at prosecuting hate speech on the Internet. Rafal Pankowski and Marcin Kornak detail at least three investigations – in Kielce, Łódź, and Rzeszów – regarding anti-Semitic material on the Internet. One, in October 2000 in Kielce, ended with a trial and a ten-month suspended sentence for the perpetrator. Nonetheless, the

---

84 Uchwała, Sąd Najwyższy I KZP 5/02 (28 March 2002).

85 *Propagowanie, w rozumieniu art. 256 k.k., oznacza każde zachowanie polegające na publicznym prezentowaniu faszystowskiego lub innego totalitarnego ustroju państwa, w zamiarze przekonania do niego.*

86 Wyrok Trybunału Konstytucyjnego, K 5/07 (19 September, 2008). The present study limits itself to 2010, therefore the subsequent 2011-judgement of the Polish Constitutional Tribunal is not mentioned. For the account of the most recent developments of the Constitutional Tribunal on hate speech (in particular, Judgement K 11/10, 19 July 2011), see BELAVUSAU, FREEDOM OF SPEECH, op. cit. *supra.*

authors argue that there have been no coordinated efforts to date to curb hate speech on the Internet.[87]

E. Anti-Gypsyism in Poland

Lisa Morrisson Pucket gives a striking description of how it feels to be Romani in the Polish transition to democracy as "the devil replac[ing] Satan":

> "As liberalization has allowed the expression of diverse views, an increase in overt racism has resulted. More freedom, such as the increase in Romani newspapers, magazines and other publications, have been accompanied by harassment and attacks [...] Such discrimination is not surprising given a recent public opinion poll that reported 69% of Poles dislike Roma, while only 10% reported liking them. Treatment of Roma in Poland falls under the Ministry of Culture and Arts, which suggests that the government believes that Roma have a problem with cultural preservation. This perception fails to acknowledge the full extent of the problem such as housing and employment are not adequately addressed by the government."[88]

Prior to the EU enlargement eastward, Polish authorities had managed, to a large extent, to ignore the whole issue of virulent anti-Gypsyism in Poland. Instead they justified their lack of action to combat it by reference to the small number of Roma in Poland and the claim that the situation of Roma was much better than in other CEE countries.[89] Indeed, several violent anti-Roma pogroms throughout 1990s were overlooked by the authorities.[90] Since

---

87 Rafal Pankowski & Marcin Kornak, *Poland*, in RACIST EXTREMISM IN CENTRAL AND EASTERN EUROPE 156 (Cas Mudde ed., 2005). The present study limits its scope to the year 2010. Yet the situation may change since recently hate speech on the Internet became the focus of government debate. In 2011, Radosław Sikorski, the Minister of Foreign Affairs, brought a suit against the editors of the Internet forums "Fakt" and "Puls Biznesu", invoking the criminal provision on hate speech. The outcome of the case is unclear. See Ewa Siedlicka & Paweł Wroński, *Minister Sikorski walczy z internetowym chamstwem*, Gazeta wyborcza (May 2011), available electronically at: http://wyborcza.pl/1,75478,9526299,Minister_Sikorski_walczy_z_ internetowym_chamstwem.html; on the recent NGO initiative to use the electronic filter identifying hate speech on the Internet, see also Joanna Klimowicz, *Obieg mowy nienawiści w internecine*, Gazeta Wyborcza (April 2010), available electronically at: http://wyborcza.pl/1,75478,9459039,Obieg_mowy_nienawisci_w_internecie.html.
88 Morrison Puckett, *Barriers to Access: Social Services and the Roma of Poland*, 48 INTERNATIONAL SOCIAL WORK 621, 623 (2005).
89 *Ibid.*
90 Eva Sobotka, *The Limits of the State: Political Participation and Representation*

the 2000s, official recognition of anti-Roma discrimination has somewhat improved, with the authorities acknowledging that problems exist and creating a special Ministerial program for the protection of Roma. However there are far fewer cases before the courts in which Roma claim protection of the law in Poland than there are in the Czech Republic and Hungary. One of the rare judgements affecting Roma rights came from a regional court in Poznań, where (similarly to an analogous Czech case) a segregation practice with regard to Romani visitors in a restaurant was deemed to be direct discrimination.

In synthesis, the hate speech clause in Poland is in line with the dominant continental vision of militant democracy. Unlike in Hungary and the Czech Republic, the incitement clause *à la polonaise* in the criminal code has been constructed with no involvement of the Constitutional Tribunal. The history of that construction illustrates the handicaps of political populism in Poland, nourished by the sensitivity of the unsettled relations with the communist past, Catholic obscurantism, politically instrumentalised homophobia, as well as long traditions of anti-Semitism and anti-Gypsyism. The stereotyping and virulent rhetorical stigmatizing of Roma communities are common both in social, political and media discourses. Authorities have used the relatively low percentage of Roma in Poland as an excuse for non-intervention in the cases of anti-Gypsyism; and the incitement clause remains essentially under-enforced.

V. Conclusions: Avenues for Legal Mobilisation against Anti-Roma Hate Speech – Coffee Grounds or Life Chances?

> *"Chance and chance alone has a message for us. Everything that occurs out of necessity, everything expected, repeated day in and day out, is mute. Only chance can speak to us. We read its message much as gypsies read the images made by coffee grounds at the bottom of a cup."*
>
> (Milan Kundera, *The Unbearable Lightness of Being*)

---

of Roma in the Czech Republic, Hungary, Poland, and Slovakia, 1 JOURNAL OF ETHNOPOLITICS AND MINORITY ISSUES IN EUROPE 12-13 (winter 2001/2002).

The case of anti-Romani hate speech in the region has country specificities that need to be taken into account by social movements. Zoltan Barany deduces three factors that have underscored the lack of success in political mobilisation of Roma in CEE:

(1) the weakness of Romani identity;
(2) the lack of past experiences;
(3) the shortcomings of their political organizations.[91]

In a situation of weak political mobilisation and lobbying forces for Romani rights before the institutions in Brussels and Strasbourg, legal mobilisation via transnational law becomes ever pertinent. The European system of human rights protection, via the possibility of individual claims before the Strasbourg Court and the preliminary reference procedure of the Luxembourg Court, provide two judicial mechanisms for taking anti-Gypsy expression seriously.

The first (Strasbourg) scenario is not without pitfalls. Hate speech cases have been reaching Strasbourg via individual complaints from perpetrators of racist utterances alleging a violation of their right to freedom of expression (Article 10 ECHR). Those cases vary, *inter alia*, from anti-Semitic leaflets, anti-Muslim book, *apologie du terrorisme*, xenophobic calendars, to, most recently, homophobic hate speech.[92] The technique of the Court has been more or less consistent. In some cases, it has found that the cases represent a straightforward contradiction of the democratic values protected by virtue of Article 17 ECHR. In the majority of cases, the Court has applied a proportionality test within the two parts of Article 10 ECHR, finding that prosecution for virulent hate speech falls within the margin of appreciation enjoyed by state parties. In all of Strasbourg's judgements, it was the perpetrators of hate speech that have initiated the Court's proceedings. Within this conventional paradigm, it is impossible to indict state authorities for a failure to launch proceedings against the perpetrators of anti-Gypsy hate speech.[93] Therefore, the Strasbourg mechanism leaves only soft law and

---

91 Zoltan Barany, *Ethnic Mobilisation and the State: The Roma in Eastern Europe*, 21 ETHNIC AND RACIAL STUDIES 208 (1998). By citing this author, I do not subscribe to the somewhat controversial views of Barany on Roma mobilization.

92 For a detailed account of the recent Strasbourg cases on hate speech, see Uladzislau Belavusau, *A Dernier Cri From Strasbourg: An Ever Formidable Challenge of Hate Speech*, 16 EUROPEAN PUBLIC LAW 373 (2010).

93 See also the unsuccessful attempt to accuse the state of sponsoring anti-Roma burlesquing via an alleged violation of Article 8 ECHR in the most recent grand chamber case, Eur. Court H.R., *Aksu v. Turkey*, Judgement of 2012, Application nos. 4149/04 and 41029/04.

monitoring recourses for potential anti-hate speech mobilisation avenues in CEE.[94]

The second (Luxembourg) scenario has become very promising in light of the so-called EU Race Equality Directive 2000/43. This Directive prohibits racial and ethnic discrimination in the areas of employment and occupation; vocational training; membership of employer and employee organisations; social protection, including social security and health care; education; and access to the goods and services available to the public, including housing.

In 2008, in the *Feryn* judgement, the ECJ held the utterances of a Belgian employer, who suggested that he will never hire Moroccans due to their unreliability, to constitute direct discrimination.[95] This xenophobic statement sufficed to invoke the Directive and sent a powerful signal about hate speech in EU law. Most importantly, the case was brought by a Belgian non-discrimination NGO in the absence of any single complaint from a Moroccan individual. The *Feryn* example offers a possible mechanism for overcoming the absence of individual plaintiffs and ambiguous stance of the national legislature in "Roma cases". As far as the vigorous rhetorical anti-Gypsyism could be framed into a claim under the "Race Directive" (e.g., employment or education grounds), it is sufficient to launch proceedings in a national court by an NGO.

Since vicious anti-Gypsyism is very often reproduced via TV, radio, newspapers, and web space, it is indispensable to safeguard the avenues for "affirmative action" in the media. An explicit incentive for positive (or at least, neutral) representation of Roma is badly needed in CEE. Similarly, there is a need for an alternative narrative about Roma, perhaps through a window of neglected histories and episodes of victimhood that emphasises the rights of Roma as members of the wider community and national cultural landscape. Moreover, it is important to ruin the mythology of the essentialist character of Roma minorities. As observed by Peter Vermeersch, by taking the cultural identity of the marginalised community uncritically and putting it into the centre of advocacy, social movements often construct a particular sectional minority identity. The latter not only ignores individual identities but also contributes to greater stigmatisation. However, the essentialist

---

94 For a scrutiny of the non-discrimination discourse towards Roma in Strasbourg, see Emanuela Ignătoiu-Sora, *The Discrimination Discourse in Relation to the Roma: Its Limits and Benefits*, Ethnic and Racial Studies 1697 (2011).

95 See Case C-54/07, *Centrum voor gelijkheid van kansen en voor racismebestnijding v. Firma Feryn NV*, 2008 ECR I-5187. See Belavusau, *Fighting Hate Speech through EU Law*.

categorisation schemes lie at the heart of Roma oppression.[96] Moreover, the discursive marginality of Roma can be separated from political, social, and economic aspects. In this context, Zoltan Barany offers an example of the Chinese in Indonesia and Malaysia and people of Indian ancestry in Trinidad and Tobago. Although economically influential they remain politically marginalised.[97] Therefore, the press constitutes an often-underestimated medium for the de-marginalisation of Roma, despite their socio-economic marginalisation. In this respect, the media could play a positive role in fostering a semiotic space of tolerance, while demystifying the rhetorical anti-Gypsyism and promoting counter-xenophobic identities.

Another strategy for the mobilisation of Roma social movements should focus on incitement to anti-Gypsyism by state officials, such as the police, administration, and government members. Considering the threat of pogroms, the *perfomative* potential of such hate speech against Roma should be deconstructed in light of the respective criminal clauses (as demonstrated in this study, available in all three scrutinised countries). The concrete threat of violence to Roma remains enigmatic for judges and prosecutors unless it is brought into a double rhetorical framework of victimhood accounts and histories of persecutions. Moreover, social movements should not ignore the representation of Romani individuals in the media in terms of the "genetic propensity for crime". Even if the judicial challenge to hate speech allegations remains unsuccessful, they should be ready to contextualise and invoke those rhetorical stigmas with stories of anti-Roma discrimination and pogroms.

In the popular rhetorical context of Central and Eastern European countries, the Roma remain undoubtedly the most marginalised, mystified, stigmatised and misunderstood community of the region. The democratic changes after communism saw freedom of expression installed at the apex of civil rights protection. Yet free speech also exposed Roma to omnipresent vituperation. The neglected avenues identified above for the fight against anti-Roma hate speech (in particular, via EU law) should become the focal point of CEE non-discrimination agendas.

---

96 Peter Vermeersch, *Marginality, Advocacy, and the Ambiguities of Multiculturalism: Notes on Romani Activism in Central Europe*, 12 IDENTITIES: GLOBAL STUDIES IN CULTURE AND POWER 451 (2005).

97 Zoltan Barany, *Orphans of Transition: Gypsies in Eastern Europe*, 9 JOURNAL OF DEMOCRACY 142, 143 (1998). See also Morag Goodwin, *Viewing Romani Marginalization through the Nexus of Race and Poverty*, in EUROPEAN UNION NON-DISCRIMINATION LAW: COMPARATIVE PERSPECTIVES ON MULTI-DIMENSIONAL EQUALITY LAW 137 (Dagmar Schiek & Victoria Chege eds., 2009).

Chapter 8

Roma as a Discrete and Insular Minority in Poland: In a Quest for Effective Rights Protection Mechanisms

Anna Śledzińska-Simon*

I. Introduction

The estimated population of Roma in Poland sits, depending on the source, between 12,000 and 35,000 people, and thus Roma constitute between 0,05% and 0,16% of the Polish population, respectively.[1] Notwithstanding the insignificant size of the group, persons of Roma origin in Poland are subject to widespread discrimination and exclusion in various fields of life, including employment, housing, education, healthcare and social protection.[2] Thus, the Roma problem in Poland exists and should not be marginalized[3] just because Roma minority lacks political power or a critical mass. Quite to the contrary, the level of protection given to the most disempowered minority is a measure of a mature democracy that Poland aspires to be.

---

*   LL.M., S.J.D., Assistant Professor, Department of Law, Administration and Economics, University of Wrocław, Poland. I am thankful to Morag Goodwin for her insightful comments on the first draft of this chapter.

1   In the 2011 National Population Census 16,000 persons declared their Roma ethnic identity. Available at: http://www.stat.gov.pl/cps/rde/xbcr/gus/LUD_raport_z_wynikow_NSP2011.pdf Some sources, including the World Bank, indicate however that there are up to 60,000 Roma in Poland. Available at: http://web.worldbank.org/WBSITE/EXTERNAL/COUNTRIES/ECAEXT/EXTROMA/0,contentMDK:20339787~menuPK:904252~pagePK:64168445~piPK:64168309~theSitePK:615987,00.html

2   *The situation of Roma in 11 EU Member States – Survey results at a glance*, European Union Fundamental Rights Agency and United Nations Development Programme 2012. Available at: http://fra.europa.eu/fraWebsite/research/publications/publications_per_year/2012/pub_roma-survey-at-a-glance_en.htm

3   Poland does not participate in the Decade for Roma Inclusion 2005-2015. The Decade is an international initiative that brings together governments, intergovernmental and nongovernmental organizations, as well as Romani civil society, to accelerate progress toward improving the welfare of Roma in the region. See http://www.romadecade.org

The purpose of this chapter is to explore and critically assess whether the existing mechanisms of rights protection in Poland provide adequate tools to prohibit discrimination and safeguard specific minority rights for Roma. It is well recognized that fight against discrimination of Roma is likely to improve the social and economic position of this group and to put an end to the vicious circle of exclusion, resulting mainly from lack of education, marketable professional qualifications and employment.[4] Moreover, in the European Union a right-based approach is suggested as the best response to inequality that many Roma face nowadays.[5] While there is a significant degree of convergence between Member States of the European Union in the context of anti-discrimination law, the level of minority protection is determined at the state level. Thus, the reasons why certain rights do not work for Roma in practice may be to some extent country-specific and depend on the implementation of EU equality law and international minority protection standards.[6]

The chapter posits that the problem with the minority protection in case of Roma in Poland is rather complex. It is thus not solely the question of a law, although the first strand of analysis indicates that Roma do not utilize certain group rights due to failures of law. To such failures count erroneous conceptions implied in the law on national and ethnic minorities, which make specific minority rights either irrelevant or inapplicable to Roma due to their group characteristics.[7] Another legal failure follows from bad drafting of the

---

4   See e.g. Tammie O'Neil, Laure-Hélène, *Rights-Based Approaches to Tackling Discrimination and Horizontal Inequality*, Background Paper, Overseas Development Institute 2003. The authors argue that "lack of respect for equal rights and difficulties in claiming entitlements, in particular for social groups subject to legal, political, social or cultural discrimination, is a major factor underlying poverty, associated with high levels of inequality and contributing to economic and social exclusion" (3).

5   *Roma Inclusion: A Progressive and Rights-Based Approach*, European Network Against Racism, General Policy Paper no. 7, 2012. Available at: http://cms.horus.be/ files/99935/MediaArchive/policy/GPP_7_Roma%20FINAL%20adopted.pdf.   Frank Stewart, *Horizontal Inequalities: A Neglected Dimension of Development*, Working Paper No. 81 (2002). Available at: http://www3.qeh.ox.ac.uk/pdf/qehwp/qehwps81. pdf (arguing that in pluralistic societies, in addition to inequality between individuals (vertical inequality), there is also horizontal inequality, resulting from a different standing of culturally defined (e.g. ethnic) groups).

6   Like Framework Convention on National Minorities, 1 February 1995, CETS, vol. 157 (ratified by 39 States) or European Charter for Regional or Minority Languages, 5 November 1992, CETS, vol. 148 (ratified by 25 States)

7   Iskra Uzunova, *Roma Integration in Europe: Why Minority Rights are Failing*, 27 Arizona Journal of International & Comparative Law 283, 286-287 (2010) (discussing the ineffectiveness of the minority rights legal framework with regard to the social tension between Roma and non-Roma and arguing that socio-ethical norms are stronger forces of social behavior than minority rights laws).

law on equal treatment that diminishes its practical value for any victim of discrimination, not only of Roma origin.

The second strand of analysis evaluates the potential to protect Roma rights in Poland through the means of political participation, government programs and judicial process. It argues that limited prospects of Roma in Poland to successfully enforce their rights depend also on such factors as the lack of strong public interest law organizations specialized in strategic litigation or advocacy of Roma rights, the lack of internal group mobilization and resources (including human resources such as generation(s) of Roma law graduates or people with higher education qualifications) and the lack of political representation. It also inquires why no Roma has ever effectively used subsidiary human rights instruments like individual applications to an international human rights court or body (*e.g.* the European Court of Human Rights, the Human Rights Committee or the Committee on the Elimination of Discrimination against Women) against Poland. Notably, Poland has not yet signed or ratified the 1996 revised European Social Charter and thus, it has not accepted the colective complaint procedure to the European Committee of Social Rights. Would it be because of their lacking ability to protect their rights and low rights-awareness or rather because of preference for different forms of conflict resolution?

The reference to 'discrete and insular minorities' in the title recalls the plurality opinion written by Justice Stone for the US Supreme Court in *Carolene Product* case.[8] In the famous footnote to this opinion Justice Stone stands as a great defender of minorities who are excluded from the political process and their interests are not adequately represented in the legislatures. Drawing a difference between legislation that regulates ordinary economic activities and legislation that restricts constitutional liberties, he insisted on rejecting the presumption of constitutionality of laws curtailing the ordinary democratic process, discriminating against the minorities or contravening rights specifically enumerated in the Constitution. Thus, in his opinion, legislation aimed at racial, ethnic, and religious minorities that lack the protection of political processes should not be subject to a rational basis analysis, but a heightened standard of judicial review. In result, the *Carolene Product*'s Footnote Four opened a new era of the Supreme Court jurisprudence, which required the government to show a compelling state interest anytime it regulated against a minority (suspect class) or limited constitutional liberties.[9]

---

8   *United States v. Carolene Products Co.*, 304 U.S. 144 (1938).

9   See e.g. Marcy Strauss, *Reevaluating Suspect Classifications*, 35 SEATTLE UNIVERSITY

The chapter applies the Footnote Four's rationale to the case of Roma in Poland in order to show that they are an ethnic minority unable to defend their interests through the democratic process and the responsibility to protect them falls *inter alia* upon the courts.

The chapter ends on a more positive note with an example of a successful strategic litigation case in the area of discrimination in access to publicly available services. It provides evidence that rights can be successfully enforced once legal assistance is offered to Romani victims of discrimination. Otherwise victims who are aware of their rights and existing redress mechanisms, but have no access to legal aid, might choose not to report discriminatory treatment and human rights abuse and not to recourse to courts. Once their access to courts is not hindered, Roma might be interested to litigate and see that the right not to be discriminated against is not a luxury good available only to members of more politically and socially empowered groups. Thus, this isolated success story of Roma discrimination case in court can help to increase confidence of Roma in the justice system and in justice in general.

II. Failures of the Legal System of Minority Protection

Having accepted that a right-based approach is a preferable strategy for achieving greater social integration and empowerment of Roma, the following paragraphs examine the failures inherent in the legal system of minority protection. They include instances of such formulation, interpretation and application of law, which turn the protection offered in general to minorities or in particular to Roma insufficient.

There is a broad consensus that an adequate system of minority protection consists of two interrelated elements: (1) the general prohibition of discrimination in enjoyment of human rights and (2) special rights for persons belonging to minorities.[10] It is also argued that the general anti-discrimination law is not minority-specific, but it should be interpreted and

---

LAW REVIEW 135 (2011); David A. Strauss, *Is Carolene Products Obsolete?*, 2010 U. ILLINOIS LAW REVIEW 1251, 1253 (2010); Bruce A. Ackerman, *Beyond Carolene Products*, 98 HARVARD LAW REVIEW 713, 724 (1985); Lewis F. Powell, *Carolene Products Revisited*, 82 COLUMBIA LAW REVIEW 1087 (1982)

10 Kristin Henrard, *An E.U. Perspective on New versus Traditional Minorities: On Semi-Inclusive Socio-Economic Integration and Expanding Visions of "European" Culture and Identity,* 17 COLUMBIA JOURNAL OF EUROPEAN LAW 57, 61 (2010/2011).

applied in a minority conscious way for the sake of protection of important identitarian interests (related to exercise of freedom of speech, association, religion or the right to education).[11] The second category is minority-specific. The law in Poland provides protection against discrimination, including ethnic discrimination, and safeguards special minority rights. The fact that law recognizes Roma as an ethnic minority is important in the context of a rather homogenous nationality of the population leaving on the Polish territory.[12]

A. *Protection of ethnic minority rights*

According to one interpretation the Polish Constitution[13] adopts an ethnocentric perspective since references to 'the Polish Nation' and 'the common good – Poland' are made already in its Preamble and to 'national heritage', 'products of culture as a source of Nation's identity' and 'national cultural heritage' in the following articles regarding the core principles of the Republic. To say the least, the concept of the Nation emerging from the constitutional provisions is not coherent, in particular when it links the Nation with the idea of 'Motherland' and not the State, using such terms as 'our ancestors' or 'our compatriots' or referring to a confessional and cultural community.[14] In this context Roma hardly fall in the meaning of 'the Polish Nation'. Nevertheless, the dominant view of the constitutional theory[15] and the Constitutional Tribunal[16] accepts that the Nation as a source of the sovereign power denotes a political category of people who are Polish citizens, notwithstanding their ethnicity.

The Constitution guarantees that Polish citizens belonging to national or ethnic minorities enjoy the freedom to maintain and develop their own language, to maintain their customs and traditions, and to develop their own

---

11   *Id.*

12   In the 2011 National Population Census 93,9% person declare exclusively the Polish national identity, 2,19% – jointly the Polish and non-Polish identity and 1,46% – exclusively the non-Polish identity.

13   Constitution of the Republic of Poland (further as the Constitution of Poland) adopted on 2 April 1997, Journal of Laws 1997, No 78, Item 483.

14   Artur Ławniczak, Kwestia modyfikacji treści lub usunięcia preambuły do Konstytucji RP, in KONIECZNE I POŻĄDANE ZMIANY KONSTYTUCJI RP Z 2 KWIETNIA 1997 ROKU, 127-151 (Bogusław Banaszak, Mariusz Jabłoński eds. 2010).

15   L. Garlicki, Polskie prawo konstytucyjne. Zarys wykładu 55 (2011).

16   Judgment of the Constitutional Tribunal (further as CT judgment) of 4 May 2005, K 18/04.

culture. Moreover, it provides that national and ethnic minorities have the right to establish educational and cultural institutions, institutions designed to protect religious identity, as well as to participate in the resolution of matters connected with their cultural identity.[17] The way the Constitution recognizes special needs of national and ethnic minorities follows a model of protection for traditional minorities, which did not choose to become minorities and therefore tend to resist assimilation and exhibit the desire to use their language and preserve their cultural distinctiveness.[18] In this respect it excludes from the constitutional protection non-Polish citizens, even if they belong to the same ethnic group that benefits from such protection. It follows that new migrants are not included in the constitutional concept of minority inasmuch as they are not included in the concept of a sovereign.[19]

Paradoxically the Constitution is not consistent in providing equal guarantees to national and ethnic minorities. Whereas Article 35 addresses both categories, Article 27 refers only to national minorities, whose language rights resulting from ratified international agreements should not be limited by the recognition of Polish as the official language in the country.[20]

The legal definitions of a national and ethnic minority are provided in a statutory law, which implements the Framework Convention on National Minorities and the European Charter for Regional or Minority Languages. Ethnic minority is a group of Polish citizens that jointly fulfils the following conditions:

---

17 Article 35 of the Constitution of Poland.

18 WILL KYMLICKA, MULTICULTURAL CITIZENSHIP: A LIBERAL THEORY OF MINORITY RIGHTS 61 (1995).

19 It remains the power of the state (the constitution-makers) to define the confines of the nation and determine who the insiders are that are eligible for benefits of membership. Lua Kamál Yuille, *Nobody Gives a Damn About the Gypsies: the Limits of Westphalian Models for Change*, 9 OREGON REVIEW OF INTERNATIONAL LAW 389, 392 (2007).

20 Marek Safjan, Pozycja mniejszości w Polsce w świetle orzecznictwa Trybunału Konstytucyjnego, available at: http://www.trybunal.gov.pl/wiadom/Komunikaty/20031003/20031003.pdf. See also the Resolution of the Constitutional Tribunal of 14 May 1997, W 7/96 (underlining that a citizen is obliged to use the official language in relations with public authorities unless s/he is entitled to use a minority language in order to realize such fundamental rights like the right to defense or the right to information).

1) is less numerous than the rest of the population of Poland;
2) significantly differs from other citizens with regard to language, culture and tradition;
3) strives to maintain its language, culture and tradition;
4) is aware of its own historic national community and is inclined to express and protect it;
5) its ancestors have been living on the present territory of the Republic of Poland for at least 100 years;
6) does not identify itself with a nation organized in its own state.[21]

The law lists Roma, Karaims, Lemks and Tatars as ethnic minorities that satisfy the above-mentioned criteria.[22] The law recognizes also nine national minorities: Armenians, Belarusians, Czechs, Germans, Jews, Lithuanians, Russians, Slovaks and Ukrainians. The law defines them as groups which, in addition to the above characteristics ((1)-(6)), identify with a nation organized into its own state.[23]

However, the Minorities Act applies only to Roma with Polish citizenship. It stipulates certain individual rights like the right to identify or not with a minority, the right not to disclose information about one's identity, the right to enjoy rights and freedoms individually and with other members of the minority, the right not to be forcefully assimilated or subject to measures aimed at a change of the national or ethnic proportions in the population, as well as the right to equal protection of laws and non-discrimination with regard to the minority status.[24] Individuals have also certain language rights like the right to use the minority language in private and in public, to spell the names according to the minority language, to learn or to be instructed in the minority language, and also to education of the minority history and culture. It is also possible to use the minority language as supporting before the local authorities under certain conditions.[25] They can also use their minority language in courts and require information in the

---

21 Article 2 (3) of the Act of 6 January 2005 on national and ethnic minorities and the regional language (further as the Minorities Act), Journal of Laws 2005, No. 17, Item 141.

22 It is important to note that Karaims, Lemks and Tatars are even less numerous than Roma, but they are not so territorially dispersed.

23 Article 2 (1) of the Minorities Act.

24 Articles 4-6 of the Minorities Act.

25 Articles 7-16 of the Minorities Act.

minority language and interpreter in the criminal, civil and administrative proceedings. Minority organizations and cultural organizations might also receive government support for protection, preservation and development of cultural identity.[26] Further, national and ethnic minorities have also the right to access public means of communication through minority programs in the public radio and television and to set up their own radio and TV stations.[27] Members belonging to national and ethnic minorities can also establish private educational institutions and choose them as the place of education for their children.[28]

In fact, many guarantees of language, cultural and educational rights are of little practical relevance for Roma due to the size and characteristics of this group. Like everywhere in Europe, Roma in Poland are not a homogeneous category.[29] They consist of a number of groups and subgroups[30] that do not share a single common language but speak different dialects. Moreover, they are 'geographically detached', living in many different regions of Poland. Consequently, they do not share the same customs and traditions and differ also with regard to their social and economic situation. Finally, they are represented by many small organizations,[31] which have different aims and priorities or occasionally even compete with one other for recognition by the government as the representation of all Roma interests.[32]

It is clear that the law does not adequately take all these group characteristics in account. Thus, it commits 'the sin of essentialization', while wrongly assuming that all Roma are the same. In consequence, the law requires Roma to mobilize and unify as if they had one shared identity, whereas in practice Roma seem to have multiple ones. For this reason more

---

26 Articles 18 of the Minorities Act.

27 Article 21 (1) 8a of the radio and television Act of 29 December 1992, Journal of Laws of 1993, No. 7, Item 34.

28 Regulation of the Minister of National Education of 19 November 2009, Journal of Laws of 2009, No. 200, Item 1537.

29 The Polish population also includes a small group of Sinti, although their exact number is not known.

30 The main Romani groups in Poland include: Polska Roma (with its subgroups like the Sasitka Roma/German Roma and Haladitka Roma/Ruska Roma), Kelderara, Lovara and Bergitka Roma.

31 The Roma community portal publishes the lists of more than 40 local Roma organizations, available at: http://harangos.pl/organizacje-romskie/. The most prominent are: the Central Roma Council (Białystok), the Association of Roma in Poland (Oświecim) and the Union of the Polish Roma (Szczecinek).

32 One area of competition is the access to government subsidies or special funds from the state budget and the European Union dedicated for Roma integration.

numerous, concentrated minorities with stronger sense of common identity, in particular the Germans, have more real chances to make use of certain rights provided in the law. For example, ethnic communities like Roma hardly ever constitute the 20% of the local population in order to demand the use of a minority language as a supporting language before local authorities.[33]

Apart from the lack of a critical mass and a shared identity, some Roma have perhaps no interest in particular minority rights provided by the law. The law concerning the use of minority languages in education allows the minority language to be the only language of instruction, one of the two languages of instruction (in bilingual schools) and the language taught in an additional school course.[34] The use of Romani dialects in the context of education is problematic due to objections to the popularization and the traditional use of Romani as a secret language (argot) without a unified standard form or codification. Finally, there are also few Romani language teachers. Therefore, the European Commission against Racism and Intolerance (ECRI) noted in its 2010 report on Poland that Roma could claim the use of the Romani language in schools, kindergartens or even in universities,[35] but that there was no interest in pursuing such claims.[36] Still, other sources show there is a growing interest in introducing Romani language in schools.[37] Moreover, at least one Roma community established a private kindergarten in order to teach their children Romani from an early age.

Another important reason why minority-specific group rights provided by law are of little relevance for Roma relates to human and material resources. For Roma (as compared to the German or even Jewish minority), it might be particularly difficult to enforce rights, which require significant financial

---

33 In Poland only German, Lemko and Kashubian languages are used in official relations with local authorities. See the list of municipalities with a minority supporting languages available at: http://mac.gov.pl/wp-content/uploads/2011/12/Lista-gmin-wpisanych-do-Rejestru-gmin-na-kt%C3%B3rych-obszarze-u%C5%BCywane-s%C4%85-nazwy-w-j%C4%99zyku-mniejszo%C5%9Bci1.pdf

34 Regulation of the Minister of National Education of 14 November 2007, Journal of Laws of 2007, No. 214, Item 1579.

35 In Poland the European Charter on the Regional and Minority Languages came into force on 1 June 2009.

36 ECRI Report on Poland, CRI(2010)18. Available at: http://www.coe.int/t/dghl/monitoring/ecri/country-by-country/poland/POL-CbC-IV-2010-018-ENG.pdf

37 Wiktor Osuch, Agnieszka Dwojak, *Szkolnictwo mniejszości narodowych w Polsce, ze szczególnym uwzględnieniem Romów małopolskich* (2009). Available at: http://www.ap.krakow.pl/ptg/index_pliki/czasopismo/tom_4/artykuly_4/osuch_szkolnictwo.pdf

investment or organizational effort. Additionally, national minorities have other alternatives than the government grant programs to receive financial support. They can possibly request funding from their 'Motherland' through various public or private institutes or foundations promoting national culture abroad.

As already mentioned, the Minorities Act does not apply to minorities without Polish citizens. In this category fall Roma migrants from East European countries that travelled to Poland starting from the early 1990s,[38] unless they acquired Polish citizenship.[39] The second wave of Roma migrants came to Poland mainly from Romania and Bulgaria following EU enlargement in 2007[40] and they can enjoy the status of short-term residents without fulfilling any additional requirements.[41] Consequently, there are four categories of Roma migrants in Poland: (1) who are EU citizens with the long-term resident status;[42] (2) who are EU citizens without the long-term resident status due to lack of legal employment or other entitlement enlisted in the Citizens Directive; (3) who are non-EU citizens (third country nationals) and reside in Poland legally[43] (4) who as third country nationals reside in Poland illegally. It is likely that the number of new Roma migrants exceeds the number of Roma with Polish citizenship, although at the moment no official statistics show the exact number of Roma in the above categories. Moreover, the socio-economic situation of illegal migrants is likely to be worse than of

---

38 Usually the first wave of Romani migrants travelled to other European countries or returned back to their home countries. However, it is estimated that up to 500,000 Romanian citizens, mainly of Roma origin, were temporarily present in Poland in 1990s. Paweł Lechowski, Migracje Romów rumuńskich in Romowie, in HISTORIA I KULTURA, 22-32 (Agnieszka Caban, Grzegorz Kondrasiuk eds. 2009).

39 Elena Marushiakova and Vesselin Popov estimate that there are between 50,000 to 100, 000 Roma migrants, although some sources say it is up to 200,000 persons. Elena Marushiakova and Vesselin Popov, *Poland*, in ROMA AND THE ECONOMY: OVERVIEW REPORTS 52-56 (2004).

40 Still 7 years after the accession of Bulgaria and Romania to the European Union other Member States can apply additional conditions restricting the free movement of workers from, to and between these Member States.

41 At the same time many Polish Roma immigrated to other Member States following the accession of Poland to the EU.

42 EC Directive of 29 April 2004 (further as the Citizens Directive), O.L 2004, L 229/35.

43 In accordance to the Alliens Act of 13 June 2003, Journal of Laws of 2003, No 128, Item 1175.

Roma with Polish citizenship.[44] The same can be expected with regard to the situation of their rights protection.[45]

B. Prohibition of discrimination

In contrast to minority rights, which have predominantly a group character, prohibition of discrimination protects individuals. Yet, discrimination usually concerns individuals belonging to a particular minority and originates in prejudices and stereotypes about this minority group. Therefore, the effective elimination of discrimination has important implications for the protection of the entire group. In short, the general goal of anti-discrimination law is to provide remedies against unlawful actions of public authorities and private persons who treat an individual unevenly on the basis of particular, usually inborn or permanent, characteristics like ethnic origin or skin colour. Although the aim to reach "the equilibrium that would exist in the counterfactual world in which every individual retained his or her same abilities but the employer (or purchaser) was somehow prevented from observing any of the prohibited traits (such as race or sex)"[46] is rather unattainable, anti-discrimination law helps to break the cycle of disadvantageous treatment and fight prejudices. To some extent, it should also allow for reverse discrimination (positive actions) in order to provide equal opportunities and more fair outcomes. Summing up, anti-discrimination law plays three main functions: it redresses the wrongs, breaks the cycle of disadvantage and accommodates the difference.[47]

---

44 Claude Cahn and Elspeth Guild, *Recent Migration of Roma in Europe* 17 (2010), available at: http://www.osce.org/hcnm/78034 The authors note that the EU enlargement 'created a situation in which, in countries of immigration, superficially unitary Romani communities may include persons with differing status and potentially differing legal entitlements, particularly as concerns EU rights, as well as rights under the Council of Europe's European Social Charter and Revised Charter'.

45 Now and again their presence receives public attention in the media, but mass expulsion of illegal migrants of Roma origin has never been discussed or enforced. See e.g. Jacek Harłukowicz, *Wrocław bezradny wobec nielegalnych koczowisk Romów* (*The city of Wrocław helpless with illegal Roma camps*), Gazeta Wyborcza of 1.3.2012. Available at: http://wyborcza.pl/1,75248,11260380,Wroclaw_bezradny_wobec_nielegalnych_koczowisk_Romow.html

46 John J. Donohue, *The Law and Economics of Antidiscrimination Law*, John M. Olin Center for Studies in Law, Economics, and Public Policy Working Papers, Paper 290, 33, 45. Available at: http://digitalcommons.law.yale.edu/lepp_papers/290

47 Sandra Fredman, Introduction: Combating Racism with Human Rights: The Right to Equality, in Discrimination and Human Rights: Case of Racism (Sandra Fredman eds. 2001), 15.

In the social perception it also has a symbolic value sending a clear message that discrimination is unacceptable.

In the EU legal order equality has been recognized as a fundamental principle of law.[48] It is now enshrined in the Treaty of the European Union both as a core value (Article 2) and as one of the aims of the Union (Article 3 (3)).[49] On this basis, the European Commission has the power to initiate proceedings against a Member State infringing the principle of equal treatment.[50] Since the Amsterdam Treaty both the personal and material scope of the principle of equal treatment was extended.[51] In result, the core of today's EU anti-discrimination law constitute directives adopted on *ex* Article 13 of the Treaty establishing the European Community like the Racial Equality Directive,[52] the Framework Equality Directive,[53] the Recast Equal Treatment Directive[54] and the Goods and Services Directive.[55]

Within the framework of EU anti-discrimination law the principle of equality is primarily realized through guarantees of equal treatment that "precludes comparable situations from being treated differently and different situations from being treated in the same way, unless the treatment is objectively justified".[56] In fact, equal treatment and prohibition of discrimination need to be seen as obverse and reverse of the same coin.

---

48 Cases C-117/76 and C-16/77 *Ruckdeschel and others v Hauptzollamt Hamburg-St. Annen* [1977] ECR 1753.

49 Treaty on European Union, O.J. 2010 C 83/13.

50 However, it might not do so for political reasons like in the case of mass expulsion of Roma in summer 2010 by France when the European Commission choose not to institute proceedings against France for infringement of the Racial Equality Directive. Gráinne de Búrca, *The Trajectories of European and American Antidiscrimination Law*, 60 AMERICAN JOURNAL OF COMPARATIVE LAW 1, 9 (2012).

51 The Treaty of Amsterdam introduced Article 13 as a general competence norm entrusting the European Community the power to adopt measures to combat discrimination on a number of grounds. Article 13 gave the impulse for adoption of new anti-discrimination directives.

52 EC Directive 2000/43/EC of 29 June 2000, O.J. 2000 L 180/22.

53 EC Directive 2000/78/EC of 27 November, O.J. 2000 L 303/16.

54 EC Directive 2006/54/EC of 5 July 2006, O.J. 2006 L 204/23.

55 EC Directive 2004/113/EC of 13 December 2004, O.J. 2004 L 373/37.

56 Christopher McCrudden and Sacha Prechal (eds.), *The Concepts of Equality and Non-Discrimination in Europe: a Practical Approach*, European Commission, Directorate-General for Employment, Social Affairs and Equal Opportunities, Unit G.2, November 2009, 4. See also European Union Fundamental Rights Agency and European Court of Human Rights, *Handbook on European Non-Discrimination Law*, (Council of Europe, 2011).

Moreover, it also encourages positive actions and in this way it responds to the concept of substantive equality.

On the national level, the Constitution of Poland states in general terms that "all persons shall be equal before the law and have the right to equal treatment by public authorities".[57] It means that subjects who can be distinguished with regard to one relevant feature in a particular normative context must be treated equally.[58] However, even under the equality principle certain departures from equal treatment are permissible provided that (1) unequal treatment is directly related to the aims and content of a challenged norm; (2) the interest to be protected by means of unequal treatment are in proportion to the interests of the subjects against whom it will operate, and whose interests will be infringed by unequal treatment; and (3) the challenged norm remains in conjunction with other constitutional norms, principles and values that justify unequal treatment of similarly situated subjects. Among the constitutional principles that justify departures from equal treatment is the principle of social justice.[59] The Constitution prohibits also discrimination on any ground in political, social or economic life.[60] However, the challenge of discrimination is limited "to enjoyment of other constitutionally protected rights" in cases filed as constitutional complaints.[61]

In the field of employment discrimination with regard to ethnicity is prohibited by the Labour Code.[62] According to its provisions all employees need to be treated equally with regard to conclusion and termination of employment contracts, establishing the conditions of work, as well as promotion and access to vocational training.[63] Important to note that the anti-discrimination chapter (Chapter IIa) of the Labour Code was introduced in 2003 in anticipation of Polish accession to the European Union as part of the implementation of the EU directives concerning equal treatment in occupation and employment.[64] However, this aim was only partially attained.

---

57   Article 32 (1) of the Constitution of Poland.
58   The Constitutional Tribunal refuses to hold however that unequal subjects must be treated unequally or unequal subjects must not be treated equally. See e.g. CT judgment of 19 April 2011 (P 41/09).
59   See e.g. CT judgment of 18 January 2011 (P 44/08)
60   Article 33 of the Constitution of Poland.
61   See e.g. CT decision of 24 October 2001 (SK 10/01).
62   Act of 26 June 1974 – Labour Code, Journal of Laws of 1998, No 21, Item 94; and Act of 20 April 2004 on promotion of employment and institutions of employment market, Journal of Laws of 2004, No. 99, Item 1001.
63   Article 18.3(a) of the Labour Code.
64   EEC Directive of 9 February 1976, O.J. 1979 L 6/2 and EC Directive of 27 November 2000, O.J 2000 L 303/16.

A striking example of a defective implementation of the EU Racial Equality Directive is the Equal Treatment Act.[65] The Act was adopted as late as in December 2010 in order to transpose the remaining provisions of several EU anti-discrimination directives, which had not yet been implemented into the Polish legal order. It prohibits discrimination in the areas of self-employment, education, social protection and social security, health care and access to and supply of goods and services. A quick analysis of its provisions would suggest that the law achieves the aims of the directives, but a more careful examination reveals a number of serious flaws that render individual protection against discrimination illusory for all victims, not only Roma.

Nevertheless, the Act was celebrated as the finalization of the implementation process in the field of anti-discrimination and on this account the European Commission withdrew two infringement complaints against Poland.[66] Paradoxically, the European Commission accepted the fact the law on equal treatment was introduced without carrying any substantive assessment of its content. The Commission was not warned by the title that reads "Act on implementation of some provisions of the European Union concerning the principle of equal treatment", which suggests that the real legislative intention was to escape the infringement proceedings before the EU Court.

The Equal Treatment Act is based on the principle of non-discrimination, but the way it is formulated is unclear both for public authorities and persons to whom it applies. The general duty of equal treatment is weakened by too many exceptions and derogations. In its material scope the law covers prohibition of discrimination with regard to sex, race and ethnicity, age, disability, religion and sexual orientation in other areas than employment.

---

65   Act of 3 December 2010 on implementation of some of the provisions of the European Union with regard to equal treatment (further as the Equal Treatment Act), Journal of Laws 2010, Nr 257, Item 1700.

66   By the end of 2010, the Commission initiated two actions against Poland (Case C-341/10 *Commission v. Poland*, action brought on 7 July 2010 and Case C-326/09 *Commission v. Poland*, action brought on 12 August 2009. They concerned lack of adequate implementation of the Racial Equality Directive and the Goods and Services Directive (Directive 2004/113/EC). The Commission issued also two reasoned opinions regarding defect transposition of the Framework Equality Directive and non-communication of national legislation transposing the Recast Equal Treatment Directive (a reasoned opinion of 28 January 2010 and of 18 May 2010). Nevertheless, in 2011 the Court of Justice of the European Union ruled only on the failure to implement the Goods and Services Directive within the prescribed period (Case C-326/09 *Commission v. Poland*, judgment of 17 March 2011). This judgment has however merely a symbolic character and did not have to be enforced.

However, the grounds of prohibited discrimination vary in different areas. In this respect, the Act faithfully mirrors the unfair hierarchy of discrimination grounds in the EU law.[67] Accordingly, in the area of health services and education the law regulated only discrimination on the basis of nationality, sex, race and ethnicity only with regard to and omitted such criteria as age, disability, religion and sexual orientation, whereas discrimination on any ground it is outlawed in the area of employment, vocational training, self-employment and trade union activity.

Another crucial flaw in the Act follows from thoughtless translation of EU directives which univocally require that sanctions for infringement of the principle of equal treatment are effective, proportionate and dissuasive. Sanctions may comprise the payment of just compensation to the victim.[68] However, the Equal Treatment Act provides victims of discrimination the right to sue only for material damages in pursuance to the Civil Code.[69] Unlike compensation, material damages do not encompass moral damage and are insufficient to remedy discrimination if it did not inflict any material loss (like discrimination in access to services). As Professor Łętowska rightly puts it, "wearing out the shoes while walking to another shop or bar after being denied the service" could be claimed the only material damage in such cases.[70]

Furthermore, the law indicates that both the Ombudsman and the Government Plenipotentiary for Equal Treatment are the equality bodies in the light of EU anti-discrimination directives. However, their competence is limited just to intervention in cases of discrimination by public authorities and does not cover the most frequent instances of discrimination in the private sphere. Moreover, the Government Plenipotentiary does not fulfil the criterion of an independent body since it belongs to the organizational structure of the Chancellery of the Prime Minister and depends on the governmental approval.[71]

---

67 See e.g. Erica Howard, *The Case for a Considered Hierarchy of Discrimination Grounds in EU Law*, 13 MAASTRICHT JOURNAL OF EUROPEAN AND COMPARATIVE LAW 445-470 (2006).

68 Article 15 of Directive 2000/43/EC.

69 Article 13 of the Equal Treatment Act.

70 E. Siedlecka, *Dyskryminacja ma się, niestety, dobrze*, Gazeta Wyborcza, 12.12.2011 (refering to prof. E. Łętowska's presentation at the conference 'Effective Legal Protection against Discrimination of Women'), available at: http://wyborcza.pl/1,76 842,10797587,Dyskryminacja_ma_sie__niestety__dobrze.html

71 Article 21 of the Equal Treatment Act.

Difficulties with regard to enforcement of the right to non-discrimination are illustrated in the court statistics for 2011. In the first year after the Equal Treatment Act came into force only 30 cases were filed with the regional and district courts on its basis.[72] Taking into account that the personal scope of the law was rather broad since it applies to all types of victims of discrimination with regard to their skin colour, nationality and ethnicity, religion, sexual orientation, disability, age or gender, the number of complaints is very low. In the course of 2011, courts decided 17 cases, out of which 9 were dismissed, 3 remanded, 1 rejected and 2 discontinued. 13 cases were pending in 2012. The fact that the majority of complaints were not decided on the merits demonstrates that the plaintiffs were not able to properly utilize the law. However, the statistics do not show exactly the prohibited ground of discrimination alleged in these cases; therefore it is not possible to conclude whether they concerned any person of Romani origin.

Although it goes beyond the scope of this chapter to evaluate the impact of the anti-discrimination law on particular categories of victims, the protection of sensitive data in Poland obstructs any scientific analysis of this sort. Currently, no public authority in Poland collects ethnic data: the police, prosecutors, courts and even the Ombudsman[73] do not disaggregate complaints according to race or ethnicity of individual applicants even if processing such anonymous data is legal under the international standards.[74] In this regard, a categorical approach to data protection assumes that race or ethnicity is not relevant in seemingly ethnicity-neutral legal problems. Consequently, it is impossible to gauge the extent of discrimination, in particular structural or indirect discrimination, which is often 'invisible'.

Summing up the characteristic features of the legal framework for minority protection in Poland, it is clear that neither the recognition as an ethnic minority, nor guarantees of certain minority-specific rights, or even anti-discrimination law does significantly change the situation of Roma and improves the enjoyment of their rights. The next parts of this chapter

---

72 The Ombudsman associates such small number of cases with low awareness f the rights guaranteed in the law. See the general statement of the Ombudsman to the Minister of Justice of 29 March 2012, available at: http://www.sprawy-generalne. brpo.gov.pl/pdf/2012/01/693226/1635149.pdf

73 The Ombudsman registers race and ethnicity only in cases that directly concern the rights of national and ethnic minorities.

74 See e.g. Peter Simon, *"Ethnic" statistics and data in Council of Europe countries*, Study Report 2007, http://www.coe.int/t/dghl/monitoring/ecri/activities/themes/ Ethnic_statistics_and_data_protection.pdf

assess the potential to protect Roma rights through the means of political participation, government programs and judicial process.

III. Minority Protection Through the Political Process

The political representation and participation of a minority is undoubtedly "a condition for healthy functioning of a democratic political system and a measure for increasing human security".[75] However, the political participation discourse have also two other dimensions than conflict-prevention related to non-discrimination and legitimacy of the state.[76] Certainly, the mere recognition of a group as a national or ethnic minority does not automatically bring about its visibility and presence in the political realm. In Central and Eastern Europe the post-communist transition to democracy was important for creating the opportunities for Roma organizations to develop, mobilize and promote their culture, but in Poland it did not contribute to the emergence of Romani political representation. As Eva Sobotka rightly observes, the meaning of a Romani representative in the Polish context indicates rather a traditional community leader or an NGO activist than a party man.[77]

Roma in Poland do not have their representatives in the national or local level. This situation persists since the first democratic elections in 1990s and it can be attributed both to the highly divided character of Romani communities and negative social stereotype of Roma.[78] The fact that Roma settlements are scattered all over the territory of Poland makes it practically impossible for Roma voters to become a dominant majority in any of the electoral districts.

---

75   Eva Sobotka, *Political Representation of the Roma: Roma in Politics in the Czech Republic, Slovakia and Poland*, International Policy Fellowship Programme 2003. Available at: http://pdc.ceu.hu/archive/00001870/01/sobotka.pdf

76   See Marc Weller, Introduction – Democratic Governance and Minority Participation: Emerging Legal Standards and Practice, in POLITICAL PARTICIPATION OF MINORITIES: A COMMENTARY ON INTERNATIONAL STANDARDS AND PRACTICE lvii (Marc Weller, Katherine Nobbs eds. 2010).

77   Sobotka, *Political Representation of the Roma: Roma in Politics in the Czech Republic, Slovakia and Poland* (Note 75).

78   In the context of the Central Europe it is suggested that the main impediment to the emergence of a legitimate Romani representation derives from their dependence on the recognition by the government and the government support for their organizations, as well as from the tradition of non-democratic selection of Roma representatives. Ilona Kilimova, *Romani Political Representation in Central Europe. A Historical Survey*, available at: http://academos.ro/sites/default/files/biblio-docs/341/plugin-luprsv012p02a00103.pdf

Additionally, the election law in Poland distinguishes national minorities from ethnic minorities for the exemption from the electoral threshold.[79] In this regard it wrongly assumes that ethnic minorities do not have interest to take part in the political process and connotes them mainly with the preservation of language and culture.[80] Singling out national minorities for the special treatment in the parliamentary elections, the law acknowledges that organization of national minorities might have a political nature due to the existence of a nation state with a policy concerning its minorities living abroad.

Furthermore, among all recognized national minorities in Poland only the Germans have been able to obtain a parliamentary seat in in the Sejm (the Lower Chamber). In consequence, other national minorities and all ethnic minorities are *de facto* excluded from the democratic decision-making processes. Indeed this particular privilege to be included in the distribution of parliamentary seats notwithstanding the fact that an electoral committee registered by a national minority organization did not reach 5% of votes in the country is the most desired by groups not recognized as a national minority, in particular the Silesians.[81] Importantly, the Constitutional Tribunal upheld the electoral threshold exemption arguing that it is a legitimate exception from the principle of equal treatment and at the same time from the substantive equality principle governing democratic elections since it enhances the political opportunities of national minorities.[82]

In local government elections in 2006 and 2010, a small number of Roma ran for office, however, none were elected. Thus, no person who officially identified as Roma was elected to a legislative body in Poland. The failure

---

79   Article 197 of the Act of 5 January 2011 – Electoral Code, Journal of Laws 2011, No 21, Item 113.

80   In the local elections of 2002 four Romani candidates ran from the Democratic Left Alliance's lists in the Malopolska region. Although none of them was elected, the turnout of the registered Romani electorate reportedly reached 95-100 percent, compared to 35 percent of all registered voters. Sobotka, *Political Representation of the Roma: Roma in Politics in the Czech Republic, Slovakia and Poland* (Note 75). This case evidently shows there is a political interest of the Romani communities and the potential to mobilise their electorate.

81   Eur. Court H. R, *Gorzelik v. Poland*, Judgment of 17 February 2004, Reports of Judgments and Decisions 2004-I (GC) (finding no violation of Article 11 of the European Convention of Human Rights in a case concerning an association called 'the Union of People of Silesian' denied registration as a national minority organization. The ECHR agreed with the national courts that the denial of recognition for the Silesian minority was justified historically and necessary to prevent wrongful acquisition of electoral privileges restricted for national minorities).

82   CT Resolution of 30 April 1997 (W 1/97) and (W 14/95)

of Roma candidates to win in local elections can be perhaps explained by negative social attitudes towards Roma. Moreover, Roma issues are also not debated in the mainstream politics or political campaigns of any of the political parties. In this context, Roma appear to be discrete and insular minority and prejudice against them may be "a special condition curtailing the operation of political processes ordinarily to be relied upon to protect minorities"[83] as Justice Stone suggests. In result, Roma are to be treated as a suspect class and their cases call for a correspondingly more searching judicial inquiry.

With regard to Roma NGOs, their participation in the democratic process was somewhat obstructed by the lack of inter-Roma community unification. Currently, Roma are represented in the Joint Commission of the Government and National and Ethnic Minorities within the Roma Group. The Commission started operating in September 2005 and has mainly a consultative character. However, only recently the Minister of Administration and Digitalization determined the rules on selecting Roma representatives to the Commission and the Roma Group.

IV. Minority Protection through Government Programmes

Except specific rights guarantees entailed in the minority and anti-discrimination legislation, Roma in Poland can also take advantage of special government measures aimed at the improvement of their socio-economic condition. Given the existing nexus between ethnic origin and poverty, it is necessary to addresses the causes of discrimination and exclusion. In case of Roma it is their grim social and economic circumstances (segregation in housing and education and unemployment) that usually hinder the full enjoyment of rights and contribute to marginalization, exclusion and discrimination.[84] For this reason the government needed to develop a special program for the benefit of Roma community as a positive measure that complements the protection provided by law, or rather compensates the failures of legal and political mechanisms to protect this group. However,

---

83 See, *United States v. Carolene Products Co.*, 304 U.S. 144 (1938), FN 4 153.

84 Morag Goodwin, *Multidimensional exclusion. Viewing Romani marginalization through the nexus of race and poverty*, in EUROPEAN UNION NON-DISCRIMINATION LAW. COMPARATIVE PERSPECTIVES ON MULTI-DIMENSIONAL EQUALITY LAW 137 (Dagmar Schieck/ Victoria Chege eds. 2009).

like any type of positive action, the government program is a double-edged sword, which can also have a negative impact on those it intends to privilege.

The first pilot program for the Roma community was developed for 2001-2003 in the Małopolska region to provide better conditions of Roma in education, employment, health, sanitary conditions and housing. It aimed also to gradually abolish separate education for Roma children in so-called Roma classes, which continued after 1991. Within the pilot program public schools could get funding for teachers specially trained to facilitate the education of Romani children, as well as Romani assistants who work with Romani children in their communities and build relations between Romani parents and school authorities. The pilot program was also important for the positive evaluation of Poland as a EU candidate country by the European Commission.

The pilot program served as a model for a nation-wide government program for the period 2004-2013.[85] The Program for the Benefit of Roma Community in Poland assigned approximately 100 million PLN (25 million EUR) over 10 years[86] and the Roma Group within the Joint Commission plays an important consultative role in its implementation. The aim of the Program is to achieve greater social inclusion and integration of Roma mainly through education and the improvement of living conditions. It is addressed to members of Romani communities, and to local government and other organizations active in the promotion of Romani rights. It supports local projects in the area of education, civic society, employment, health, living conditions, security and prevention of racially-motivated crimes, preservation and promotion of Romani culture and raising awareness about Roma in the wider society and civic education of Roma.[87] Importantly, the Program envisions also the participation of other disadvantaged groups e.g. non-Romani groups, in order to prevent conflicts and tensions related to the distribution of these public funds. Nevertheless, such conflicts and tensions do arise[88] and in some localities the availability of government funding for Roma integration has paradoxically sharpened anti-Roma attitudes.[89]

---

85 Adopted as Resolution of the Council of Ministers of 19 August 2003.

86 In addition there are also EU funds available for Roma.

87 http://www.mswia.gov.pl/portal/pl/181/Program_na_rzecz_spolecznosci_ romskiej_w_Polsce.html

88 Information on the activities of the Ombudsman available at: http://www.rpo.gov. pl/pliki/12421286860.pdf

89 The evaluation of the Program is available at: http://www.ewaluacja.gov.pl/Wyniki/ Documents/6_064.pdf. See also the government report on the implementation of

The Program was welcomed by the European Commission against Racism and Intolerance, which noted with approval several initiatives like the regional minority plenipotentiaries, reference persons for Roma in the police, joint police-Roma training sessions, health visitors and legal assistance.[90] However, there are also problems encountered by the beneficiary community regarding access to and spending of the government funds. When the funds are availed to the local government there have been instances that they had not been spent on purposes directly linked to Roma integration. For example in a case taken up by the Ombudsman, the financial means provided for educational support of Roma children and youth were used instead to renovate the school building.[91] In a similar case the local authorities failed to install running water in Roma houses due to the problems with their illegal construction although it availed of a grant for the improvement of living conditions of Roma.[92] In sum, the misuse of the funds and differences with regard to the implementation of the program often relate to the approach to Roma issues of the local authorities.

Compounding the unwillingness of local authorities to spend specially-allocated funding on improving the socio-economic position of Roma, Romani organizations are unable to compete with local authorities in the allocation of such funding. Although Roma NGOs receive training how to submit projects, only 30% of their applications was accepted for funding in 2010.[93] Roma NGOs find that the share of the program funds allocated to them is too low. Additionally, many of the participating organizations lack expertise in project management and complain about the rigidity of the project evaluation. Even if the rigid standards of grant application, implementation and evaluation are not a form of discrimination, Roma NGOs experience difficulty in compliance with the program criteria.

---

the Program for 2011 available at: http://mac.gov.pl/wp-content/uploads/2011/12/Sprawozdanie-z-realizacji-Programu-na-rzecz-spoleczno%C5%9Bci-romskiej-w-Polsce-2011.pdf

90   ECRI Report on Poland (note 36).

91   http://www.rpo.gov.pl/pliki/12421286860.pdf

92   Agnieszka Mikulska, *Ksenofobia i dyskryminacja na tle etnicznym w Polsce – zarys sytuacji* (Helsinki Foundation of Human Rights 2008), available at: www.msw.gov.pl/download.php?s=1&id=4088

93   The evaluation of the Program available at: http://mac.gov.pl/wp-content/uploads/2011/12/Raport-z-badania-ewaluacyjnego-Programu-na-rzecz-spolecznosci-romskiej-w-Polsce.pdf

V. Minority Protection through Judicial Process

As it was demonstrated above, Roma in Poland are excluded from the political process and they should be treated as a discrete and insular minority that needs special protection of judicial process. In the following part it will be inquired whether judicial process can correct the failures and inadequacies of law, political process and government programs in securing the protection of Roma rights. In contrary to the legislative and executive branch of government, the judiciary seems to be particularly designed to safeguard the minority from the majority's rule and serve as the last resort for people whose rights have been violated by public authorities or private citizens. While the main challenges to the effective rights enforcement through courts in case of Roma are similar for all surveyed countries in Europe and they include problems with rights awareness, reporting and access to court, [94] there are clearly certain barriers that are country-specific. For example, what is specific for Poland in comparison to other countries in the region is lack of a single Roma discrimination case, which would be submitted, accepted as admissible and decided on the merits by an international court or body. Arguably, the insignificant number of persons belonging to Roma communities in Poland may explain this fact. However, it is also plausible to maintain that this situation is due to the weakness of Roma and non-Roma NGOs specialized in strategic litigation, or the preference of Roma for other methods of conflict resolution, or a combination of the above factors.

The Data in Focus Report reveals that the majority of Roma in Poland is not aware that discrimination is illegal (63% either do not know that it is illegal or think that it is legal) and cannot name organizations that provide support in such cases (78%). 71% respondents in Poland declared that their experience of discrimination was unreported, while the main reasons given for not reporting discrimination range from "nothing would change by reporting", "did not know how to go about reporting" to "too trivial/not worth reporting" and "concerned about negative consequences". [95]

---

94 *The Racial Equality Directive: application and challenges* (further as Synthesis Report), European Union Agency for Fundamental Rights 2012. Available at: http://fra.europa.eu/fraWebsite/attachments/FRA-RED-synthesis-report_EN.pdf   The report asserts that the main challenges to the fight against racial discrimination through litigation include "legal costs, a lack of rights awareness, a reluctance to report incidences, and a tendency towards denial of discrimination as a problem" (19).

95 *Id.,* 7.

Such low reporting level sends a wrong message that Roma are not interested to sue for damage in cases of discrimination. Although many Roma might indeed seek to secure their living in the first instance or solve some critical legal problems like challenge eviction or demolition orders, request building permissions or get access to social housing, social benefits and social aid and finally prepare their defence in criminal cases, filing a discrimination claim can be also essential for their well-being. Given a widespread scale of discrimination many seemingly neutral legal problems concerning housing, social protection or even criminal charges result from different forms of discrimination, including harassment or ethnic profiling.

Nevertheless, the initiation of court proceedings in a pursuit of an individual discrimination claim usually bears high personal costs. For Roma it can additionally entail overcoming cultural or psychological barriers related to their traditional, culture-based distrust of the institution of a state and courts as rights defenders. Roma may also fear that the justice system is hostile to Roma and prefer not to litigate. Furthermore, they might intuitively feel that the judicial process does not eradicate the causes of discrimination since any litigation of racial discrimination creates an opportunity only for *ad hoc* intervention.[96] The lack of systemic change following from a judgment might be thus another reason why such cases do not reach the court level.

It seems that the process of becoming 'victim in court' is not automatic for a victim of discrimination. Even if a plaintiff 'only' needs to make probable that a discriminatory act was unlawful and "establish facts from which it may be presumed that there has been direct or indirect discrimination",[97] she or he must develop a certain personal attitude to build the case for litigation. This is why, notwithstanding the shifted burden of proof, a victim without professional representation may have fewer chances to prevail over a defendant who is not in a socially and economically disadvantaged position or is a legal person represented by an attorney. In other countries these problems are overcome by *actio popularis*[98] or evidence from discrimination testing.[99] Such procedural advancements are still missing in the Polish legal system.

---

96 Sandra Fredman, Combating Racism with Human Rights. The Right to Equality 15 (2001).

97 Council Directive 2000/43/EC (Note 52) Art. 8

98 See Case-54/07 *Centrum voor gelijkheid van kansen en voor racismebestrijding v. Feryn NV* [2008] I-5187.

99 Isabelle Rorive, *Proving Dicrimination Cases – The Role of Situation Testing*, Centre for Equal Rights and Migration Policy Group 2009, available at: http://www.equal-jus.eu/sites/equal-jus.eu/files/Situation_Testing.pdf

Moreover, in Poland there are no powerful organizations which specialize in Roma litigation and lead strategic litigation in this area.[100] The European Roma Rights Centre is one example of such public interest law organisation "working to combat anti-Romani racism and human rights abuse of Roma through strategic litigation, research and policy development, advocacy and human rights education".[101] However, the ERRC has not supported any cases concerning Roma in Poland on the national or international level. Recently, one case was successfully litigated before domestic courts by the Polish Helsinki Foundation of Human Rights. Besides, legal aid provided by local Roma NGOs for members of their community is still developing and does not satisfy the demand at the moment.[102]

A. Minority-conscious adjudication: discrimination in access to service

The main argument following from the Justice Stone's opinion calls for a heightened judicial inquiry in cases concerning a suspect class. In this case the judiciary should depart from the presumption that the challenged law or practice is unlawful and demand from the defendant showing the compelling reasons to justify it. In particular in the area of discrimination, the courts should adopt broad conception of rights and offer victims a fair remedy. Such an approach requires however that judges are aware of the difficulties experienced by Roma in enforcing their rights.

In the light of the Equal Treatment Act discussed above persons who were unfavourably treated but did not suffer any material loss, or persons who were unfavourably treated not on the prohibited ground or in the area which is not particularly covered by the prohibition of discrimination, or persons who were unfavourably treated before the law entered into force are apparently without any legal remedy. A layman will probably have difficulty to find a different legal basis for a discrimination claim, but a trained lawyer knows how to use the potential of the general provisions of the Civil Code[103] to institute a claim for protection of personal rights.[104] The notion of personal

---

100 Jim Goldston, *The Struggle for Roma Rights: Arguments that Have Worked*, 32 Human Rights Quarterly 310 (2010).

101 http://www.errc.org/about-us-overview

102 ECRI Report on Poland (note 36), 31.

103 Act of 23 April 1964 – Civil Code, Journal of Laws 1964, No 16, Item 93.

104 The Civil Code does not contain an exhaustive list of personal rights. This open-ended catalogue is supplemented by case law, which mirrors changing social relationships, consciousness and morality.

rights is the emanation of the general right to personality and serves as a proxy for almost all rights guaranteed in the Constitution, including the right to equal treatment and non-discrimination. In case personal rights are violated, the Civil Code envisages both compensation for material and moral damage.[105] The plaintiff has to prove only that her or his personal rights were endangered or infringed, while the court has to establish which personal interest was violated. A reference to Article 32 of the Constitution should suffice to prove that discrimination on any ground is unlawful, while the Equal Treatment Act only strengthens this claim.

On this legal basis a Romani man sued the club-owner for denying him access to a club. His case was first described in the local edition of the national daily newspaper "Gazeta Wyborcza" and a short film made by the plaintiff on the spot posted on its website. Based on this information, the Helsinki Foundation of Human Rights contacted the local Romani organization (*Wielkopolskie Stowarzyszenie Romów*) and inquired the personal details of the man in order to offer him legal assistance in the court. The case would not have reached the court without the intervention of the strategic litigation program coordinator.[106]

In this case the denial of access to services offered to the public undoubtedly constituted unlawful discrimination with regard to ethnic origin, but it happened before the Equal Treatment Act entered into force, so that the civil law protection of personal rights was the only available remedy. Nevertheless, the court of the first instance rejected the discrimination claim in absence of a causal link between actions of a security guard and the club-owner. It ruled that the club-owner should not be responsible for an incidental discriminatory conduct and comments of a security guard employed by a different company and thus not directly supervised by the defendant. Clearly, the court did not

---

105 Article 23, 24 and 448 of the Civil Code. The Civil Code stipulates that any person whose personal rights are endangered or violated by others is protected by law and can demand that the unlawful action is ceased. If an infringement of personal interests already occurs, the person can demand that the perpetrator undertakes an action to remove the consequences of infringement, in particular by making an adequate declaration, or payment of compensation or a sum of money for a social purpose. In an action for protection of personal interests the burden of proof is also on the defendant who needs to show that her or his acts were not unlawful. The acts are presumed to be unlawful unless it is proven otherwise. Importantly, the concept of unlawfulness in the civil law covers not only acts contrary to law, but also to the principles of social coexistence and bones mores.

106 Dorota Pudzianowska, the coordinator of 'Article 32', the Anti-Discrimination Program of the Helsinki Foundation of Human Rights. See http://www.hfhrpol.waw. pl/dyskryminacja/litygacja/dyskryminacja-pochodzenie-narodowe-i-etniczne/

attach enough value to the evidence presented by the plaintiff showing that the club-owner openly admitted to keep her club free of Roma. In the first instance the court accepted arbitrarily only the evidence presented by the defendant who maintained that the request to leave the club and the denial of entrance to the plaintiff and persons of Roma origin who accompanied him were not related to ethnic origin, but to their drunken behaviour. The decision of the first instance was however overturned on appeal. The Court of Appeal noticed that restrictions to enter a club or a restaurant can be only justified on the grounds of public security, whereas restrictions based solely on someone's ethnic origin are unlawful. It held respectfully that exclusion on the basis of ethnicity breaches the principle of equal treatment and criticized the one-sided assessment of evidence in the first instance. The arbitrariness of this assessment included disregarding of testimonies made by a journalist of "Gazeta Wyborcza" and the regional plenipotentiary for national and ethnic minorities. Not only did the Court of Appeal find that the civil law protection of personal interests applies in this case, but also that the defendant violated dignity and the right not to be discriminated against of a Roma men who wanted to visit the club. The Court of Appeal emphasized also that the liability of the club owner extends also to such instances when the security guards are the only initiators of a discriminatory conduct and do not act upon the manager's instruction. Consequently, the Court of Appeal ordered the club-owner to apologize to the plaintiff in the press and on the Internet site of the club and to pay 10,000 PLZ compensation to the local Romani organization.

In the context of this unprecedented victory, it needs to be underlined that the preparation of this case took several months and involvement of a pro bono lawyer. Moreover, the uniformed front presented by the media, the parliamentary Committee of National and Ethnic Minorities, the Ministry of Internal Affairs and Administration, the Ombudsman, the Government Plenipotentiary for Equal Treatment and the regional plenipotentiary for national and ethnic minorities and the Helsinki Foundation who convincingly argued there had been a case of discrimination played an important role in leading this claim through the judicial process. Importantly, before the case reached the court they offered mediation, but it was not accepted by the club-owner. It is quite obvious that the outcome of the case would probably not be the same without such an institutional engagement of many human rights' defenders. Although this is yet another individual victory, which does not eliminate the causes of discrimination, it sends a clear message to the society

– racial discrimination is bad *per se* and a Roma cannot be removed from a club unless for serious reasons related solely to his or her behaviour.

VI. Conclusions

The above analysis shows that in result of social, economic and political disempowerment of Roma they appear to be a discrete and insular minority – a minority which cannot protect itself. The specific rights guarantees, the political process and the government programs entail several failures, which turn the mechanisms of rights protection to some extent ineffective or irrelevant for Roma or generate additional tensions and potential for abuses. However, even if they are not the most effective, they should not be discredited, but improved and strengthened to address more adequately the needs of Roma. As the recent example of a successful strategic litigation concerning discrimination with regard to ethnic origin demonstrates Roma need institutional support and the cooperation of various entities – the government, the equality bodies, notwithstanding their limited competence, the civil society including Roma and non-Roma organizations and finally, the media. In such a uniform approach to racial discrimination the conditions for rights enforcement are more favourable. For this reason, the right not to be discriminated against should not be viewed either by the government or by Roma as a luxury good available only to members of more politically and socially empowered groups. Furthermore, even an isolated success story of a Roma might change the distrust of this minority of the state and its justice system.

Chapter 9

Roma in Romania:
From Law to Practice

*Emanuela Ignatoiu-Sora**

I. Introduction

The institutional and media outcry in response to France's expulsion of Romani individuals in 2010 led to a great deal of questions about the situation of Roma in Romania.[1] The French authorities accused the Romanian government of avoiding their responsibilities by suggesting that Roma constitute a 'European problem', and hinted that they might block Romanian's access to the Schengen Agreement as a response. The Romanian government insisted that Roma are not only a 'transnational minority' but also European citizens with the right of free movement. The European Union reacted slowly to the French expulsions but formulated an institutional response in the form of a strategy, proposed by the Commission, that makes the various Member States responsible for the integration of their Roma communities, under EU supervision.[2] In brief, the French decision to expel foreign Roma

---

* Emanuela Ignatoiu-Sora is a post-doctoral researcher at the Vrije Universiteit Brussel, Belgium. She has a Ph.D. from the European University Institute on the topic of 'The construction of a legal regime for the protection of Roma minority'. She is working on equality and non-discrimination, minorities and rights of children.

1 The situation of Roma in Bulgaria also came under close scrutinity. For instance, Bernard Valéro, the spokesperson for the Quai d'Orsay, said that: "Nous avons pris des mesures énergiques contre les trafiquants d'êtres humains et les délinquants qui utilisent la communauté rom pour enfreindre la loi. C'est pour cela que, avec nos partenaires bulgares, nous faisons tout pour améliorer le sort de la population rom et pour combattre ceux qui abusent d'elle". Vesselina Sedlarska, A l'égard des Roms, une hypocrisie sans frontiers, 16.08.2010, www.courrierinternational.com However, the situation of Roma in Romania is the focus of the paper.

2 European Commission, *An EU Framework for National Roma Integration Strategies up to 2020*, COM(2011) 173/4 final, Brussels, http://eurlex.europa.eu/LexUriServ/LexUriServ.do?uri=CELEX:52011DC0173:en:NOT

in the summer and autumn of 2010 led to considerable discussion about the situation of Romanian Roma in their home country.[3] This chapter goes beyond these discussions and will attempt to assess the current situation of Romanian Roma.

This chapter will examine legislation and policy measures, and in particular their implementation. It will begin by outlining the major legal developments in Romania in relation to Roma and will then analyse their implementation by reference to education. Romania is an important case-study for Romani integration for several reasons. In the past decades, Romanian Roma have received a lot of attention. Since the mid-1990s, Romania has been closely scrutinized by European and international organisations and been encouraged to adopt measures to promote Romani integration; yet although Romania has adopted some very innovative institutions in relation to the Roma, it is still perceived as an under-achiever in this area. Moreover, Romania is an excellent case-study by which to illustrate the story of more than two decades of adopted provisions, their implementation in relation to the Roma, of the main approaches and of the major shifts of perspectives, but also of the improvements and changes that need to be made.

II. The Legal Underdog

Romania has chosen to recognise eighteen national minorities under the terms of the Framework Convention on National Minorities.[4] This list includes the Roma. However, for historical reasons, the legal framework for minorities in Romania is built around the needs of the Hungarian minority.[5] This explains why for many years Romania adopted laws responding more to the needs and

---

3   By "situation of Roma persons", I mean their legal status as well as their living conditions, economic and educational conditions.

4   See Second Report submitted by Romania pursuant to article 25 (2) of the Framework Convention for National Minorities, received on 6 June 2005, ACFC/SR/II (2005)004.

5   This is partly for historical reasons and partly for political reasons. As a result of the major geo-political shifts at the end of the First World War, large numbers of Hungarians became Romanian citizens, and the international community took an interest in their protection. Even during the communist regime, the Hungarian minority maintained a special position. Following the war in the former Yugoslavia, the Hungarian minority remained in the spotlight, as the international community feared an ethnic conflict. The Hungarian minority continue to be very much in the spotlight in Romania, thanks to the support of their kin-state and of an organization, the Democratic Union of Magyars from Romania, which functions as a political party.

the wishes of the Hungarian minority than to its other minorities: this is the case with the 2001 Act on Public Administration,[6] of the 2004 Electoral Law,[7] and of the 1995 Education Law.[8]

By possessing the status of national minority, the Roma minority is equally protected by these laws. This means that Roma have the right, *inter alia*, '(…) to preserve, develop and express their ethnic, cultural, linguistic and religious identity'.[9] They have the right to learn their mother tongue and to be taught in their mother tongue;[10] they also have the right to be represented in Parliament.[11] They have the right to use their mother tongue both orally and in writing in all reports with the public administration,[12] as well as before the courts.[13] According to law no 504/2002, the Romanian Society for Radio and TV has a legal obligation to broadcast in the mother tongue of national minorities.[14] However, one immediate consequence of this legislation not having been designed with the Roma in mind is the obligations contained therein are difficult to implement in regard to Romani communities and have therefore achieved very little. While the Hungarian minority are geographically concentrated, Roma live scattered in small groups across the country. Thus while Romani communities have the right, for instance, to use *Romanes*, both in writing and orally, in all dealings with

---

6   Law no. 215/2001 on Local Public Administration, published in the Official Gazette no. 204 of 23 April 2001 (amended by Law 86/2006).

7   Law no. 67/2004 on Election of Local Public Authorities, published in the Official Gazette, no. 271 of 29 March 2004.

8   Law no. 84/1995 on Education, published in the Official Gazette no. 606 of 10 December 1999 (amended by Law no. 1/2011 published in the Official Gazette no. 18 of 10 January 2011).

9   Romanian Constitution, art. 6(1): 'The State recognises and guarantees to persons belonging to national minorities the right to preserve, develop and express their ethnic, cultural, linguistic and religious identity'. The protection of the identity of the persons belonging to national minorities is linked to discrimination: 'Romania is the common and indivisible nation of all its citizens, without distinction of race, nationality, ethnic origin, language, religion, gender, opinion, political belonging, wealth of social origin' (art. 4(2)). See also art. 16 (1): '(Romanian) citizens are equal before the law and the public authorities, without privilege and without discrimination'.

10 Education Law no. 1/2011, section 12, article 45(1).

11 Romanian Constitution, art. 62 (2): the organisations of citizens belonging to national minorities (…) have the right to be represented by one deputy per national minority (…).

12 Romanian Constitution, art. 120 (2).

13 Romanian Constitution, art. 128 (2).

14 Law no. 504/2002 on Broadcasting, published in the Official Gazette no. 534 of 22 July 2002.

the public administration, this provision is only applicable in localities in which a minority represents at least 20% of the total number of inhabitants and upon request.[15] Given the nature of Romani communities, the application of this provision is extremely limited.[16]

The first time piece of legislation drafted with Roma directly in mind was the act transposing Directive 43/2000/EC (or the Race Equality Directive) into Romanian Law.[17] From the outset this law was considered to be most relevant to Roma, as the Hungarian minority is felt to be 'under-represented' rather than 'discriminated' against.[18] Romani NGOs were very much involved in the drafting of the transposing act, which resulted in the adoption by the Romanian authorities of a very comprehensive piece of legislation: Government Ordinance no. 137/2000. Romani NGOs were, for example, pivotal in the introduction of the concept of 'indirect discrimination' into the Romanian legal order and in the creation of the National Council for Combating Discrimination.[19] One NGO in particular, Romani Criss, has played a significant role in the implementation of this anti-discrimination law and have introduced strategic litigation, a legal method previously unknown in the Romanian legal system.[20]

---

15 Law no 215/2001, art.19 (note 6).

16 Roma persons exceed 20% of the population in a limited number of localities: in the Alba and Buzau departments, for instance, there is only one locality per department; in the Dolj department there are 9 localities. Up till now, the Roma have not exercised their right to communicate in their mother tongue in the respective localities. This is for different reasons: a traditional preference for not interacting with authorities, linguistic variety (Roma persons may represent at least 20% of the population of a locality but they may belong to different '*neamuri*' speaking various dialects) etc.

17 However, from 1997 onwards, Roma have received constant European attention in the Annual Reports monitoring the progress made by candidate countries but also in other European documents. Council Decision of 28 January 2002 on the principles and objectives in the Partnership accession with Romania (2002/92/EC), for instance, contains many recommendations regarding the Roma minority.

18 Renate Weber, *Report on Measures to Combat Discrimination in the 13 Candidate Countries* (VT/2002/47), Country Report Romania, 22, (2003).

19 According to ordinance no. 137/2000, the National Council for Combating Discrimination should have been created 60 days following publication in the Official Gazette but it was created only a year afterwards, following pressure from NGOs, who threatened to sue the Government.

20 Created in 1993, the NGO Romani Criss (Roma Centre for Social Intervention and Studies) fought against discrimination initially through studies and reports. The adoption of the 137/2000 ordinance allowed this NGO to use testing, reply on the reversal of the burden of proof and, most importantly, to make legal complaints denouncing discrimination against Romani individuals in the media, in job announcements, in access to services and facilities, or in access to education, job market.

III. The 2001 National Strategy for Improving the Situation of the Roma

Ten years before the European Commission was to propose the Framework for National Roma Integration Strategies in 2011, Romania had adopted a national strategy for improving the situation of Roma.[21]

In response to the European and international preoccupation with the situation of Roma in Romania,[22] the newly created National Office for Roma[23] began, in 1997, drafting a strategy to improve the situation of Roma.[24] The Romanian government finally adopted the 'National Strategy for improving the situation of the Roma' in April 2001. The intention was to make significant improvements to the lives of Roma and within a reasonable deadline.[25] The strategy covered 10 years (2001-2010) and was comprised of ten different areas: administration, social security, health, economy, justice, child welfare, education, housing, culture, communication and civic involvement. The one major result of this Strategy was that it built an institutional framework at all administrative levels, the main objective of which has been to implement this strategy.[26]

---

21 Government Decision no. 430/2001 on approving the Strategy for improving the situation of the Roma persons. In 2011, the Romanian Government adopted a new strategy for the inclusion of Romanian citizens of Romani ethnic origin for the period 2012-2020. The strategy was adopted by Government Decision no. 1221 of 14 December 2011 and published in the Official Gazette no. 6 of 4 January 2012. According to this strategy, 'Roma inclusion is a dual process, which involves a change in the mentality of the majority, and also in the mentality of the members of Roma community, a challenge that requires firm actions, developed in an active dialogue with the Roma minority, both at national and EU level', 5.

22 In 1997, the European Commission 'Agenda 2000' noted that integration of minorities in candidate countries was generally satisfactory except for Roma. Further pressure was placed on candidate countries and continuing EU activity can be seen through a Monitoring and Advocacy Programme (EUMAP) which reported on the position of Roma in Central and East European Countries.

23 The National Office for Roma was created within the Department for the Protection of National Minorities.

24 The document of the 2001 Strategy mentions that it is the result of a joint effort between the Romanian Government and organisations representing the Roma. It is also mentioned that the implementation of this Strategy will be done in consultation with the representatives of Roma organisations.

25 The main aims were: to fight against discrimination, to ensure quality of opportunities for a decent life, to preserve Romani culture and identity; to delegate responsibilities to local public authorities and to encourage the participation of Roma in economic, social, cultural and political life.

26 Within the Strategy, a number of projects have been adopted: 4327 houses have been built, running water installed for 42 villages, jobs created for 701 persons. Despite

The National Agency for Roma, established in 2004,[27] is the main institution in charge of implementing the strategy. A number of ministries (such as employment and education) created special ministerial committees responsible for elaborating measures to promote the goals of the Roma Strategy within their relevant domains, such as social protection, health, etc. A Joint committee was in charge of coordinating the activities of the various ministerial committees.[28] Eight regional offices (*'birouri regionale'*) were established and there is a county office (*'birouri judetene'*) in all 42 counties across the country. Roma councillors, who are usually drawn from the Romani community, work for these offices and collaborate with the schools, police, and employment agencies. Their role is to assess the situation of Roma in the respective counties, to ensure that Roma have access without discrimination to education, health, employment and public services, and to improve school attendance and the access of Romani individuals to the job market.

Furthermore, in areas in which Roma exceed 5% of the population, the local authorities must employ Roma experts. These experts have the role of facilitating the communication between Roma and local authorities, of developing activities for improving the situation of Roma locally and to ease possible tensions and conflicts between the Roma and the majority population.[29] In addition to these territorial institutions, the authorities

---

these results, the implementation of the strategy has been difficult: deadlines were not respected; there were frequent changes in the institutions in charge of implementation; politicization (due to an agreement between the Social Democrat Party and the Roma Party, the Roma Party was the only NGO involved in the selection of the staff for departmental offices).

27 The National Agency for Roma is a central public institution, under the subordination of the Government. It is charged with the implementation of the 2011 Strategy for the Inclusion of Roma.

28 In 2011, the Romanian Government adopted a new national strategy for the Roma: Strategy of the Romanian Government for the inclusion of Romanian citizens of Roma ethnicity for 2012-2020, published in the Official Journal, no. 6 of 4 January 2012. This new strategy introduces some changes at the level of implementation structures in light of the European Roma Framework-Strategy. The Joint Committee was replaced by a Central Unit for Implementation and Evaluation, which will act as a national contact point in relation to the European Commission. The Unit will also assume the inter-institutional coordination and communication between the various ministerial committees and it will be responsible for drafting an annual report on the progress of implementing the Strategy. The county offices and the institution of local Roma experts have remained unchanged. However, the regional offices have been abolished.

29 It was rather difficult to satisfy this requirement because of scarce human resources with the necessary qualifications. In order to qualify for the position of Roma expert,

have also created thematic structures for implementing the strategy: school mediators and health mediators.[30]

IV. Implementation

But to what degree have Roma benefited from these laws and policies? I will attempt to answer this question by way of analysing the case of education.

Education is widely viewed as crucial to improving the life chances for Romani individuals and communities and in achieving integration.[31] According to the report evaluating the National Strategy for Improving the Situation of the Roma: 'emphasis should be placed on education as this leads in time to the change of mentalities (...)'.[32] Already in the mid-1990s, the Romanian authorities had adopted measures with respect to the education of Romani pupils. In the context of the international conventions adopted by Romania during that decade,[33] but also influenced by the internal debate on

---

the candidate has to hold a university degree, have experience in Roma projects and the ability to help Roma in such domains as computer literacy, language skills and clerical work. Nevertheless, there is now a significant Romani presence at local level as more young Roma complete undergraduate studies.

30   The health mediators have the task of facilitating communication between Romani individuals and medical personnel, whilst the school mediators focus on enhancing Romani access to education.

31   Education is considered by some authors as a key factor in achieving Romani inclusion and in breaking the poverty-exclusion circle. Therefore, it is not surprising that the European Roma Rights Centre decided to bring its big test-case before the European Court of Human Rights in the area of education: Eur. Court of Human Rights, *D.H. and others v. Czech Republic*, Judgment of the Grand Chamber of 13 November 2007, Application no. 57325/00. For more, see Emanuela Ignatoiu-Sora, *The discrimination discourse in relation to the Roma: its limits and benefits*, 34 ETHNIC AND RACIAL STUDIES 1697-1714 (2011). See also, Morag Goodwin, *D.H. and others v. Czech Republic: a major set-back for the development of non-discrimination norms in Europe*, 7 GERMAN LAW JOURNAL 421-432 (2006). However, this approach has received some criticism: 'education is not the ultimate answer to Roma's problems (...). This old illuminist paradigm which equals formal education with social emancipation as the only solution is not necessarily applicable to a group which has been historically and structurally marginalized, as Roma were. Education will only work as long as it will be accompanied by other means of emancipation (political, economical) (...). FLECK GABOR AND COSIMA RUGHINIS (ed.), VINO MAI APROAPE: INCLUZIUNEA SI EXCLUZIUNEA ROMILOR IN SOCIETATEA ROMANEASCA DE AZI, HUMAN DYNAMICS, 145, (2008).

32   Agency for Governmental Strategies, *National Strategy for Improving the Situation of the Roma: Voice of Communities*, (2009). However, the report adds that there is also a need for policies leading to jobs for the Roma.

33   See especially the Framework Convention for the Protection of National Minorities and European Charter for Regional or Minority Languages.

national minorities,[34] educational policies in relation to Roma focused at first on the cultural dimension.

A. *The cultural dimension of education*

According to the Romanian Constitution, 'persons belonging to national minorities' have the right to study in their mother tongue at all levels (...)'.[35] In accordance with this legal provision, Romania recognised *romanes* as a mother tongue. In practice, it meant that Romani pupils were able to study in their mother tongue at all levels of public education. In the words of minorities expert Jean-Pierre Liegeois, 'up till now Romania is the first State to practice this teaching on such a big scale'.[36] In reality, however, few Romani pupils opt for this possibility, with the majority choosing to study in Romanian or, occasionally, Hungarian. Nevertheless, progress has been registered: if in 1990 only 50 Roma children studied in their mother tongue, in the period 2009-2010, 27,000 Romani children studied in their mother tongue for 3-4 hours per week.[37]

These measures for preserving Romani cultural identity were enriched in 2005 when the study of Romani history and culture became part of the mandatory curriculum for all pupils.[38] Knowledge and the learning of Romanes has also been encouraged through various measures: the training

---

34 Id, 2.

35 Romanian Constitution, art. 32 (3). See also 2011 Education Law, section 12 (Education for persons belonging to national minorities), art. 45-47: persons belonging to national minorities have the right to study in their mother tongue and their cultural and linguistic heritage should be preserved and respected.

36 JEAN-PIERRE LIEGEOIS, ROMS EN EUROPE, 48 (2007). Learning in their mother tongue is considered to be 'un vecteur d'apprentissage decisif' especially in the process of improving the situation of Roma (2nd report of Romania, Framework – Convention for the Protection of National Minorities). Author's translation.

37 In comparison, for the 2005-2006 academic year, a total number of 24,069 pupils chose to study Romanes as well as Roma history and traditions. More specifically, 19,812 pupils studied Romanes, whilst 4257 pupils studied Romani history and traditions. 60 pupils studied exclusively in their mother tongue. LASZLO MURVAI (ed.), GENERAL VIEW OF THE EDUCATION FOR NATIONAL MINORITIES IN ROMANIA DURING 2003-2006, 57-63, (2006). In addition to the mandatory classes, school management can allocate supplementary hours for the study of the mother tongue or/and for the study of the history and traditions of the respective minority. The curriculum for romanes as mother tongue places a particular emphasis on oral communication and knowledge of the specific values of the Romani community.

38 This encompasses: Romani history, relations between Roma and Romanians, promotion of inter-ethnic trust and respect.

of teachers working in classes where Roma pupils are numerous;[39] and classes for teachers to learn or improve their knowledge of Romanes. In 1998, a department of Romanes language and literature was set up at the Faculty for Foreign Languages at the University of Bucharest, and each year ten places are reserved for the study of this language. The study of Romanes is also cultivated through extra-school activities: a national contest on Romanes is financed and organised by the Ministry for Education and Research together with the County School Inspectorates. Annually, 60 to 70 Romani pupils participate in this kind of national language contest.

Despite these successes, there remain differences of opinion among Romani parents and NGOs about the study of Romanes in schools. Some parents who speak Romanes at home consider the knowledge acquired within the family sufficient; other parents consider that only study in Romanian is likely to ensure good integration opportunities for their children. This position is adopted especially by those parents who no longer speak Romanes.[40] The study of Romanes as a mother tongue also depends on a series of factors, in addition to parental consent, such as whether or not a family migrates from one locality to another, a lack of trained personal etc.[41] There are technical difficulties as well; although the Romani population is divided into different communities (*'neamuri'*) speaking various Romani dialects, the mandatory curriculum and the textbooks do not take into account this linguistic heterogeneity.[42] Because of this, Romani children often have to study Romanes as a foreign language rather than as a mother tongue. Thus, even for those children who speak Romanes at home, the study of standardized Romanes has the potential to confuse them and to affect its natural usage.

39　From 1991 onwards, such classes/groups for teachers were set up in pedagogical schools. See Orders no. 3577/1998 and no. 5083/1998 issued by the Ministry for Education and Research.

40　For many of these Roma, Romanes is no longer perceived as an identity issue. See Mihaela Jigau, Mihai Surdu (eds.), Participarea la educatie a copiilor romi: probleme, solutii, actori, 74, (2002).

41　The authorities tried to answer this problem by making it possible for Roma children to start the study of Romanes as mother tongue at any moment during the academic year. In addition, the study of Romanes is not dependent on residence in a particular locality. Furthermore, in the absence of trained staff, Romanes can be taught by Roma persons who graduated from high school. *Id.*, 73.

42　'Romanes as it is taught in schools differs from the various spoken versions. Because of this it is usually studied as a foreign language. Grammar is often the most challenging part as it is very abstract. The study of romanes at school affects its natural usage'. Gabor and Rughinis, note 31, 148. Author's translation.

B. *The social dimension of education*

With the adoption of the 2001 Strategy for Improving the Situation of the Roma, the focus began to shift from the cultural preservation perspective to the social dimension of education. Within the 2001 National Strategy, the authorities launched a new programme focusing on reintegration, drop-out prevention and positive measures with the intention of supporting Romani inclusion through education. This was, in part, triggered by very worrying data on literacy and school attendance among Romani pupils: in 2001, the participation of Romani children in pre-school education was four times lower than that of the participation of non-Romani children; 25% less Roma children than non-Romani children attended primary school and 30% less Romani children than non-Romani children attended secondary school. 40% of the adult Romani population was found to be illiterate.[43] In data from 2007 26,3% of Romani adults had never attended school in comparison to 2,3% of non-Romani adults. The ratio in participation between Roma and non-Roma for 16-19 year olds stood, in 2007, six years after the strategy began, at 1:4 (17% to 69%). More than half of those Romani pupils still in school at 18 fail their final examination at the end of secondary school.[44] However, it should be noted that problems of access to education (non-enrollment, absenteeism, high drop-out) are also a feature of education in rural areas. For now, it is not clear whether these figures are related to Romani ethnicity or to whether living in rural areas.

It is in this context that Romanian authorities decided to make schools the real agents of change. For this, a number of programmes and measures were adopted in order to prevent absenteeism, drop-outs and a lack of enrolment: the training of primary and secondary school teachers, a programme for Romani mothers (School for mothers),[45] the second chance programme,[46] the

---

43 There are different possible explanations for these differences: the socio-economic explanation (the reduced school attendance in the case of Romani children would be a consequence of their poverty), the cultural explanation (the lifestyle differences and Romani resistance to cultural assimilation); institutional failure would be another possible explanation (the failures of the educational system and educational policies). Jigau and Surdu, note 40.

44 Id., 47.

45 Grigore D. Neacşe and Gheorghe Sarău, Evaluarea politicilor publice, 139, (2009).

46 The 'second chance' programme was designed for those who dropped out of school because of socio-economic reasons or for those who had never enrolled. It was launched in 2000 as a pilot project financed by EU funds. Since then, the 'second chance' scheme has been extended nationwide and offered to all sections of the populations, with particular emphasis on literacy courses but also minimum

creation of school mediators, and the allocation of reserved places for Roma in high schools and universities.

The position of school mediator was introduced in a pilot programme in the 1990s by NGOs with the purpose of facilitating access to education and of preventing Romani children who have been enrolled from dropping out.[47] The programme was initially financed privately, by NGOs or churches; as the project was further developed, it was financed through the European Union PHARE programme.[48] In 2003, the role of school mediator was officially recognised by the Romanian authorities.[49] In practice, it means that school mediators are paid from the public local budget. However, because of low wages and insufficient financial resources at the local level, there are not enough school mediators for all the schools in the communities with large percentage of Roma population.

Where initially only 70 school mediators were trained in 10 counties, by 2007 there were 500 school mediators. The main role of a school mediator is to link schools and communities, to create among young Romani children and their parents a favourable attitude towards education and to prevent discrimination against Roma within the education process. The school mediator programme is credited with increasing school attendance of Romani children and reducing the drop-out rate.[50] The school mediator programme proved to be successful with Romani communities as the majority of the mediators are themselves Romani, which in practice made it easier to create the necessary trust.[51] The programme has also improved relations between

---

professional training. See Orders no.4780/1999 and no.5080/1999 issued by the Ministry for Education.

47   GHEORGHE SARAU, ELENA RADU, GHIDUL MEDIATORULUI SCOLAR – PENTRU COMUNITATI CU PROMI, 13 (2011).

48   PHARE RO 0104.02 Access to education for vulnerable groups; PHARE 2003/005-551.01.02 Access to education for vulnerable groups; PHARE 2004 Access to education for vulnerable groups with focus on Roma.

49   Order of the Ministry for Labour, Social Solidarity and Family, no. 338 of 16 July 2003 for Classification of Professions in Romania. See also, Order no. 1539/19.07.2007 on the classification and activity of school mediator, published in the Official Gazette no. 670/1.10.2007.

50   It has been effective especially in eastern counties (e.g. Braila, Iasi and Vaslui) where the Roma community is particularly poor.

51   Gabor and Rughinis, *supra* note 31, 148. There were only two male school mediators. One of them was beaten up in Ialomita county by Romani men. Since then, only women have been appointed as school mediators as they are accepted by both Romani men and women for discussion, entering the family house, etc. (Viliam Oaie, 'Romii ca test de viabilitate pentru politica de incluziune sociala a UE', presentation at the national conference *Accounting public policies for Roma*, May 10-11, Bucharest, 2012).

schools and the local Romani community and, as a result, the majority of schools involved in the programme have made efforts in order to continue with it even after the PHARE funding was no longer available.[52] However, the lack of funding for the training of the mediators is now putting the school mediator programme at risk.[53]

The Romanian authorities have also adopted other positive measures for Roma in order to facilitate Romani access to education and to preserve their cultural identity.[54] The intention of these measures was to create a Romani elite that could provide modern leadership to their communities. Beginning with the academic year 1992-1993, the Minister for Education allocated a number of free places to Romani pupils in both high schools and universities, which could be accessed without the completion of entrance examinations.[55] According to data from the Ministry of Education, almost 3,000 young Roma are now admitted to high school without admission exam every year, and almost 500 Roma are admitted to public universities without passing an admission exam (with places in particular focused on law, social studies and political science).

However, only about half of the reserved spots at high school places and at university faculties are filled each year. In Galati, for instance, for the academic year 2011-2012, a total number of 15 places were allocated at the University 'Dunarea de Jos' but only 8 spots were filled. The candidates were mostly interested in studying medicine and law.[56] A number of factors can explain this: for example, Romani pupils may not be aware of these possibilities; pupils may be afraid that they will not be able to cope with academic study and so prefer a vocational education.[57] Some Roma pupils, and especially girls, are married before graduating from secondary school and thus dedicate time to their family and have little time over for academic

---

52   However, a possible negative effect is the lack of direct communication between Romani parents, Romani children and school personnel.

53   Because of the lack of funding, many trained school mediators decide to leave the programme for other jobs. Elena Raducan (Radu), 'Competentele si capacitatile de imputernicire pe care le dezvolta/atribuie mediatorul scolar', presentation at the national conference *Accounting public policies for Roma*, May 10-11, SNSPA, Bucharest, (2012).

54   The allocation of free places started in 1992 but was intensified following the adoption of the National Strategy for improving the situation of the Roma in 2001.

55   See Orders no. 3577/1998, no. 5083/1999, no. 3294/2000 and no. 4542/2000 issued by the Ministry for Education and Research.

56   Domnica Negru, *Locurile pentru romi la universitate au ramas neocupate*, www.adevarul.ro, 17 septembrie 2011.

57   Gabor and Rughinis, note 31, 149.

study. It is also possible that Romani pupils are less aware of the economic advantages of education, as it is an investment over a long term before the economic results, such as better jobs and better wages, become visible.

Furthermore, the procedure for gaining such places at high school or university continues to be controversial. In order to occupy these spots, candidates only need to present a recommendation written by a Romani civic, cultural or political NGO to confirm that the candidate belongs to the Romani minority. Recent disclosures in the media have shown that some of these NGOs sell recommendations to pupils who do not belong to the Romani minority. A recent study suggests that 1 in 5 of these reserved places is actually filled by non-Romani Romanian pupils.[58] In order to prevent this happening in the future, Roma NGOs have recently asked the Ministry of Education to establish committees at the level of schools or communities to assess any candidate for a reserved spot. Nevertheless, despite these difficulties, according to Ilie Dinca, the President of the National Agency for Roma, 'since positive discrimination has been introduced in the field of education progress is clear'.[59]

Furthermore, various other programmes have been initiated to increase the participation of young Roma in education.[60] These measures had a social protection dimension as they targeted pupils whose families have low or no income: scholarships, free stationary, and the reimbursement for transportation in the case of pupils who commute. In 2002, the Romanian government introduced the programme *'Food in schools'*. According to this programme, pupils in kindergarten and secondary school receive milk and one croissant every school day; an average 2 million children benefit from this programme, although many of these are non-Roma. Although it has had some success in promoting Romani school attendance,[61] the programme is very controversial because of high costs and the poor quality of the food provided.[62] In 2010, the Romanian government created another programme,

---

58   *Locurile pentru romi din facultati sunt ocupate de romani*, www.digi24.ro, 20.08.2012.

59   Available at: http://www.ziare.com/stiri/victime/afp-desi-merg-la-scoala-rromii-din-romania-au-acces-limitat-la-locuri-de-munca-1033335

60   See, for instance, the Strategy for developing the pre-college education for the 2001-2004 adopted by the Ministry for Education and Research.

61   Available at: http://www.ziare.com/articole/program+cornul+si+laptele). Programul Laptele si cornul: pierderi anuale de cel putin 100 de milioane, published on 21 February 2011.

62   The European Commission stopped financing this programme because the milk did not correspond to the required standards. It seems that in 2009 the Romanian government lost around 10,000,000 euros because of the inefficiency of the programme.

'*Apples in schools*'. Under this programme, pupils in primary and secondary school receive a piece of fresh fruit every school day. This programme is 75% financed by EU funds.

So far the government's educational policies have shown some promising results: despite the continued existence of a wide gulf separating Roma from the rest of the population, young Roma are better educated than their parents, and many more Romani pupils attend school than in the previous generation.[63] The general tendency is positive: an increase in the level of participation in education at all levels[64] and a decrease in the drop-out rate.[65] However, it is important to highlight that success in increasing Romani access to education does not depend exclusively on educational policies. Indeed, accessibility to the educational process is influenced by various independent variables:[66] general socio-economic determinants (the presence of qualified teachers depends on the size and degree of development of a particular locality), school determinants (material facilities, the level of training of teachers, whether the teachers need to commute or not), socio-family determinants[67] (in the case of Roma, young girls are usually encouraged to marry instead of attending school, lack of motivation to continue studying because of the lack of role models in the community or because of a difficulty in perceiving the immediate economic value of education[68]), cultural determinants (a certain culture of 'living in the present' which makes it difficult to plan for the longer term as is necessary with formal education;[69] the economic value of education tends to resonate more with adult Romani men who are involved in business and trade as the knowledge acquired in schools could benefit their economic

---

63 For instance, approximately 250,000 Roma pupils enrolled for the 2005-2006 academic year in comparison to approximately 160,000 Roma pupils for the 2002-2003 academic year.

64 From 91,2% in 1990-1991 to 95,8% in 2000-2001, Jigau and Surdu, note 36, 41-43.

65 In 1990/1991: 1.8; 1991/1992: 1.5; 1993/1994: 0.6; 1994/1995:1.0; 1995/1996:0.8; 1996/1997:0.8; 1997/1998:0.8; 1998/1999:0.9; 1999/2000:0.9. Data from the National Institute of Statistics, *Id.*, 41-43.

66 LIEGEOIS (note 36).

67 A very high percentage of school units in the rural environment lack qualified teaching staff. This percentage is even higher in the case of school units where Romani pupils are more numerous. The most numerous school units with lack of qualified teaching staff are present in isolated localities, at more than 25 km away from a city. Usually the population in these localities work in agriculture; the localities are less developed and they lack infrastructure. Because of all these factors, these localities are less attractive for trained teachers. JIGAU AND SURDU, note 40, 52-62.

68 GABOR AND RUGHINIS, note 31, 147.

69 *Id.*,152-153.

activities; some Roma parents feel uncomfortable in relation to educational institutions, which they perceive as unknown territory). It is therefore important that any implementation of such measures attempt to encompass the whole social experience of Romani children and of their families.

V. Conclusions

During the heated discussions in the summer of 2010, many questioned the measures taken in regard to the Romani minority in Romania and the sincerity of their implementation. The measures taken over the last two decades in Romania in relation to Roma offer an interesting case study. What we can see from Romania is that the focus of the measures adopted changed over time: from a cultural dimension to a focus on discrimination, and finally towards a social focus on integration. The case of education was the most telling in this regard: from measures to allow Romani pupils to preserve and develop their linguistic and cultural heritage, to policies aimed at preventing and reducing drop-outs as well as to increasing the participation of Romani pupils in the educational process.

But the case of education showed more than a simple shift of perspectives at the policy-making level. It highlighted that it is not enough to adopt a provision, and that implementation, despite the best of intentions, proves to be a rather complex process. It is in this key that one should read the provision on the possibility to study in Romanes. The apparatus for its implementation is quite impressive: the training of teachers, the publishing of textbooks, free reserved spots at universities, and extra-curricular activities such as the yearly national competition on Romanes language and literature. Progress is evident: from 50 pupils studying their mother tongue in 1990 to an average of 27,000 pupils for the 2009-2010 academic year. And yet, the implementation of this provision revealed resistance to the efforts that had not been anticipated by the legislator or the policy-maker: these included a variety of opinions among Romani parents as to the utility of studying in Romanes, or the linguistic heterogeneity which is still not taken into account in the curriculum and the textbooks. It is a delicate decision to enforce a standardized and, to some degree, artificial language as this might affect its natural usage.

The policies focusing on the social dimension of education have also had interesting results. They demonstrate how well thought-through programmes – such as the school mediators – are very dependent on continued funding.

The allocation of free places for Romani pupils in high schools and colleges underlined the need for accompanying measures (pupils might still choose vocational schools instead of theoretical schools because of a lack of confidence) but also the risk of creating tensions between minorities and the majority (in the context of high costs for education, as in Romania, combined with the fact that a large part of the Romanian population is impoverished, the allocation of free places for one particular group has exacerbated existing tensions).

This brief analysis of Romania's education policies for Roma has also shown that solutions to the problem of continued attendance, for instance, require a broad approach encompassing the whole social experience; in particular, policies need to focus on the school experience for Romani children and parents and the connections between living conditions, values and expectations. It is here that policy-makers should focus, for example, by presenting the economic value of education, or in targeting their educational policies, at least initially, more at young Romani men than Romani girls, due to the traditional position of Romani women in decision-making.

Thus, in answering the initial question of this paper as to what the current situation of Romanian Roma is, it is important to underline that Roma in Romania benefit from a number of legal provisions and policies regarding their cultural and linguistic heritage, are formally protected against discrimination, and they benefit from a complex legal and policy framework for their social inclusion. However, our brief look at the implementation of these measures shows that, despite significant efforts being made by Romania in all these directions, improving the situation of Roma, as attempted by the Romanian authorities, is a rather complex and lengthy process.

Chapter 10

Positive Action for Roma in Belgium

Jozefien Van Caeneghem[*]

I. Introduction

In recent years, Romani issues have received increasing media and scholarly attention right across Europe. Belgium – along with other European Union Member states – has been struggling to find a fitting response to the various problems that this ethnic minority deal with on a daily basis. The issues range from extreme poverty to health concerns, unemployment, an uncertain housing situation and irregular education. However, the Roma topic has now finally – albeit hesitantly – been put on the political agenda; yet the measures taken so far, if any, have had little or no effect on the everyday life of Roma throughout the European Union. Existing policies are clearly falling short of what is needed to deal effectively with the complexity of the issue, a point that was emphasized in 2011 with the European Commission adoption of a 'EU framework for National Roma Integration Strategies up to 2020' that is intended to encourage Member states to adopt or further develop a specific, comprehensive and targeted approach to Romani integration in order "to make a tangible difference to Roma people's lives".[1] It is clearly time for governments to explore new options by expanding already existing mechanisms' scope of application, such as positive action measures, which so far have been used mainly to eradicate the historical differences between men and women in the workplace. Like women, Roma have – as an ethnic minority – historically been victims of systematic discrimination, both in

---

[*]   Jozefien Van Caeneghem is a Ph.D. researcher at the Fundamental Rights and Constitutionalism research group of the Vrije Universiteit Brussel.
1   COM(2011) 173 final, 5 April 2011, 3-4.

their country of origin and in other Member States. Stereotyping and negative media attention has aggravated this situation.

The hypothesis of this paper is that positive action for Roma may be the missing link that can break the vicious circle of poverty, hopelessness and discrimination in which many Roma – and Roma policies – are stuck. Firstly, this paper will examine the concept of positive action. An overview shows how organisations in the international arena, and more specifically the United Nations, the Council of Europe and the European Union interpret this concept and how their respective bodies and/or courts deal with positive action measures. Secondly, this chapter will consider the particular issues that face Roma in Belgium. The focus will be on housing, education, employment, health and poverty. Thirdly, we will consider the scope for positive action in Belgium. After examining the applicable legislation, the chapter will give an overview of positive action in relation to Roma that has been taken at the different policy levels in Belgium, with the focus on Flanders and Wallonia. Fourthly, attention will be drawn to the need for ethnic data in order to render positive action measures – and for that matter any integration policy – for Roma fully effective. Misconceptions concerning the collection and use of such sensitive data will be addressed, and an explanation attempted as to why the collection and use of ethnic data is a precondition for efficient and effective integration of Roma in Belgian – or any other – society. Finally, a conclusion will be drawn concerning the present situation of positive action for Roma in Belgium and recommendations for the future will be made.

II. What is Positive Action?

A. Concept

The term 'positive action' denotes special measures introduced in a specific situation to benefit certain persons – and not necessarily to damage others – on the basis of a specific criterion – such as ethnic origin – to remove or compensate for a difference in treatment.[2] The purpose of such measures is thus the compensation of (past) inequalities through the promotion of the participation of certain groups in key sectors of social life.[3] Positive

---

2 EU Agency for Fundamental Rights and Council of Europe, HANDBOOK ON EUROPEAN NON-DISCRIMINATION LAW (Council of Europe, 2011), 37.

3 *Id.*, 38.

action is only one of many terms used for such special measures. Others include 'temporary special measures', 'positive discrimination' and 'reverse discrimination'.[4] Irrespective of the name, the measures all have the same characteristics: they are extraordinary and are thus introduced for a limited time period in order to ensure that a certain group – that faces systematic discrimination – is able to overcome the effects of that discrimination.[5] Positive action measures are generally considered as an exception to the prohibition of discrimination, as they are introduced to correct pre-existing inequalities.[6] The measures can be legislative, executive, administrative, budgetary or regulatory instruments at any policy level, as well as plans, policies, programs and preferential systems concerning employment, housing, education, culture and participation of prejudiced group in the public sphere.[7] In the past, the concept of positive action has been used primarily to eliminate the historical discrimination of women in the workplace. The UN Committee on the Elimination of Discrimination against Women takes the view that preferential treatment, targeted recruitment, targeted promotion, numerical goals connected to time-frames and quota can be considered positive actions.[8] Policy makers and the general population have accepted positive action to enhance the position of women for years. In 2011, new legislation was created in Belgium that obliges governmental companies and stock market listed firms to ensure that one third of the seats in their Board of Directors are reserved for women.[9] Such action is considered valid for gender discrimination in the work place, but also to address the underrepresentation of ethnic minorities in the public service.[10]

---

4 General Recommendation No. 32: The Meaning and Scope of Special Measures in the International Convention on the Elimination of All Forms of Racial Discrimination, para. 12, UN Doc. CERD/C/GC/32 (2009).

5 *Id.*, para. 11,16.

6 HANDBOOK ON EUROPEAN NON-DISCRIMINATION LAW (Note 2), 37-41.

7 General Recommendation No. 32: The Meaning and Scope of Special Measures in the International Convention on the Elimination of All Forms of Racial Discrimination, para. 12, UN Doc. CERD/C/GC/32 (2009). para. 13.

8 General Recommendation No. 25: Article 4, para. 1 of the Convention (temporary special measures), para. 22, UN Doc. A/59/38 (supp.) (2004).

9 Wet van 28 juli 2011 wijziging van de Wet van 21 maart 1991 betreffende de hervorming van sommige economische overheidsbedrijven, tot wijziging van het Wetboek van Vennootschappen en tot wijziging van de Wet van 19 april 2002 tot rationalisering van de werking en het beheer van de Nationale Loterij, teneinde te garanderen dat vrouwen zitting hebben in de raad van bestuur van de autonome overheidsbedrijven, de genoteerde vennootschappen en de Nationale Loterij, B.S. 14 september 2011.

10 HANDBOOK ON EUROPEAN NON-DISCRIMINATION LAW, (Note 2) 38.

B. The international arena

Positive action measures can be used to eliminate discrimination on the basis of race or ethnic origin. In the light of persistent and structural disadvantage to Roma across the European Union, the European Commission stated in 2010 that "[a]n effective equality policy goes beyond the prohibition and punishment of discrimination and involves proactive government interventions to promote equality" and that, in this light, Member states are encouraged to take positive action measures to tackle discrimination.[11] In addition to the European Union, the competent bodies of the United Nations and the Council of Europe have also applied the concept of positive action on the basis of race and ethnic origin. What follows under this title is an overview of interpretations of the concept of positive action given by these organisations.

1. UNITED NATIONS

The International Convention on the Elimination of All Forms of Racial Discrimination provides for the possibility for positive action by stipulating in Article 2(2) that:

> "States Parties shall, when the circumstances so warrant, take, in the social, economic, cultural and other fields, special and concrete measures to ensure the adequate development and protection of certain racial groups or individuals belonging to them, for the purpose of guaranteeing them the full and equal enjoyment of human rights and fundamental freedoms. These measures shall in no case entail as a consequence the maintenance of unequal or separate rights for different racial groups after the objectives for which they were taken have been achieved".[12]

The UN Committee on the Elimination of Racial Discrimination, the body of independent experts responsible for interpreting and monitoring the implementation of the Convention by State parties, stresses that positive action should be of a temporary nature and that the measures may not – in time or in application – reach further than what is necessary to eliminate

---

11 European Commission, Improving the tools for the social inclusion and non-discrimination of Roma in the EU (2010), 21.

12 International Convention on the Elimination of All Forms of Racial Discrimination of 21 December 1965, Art. 2(2); UNTS 195 (ICERD).

the existing inequality.[13] The purpose of positive action measures must be limited to the elimination of existing inequalities and the prevention of future inequalities.[14]

2. Council of Europe

Within the Council of Europe, the possibility to introduce positive action is derived from the prohibition of discrimination in Article 14 of the European Convention for the Protection of Human Rights and Fundamental Freedoms (hereinafter ECHR).[15] Thus far in its jurisprudence, the European Court of Human Rights (hereinafter ECtHR) has only hinted at its views on positive action on the basis of ethnic origin. For example, in a recent judgement concerning an educational system in which Romani children were placed in separate classes from non-Romani children ostensibly because of their insufficient knowledge of the language, the ECtHR stated that:

> "[...] in certain circumstances such placement would pursue the legitimate aim of adapting the education system to the specific needs of the children. However, when such a measure disproportionately or even, as in the present case, exclusively affects members of a specific ethnic group, then appropriate safeguards have to be put in place".[16]

The ECtHR, however, has yet to rule directly on the compatibility of positive action with Article 14 ECHR,[17] which allows Member states to treat groups differently in order to eliminate a factual inequality between them.[18] Indeed,

---

13 General Recommendation No. 32: The Meaning and Scope of Special Measures in the International Convention on the Elimination of All Forms of Racial Discrimination, UN Doc. CERD/C/GC/32 (2009).

14 *Id.*, para. 21-26.

15 Article 14 states that "The enjoyment of the rights and freedoms set forth in this Convention shall be secured without discrimination on any ground such as sex, race, colour, language, religion, political or other opinion, national or social origin, association with a national minority, property, birth or other status". European Convention for the Protection of Human Rights and Fundamental Freedoms of 4 November 1950, CETS No.: 005 (hereinafter ECHR).

16 Eur. Court H.R., *Oršuš and Others v. Kroatië*, Judgment of 16 March 2010, Application No. 15766/03, para. 157.

17 Olivier De Schutter, The Prohibition of Discrimination Under European Human Rights Law, 6,48 (2011)

18 Eur. Court H.R., *Thlimmenos v. Greece*, Judgment of 8 April 2000, Application No. 34369/97, Reports of Judgments and Decisions 2000-IV, para. 44. Eur. Court H.R.,

the ECtHR has already held that "the right not to be discriminated against in the enjoyment of the rights guaranteed under the [ECHR] is also violated when States [...] fail to treat differently persons whose situations are significantly different".[19] From this it follows that "[...] in certain circumstances a failure to attempt to correct [factual] inequalities through different treatment may in itself give rise to a breach of the Article [14]".[20] Despite the lack of specific case law, it seems likely that positive action measures would pass the Court's test for Article 14, provided there is an objective and reasonable justification for the implemented difference in treatment and provided such difference is proportional to the aim pursued.[21]

Protocol No. 12 to the ECHR, which creates a non-supplementary non-discrimination guarantee, provides clearly for the possibility – not obligation[22] – to adopt positive action measures to promote full and effective equality.[23] The Preamble to Protocol 12 ECHR reaffirms "that the principle of non-discrimination does not prevent States Parties from taking measures in order to promote full and effective equality, provided that there is an objective and reasonable justification for those measures".[24] Even though the drafters of the Protocol remained cool on the issue,[25] the Preamble indicates that – provided the proportionality principle is respected[26] – Member states can adopt temporary measures introducing specific benefits to promote equality in situations where certain groups are injured or where de facto inequalities exist.[27]

In contrast with the ECHR and the Strasbourg Court, the European Committee of Social Rights (hereinafter ECSR) has been explicitly welcoming of positive action. The ECSR imposes a positive, due diligence duty on States

---

D.H. and Others, judgment of 13 November 2007, Application No. 57325/00, para. 175.

19 *Thlimmenos v. Greece*, para. 44; Eur. Court H.R., *Pretty v. UK*, Judgment of 29 April 2002, Application No. 2346/02, para. 88.

20 *D.H. and Others*, (note 18) para. 175.

21 DE SCHUTTER (Note 17), 31

22 Explanatory report of 29 August 2000 of Protocol No. 12 to the European Convention for the Protection of Human Rights and Fundamental Freedoms of 4 November 1950, H (2000) 11 prov., para.16.

23 Protocol No. 12 of 4 November 2000 to the Convention for the Protection of Human Rights and Fundamental Freedoms, ETS No.: 177.

24 *Id.*, third recital Preamble.

25 DE SCHUTTER (Note 17), 6.

26 Proportionality means that the difference in treatment must pursue an objective and legitimate goal by means of proportionate measures.

27 See Protocol No. 12 of 4 November 2000, third recital Preamble.

Parties to the European Social Charter to promote equality by requiring them to monitor "the impact on vulnerable groups of certain general measures or policies that are ostensibly 'neutral' [...]".[28] The European Social Charter prompts such reasoning,[29] which was demonstrated in a Decision of the ECSR demanding positive action from Bulgaria to improve the housing and accommodation of Roma.[30] The Committee decided that "[...] in the case of Roma families, the simple guarantee of equal treatment as the means of protection against any discrimination does not suffice [...]". Thus all relevant differences must be taken into consideration and the State must act accordingly, which means that "[...] for the integration of an ethnic minority as Roma into mainstream society measures of positive action are needed".[31]

3. EUROPEAN UNION

The European Court of Justice (hereinafter ECJ) has repeatedly interpreted the concept of positive action in its case law concerning employment.[32] The ECJ has introduced a strict test of proportionality of positive action measures for women introduced by the Member states.[33] In its case law, the ECJ has ruled that measures that are discriminatory in appearance but are intended to eradicate inequalities in social life are in line with the applicable rules as long as the measures are proportionate to the aim of eliminating inequalities; in other words, discretion must be built into the measures to prevent that the preferential treatment is automatic, unconditional and absolute.[34] Since 2000, Member states can also adopt positive action on the basis of ethnic origin. Directive 2000/43/EC (hereinafter Race Directive) stipulates in article 5 that the principle of equal treatment does "not prevent any Member State

---

28 DE SCHUTTER (Note 17), 6-7.

29 The principle of non-discrimination is contained in article E. European Social Charter *(Revised)* of 3 May 1996, ETS No.: 163.

30 European Committee of Social Rights, *European Roma Rights Centre v. Bulgaria*, Decision of 18 October 2006, Complaint no. 31/2005, para. 42.

31 *Id.*

32 HANDBOOK ON EUROPEAN NON-DISCRIMINATION LAW (Note 2), 39.

33 *Id.*, 37-41.

34 The most important case law of the European Court of Justice in this regard can be found in the following judgments: Case 450/93, *Kalanke v. Freie Hansestadt Bremen*, 1995 ECR I-3051. Case 409/95, *Marschall v. Land Nordrhein-Westfalen*, 1997 ECR I-6363. Case 407/98, *Abrahamsson and Leif Anderson v. Elisabet Fogelqvist*, 2000 ECR I-5539.

from maintaining or adopting specific measures to prevent or compensate for disadvantages linked to racial or ethnic origin".[35] The recital provides that:

> "[t]he prohibition of discrimination should be without prejudice to the maintenance or adoption of measures intended to prevent or compensate for disadvantages suffered by a group of persons of a particular racial or ethnic origin, and such measures may permit organisations of persons of a particular racial or ethnic origin where their main object is the promotion of the special needs of those persons".[36]

Member states have a large margin of appreciation in this matter, given that only they can decide to adopt or preserve certain measures compensating or preventing inequalities on the basis of ethnic origin in the public sphere. It is important to note that the Race Directive only introduces the *possibility* of positive action, and only in the *public* sphere.[37] It is thus up to Member states to decide whether or not to implement positive action measures. However, in certain circumstances, for example where an ethnic group is underrepresented in a segment of the labor market or in a specific position, it could be argued that Member states have a duty to introduce positive action measures to secure equality as this might be the only option to ensure that Member States comply with the overriding obligation to create equality in society.[38] In the United Kingdom, for example, public bodies have, since the Race Relations Act 2000, a duty to promote race equality that is reinforced with specific duties such as the producing and publishing of race equality schemes and action plans that are then monitored on equality and adequacy by the Commission for Racial Equality.[39] Such a "proactive approach towards ensuring equality schemes and action plans" is not only important for enhancing the transparency and accountability of public bodies but also to justify the need for and use of positive action measures.[40] In any event, it would only be logical for the ECJ to employ the same strict interpretation of positive action for Roma as it does for women.

---

35   Directive 2000/43/EC of 29 June 2000, O.J. 2000 L 180.

36   *Id.*, recital 17.

37   ICERD, 195.

38   Erika Szyszczak, Positive Action as a Tool in Promoting Access to Employment (2006).

39   *Id.*

40   *Id.*

III. Roma in Belgium

A. Introduction

Estimates on the number of Roma in Belgium vary from 15,000 to 50,000 people.[41] No official or exact data on the number of Roma in Belgium exist because ethnicity is not registered in public registers, such as the population and the foreigners' registers.[42] Registration in these registers is done on the basis of country of origin, which can be an indication of ethnicity but not, obviously, definitive. There are also other factors adding to the difficultly of mapping the Roma population in Belgium. Roma often live anonymously in closed Romani communities and prefer not to identify themselves as Roma out of fear for stigmatisation, stereotyping and discrimination.[43] In addition, Roma often move across borders, both within Belgium and across Europe, thus affecting the size of the Roma population in a given country or region.[44]

Many misconceptions exist about Roma and their lifestyle. One such misconception concerns the term 'Roma'. Contrary to what many people think, 'the Roma' are not a homogeneous group. The term is merely used as an umbrella to refer to a collection of groups of people who possess more or less similar cultural characteristics and share a history of discrimination and marginalisation in Europe.[45] The term thus not only covers Roma, but also – *inter alia* – Roms, Travellers, Manouches and Sinti. Another misconception

---

41   COM (2011) 173 final, 5 April 2011. Federale Overheid, Nationale Strategie voor de Integratie van de Roma, 9 (2012). Vlaamse Overheid, Vlaams Actieplan Moe(Roma)-Migranten 2012, 9-19 (2011). Overheid Centre de Médiation des Gens du Voyage en Wallonie A.S.B.L., Caravane et Logement: Entre Précarité Juridique et Bien-Être Social, 4 (2010).

42   Ramón Peña-Casas, Dalila Ghailani and Ides Nicaise, Promoting the Social Inclusion of Roma. A Study of National Policies, 5, 6, 16 (2011). Strategie Centrum voor Gelijkheid an Kansen en Racismebestrijding, Raxen Thematic Study on Housing Conditions of Roma and Travellers in Belgium, 7 (2009).

43   Nationale Strategie Voor De Integratie Van De Roma (2012), 11. Elias Hemelsoet, *Samenleven met Roma: fictie of realiteit?*, in Armoede en Sociale Uitsluiting (Danielle Dierckx, Jan Vrancken, Jill Coene and An Van Haarlem eds, 2011), 367. Jacqueline Fastrès and Sophie Hubert, *De Charybde en Scylla? Petites chroniques d'une intégration impensée: les Roms en Wallonie*, Intermag, 8-14 (2009).

44   *Id.*

45   The term is utilized for practical reasons in policy documents dealing with discrimination and social exclusion issues and not to deal with issues of cultural identity. SEC(2010) 400 final, 7 April 2010.

is that all Roma maintain an itinerant lifestyle. On the contrary most Roma in Belgium maintain – be it out of free will or forced because of lack of caravan plots – a sedentary lifestyle and live in fixed caravans, houses or apartments.[46] The majority of Roma in Belgium live in the cities of Antwerp, Brussels, Charleroi, Diest, Ghent, Heusden-Zolder, Liège, Namur, Temse and Tienen.[47] A smaller number of Roma live in Leuven, Ostend, Sint-Niklaas, Verviers and Waver.[48] A final misconception concerns the nationality of Roma. While a majority of the Travellers (approximately 7,000 persons), the Manouches (approximately 1,500 persons) and the Roms (approximately 700 persons) in Belgium have Belgian nationality,[49] the majority of Roma in Belgium (approximately 20,000 persons) do not. They are instead nationals of their country of origin.[50] For the purpose of this chapter, the term 'Roma' will be used to encompass all these different groups.

B. Roma issues

Over the past few years, a number of journalistic accounts have been written about Roma in Belgium. However, when Romani issues are reported upon in the news, it is often with a negative slant, generating unfavourable feelings within the majority of the population towards Roma and adversely influencing the integration of Roma in Belgium. In this section, a closer look is taken at

---

46 In Belgium, Manouches and Sinti in particular live in fixed caravans, whereas Roma live in houses or apartments and most Roma maintain a semi-sedentary lifestyle: they travel in summer and live in private or public caravan parks in winter. Nationale Strategie voor de Integratie van de Roma (2012), 7-8. Centrum voor Gelijkheid van Kansen en Racismebestrijding, information received via email on 11 April 2012.

47 Vlaams Actieplan Moe(Roma)-Migranten 2012, 11 (2011). MATTHIAS STAMPER, DE ROMA-PROBLEMATIEK TE GENT. NAAR EEN INTEGRALE EN DUURZAME OPLOSSING 10, (2011). SARAH CARPENTIER, RECHERCHE-PILOTE SURE LA SENSIBILISATION DES AUTORITÉS PUBLIQUES À LA COMMUNAUTÉ ROM ET SUR L'INTÉGRATION SCOLAIRE DES ENFANTS ROMS, 28, (2004).

48 *Id.*

49 Approximately 7,000 Travellers, 1,500 Manouches and 750 Roms are Belgian nationals. Approximately 20,000 Roma in Belgium hold the nationality of their country of origin: Nationale Strategie Voor De Integratie Van De Roma, 7 (2012). WOLF BRUGGEN, ROMA IN VLAANDERN. MINDERHEID ONDER DE MINDERHEDEN? 5, (2003). TOON MACHIELS, GARDER LA DISTANCE OU SAISIR LES CHANCES. ROMS ET GENS DU VOYAGE EN EUROPE OCCIDENTAL, 17 (2002).

50 Turkey, Poland, Bulgaria and Romania are the most important inflow countries in Belgium. The inflow from Middle- and Eastern-European countries varies from municipality to municipality. Nationale Strategie Voor De Integratie Van De Roma, 7 (2012). Bruggen, *id.*, 5. Machiels, *id.*, 17.

the main issues that many Roma struggle with in Belgium, namely housing, education, employment, extreme poverty, health, and migration. But while it is true that many Roma face such difficulties, other Roma do not face the same struggles and are well integrated into Belgian society.

1. HOUSING

For many Roma, finding housing is a priority, be it that the quality of the home is only of secondary importance.[51] Those Roma that live – or wish to live – in caravans are faced with a significant lack of caravan plots, with the available spots being very expensive.[52] It is also difficult to obtain building permits for caravans; a requirement that results in illegal stays by Roma families on other – not for caravan designated – plots and a constant fear of eviction for the families involved.[53] On existing caravan plots, infrastructure and sanitary provisions – if any – are often poor and insufficient.[54] Roma living in houses or apartments are often the victims of slum landlords or live in squats.[55] In addition, financial and social considerations often contribute to different families living in the same house, which in turn leads to neighbourhood problems.[56]

2. EDUCATION

Education forms an essential part of the successful future integration of all children. For Romani children, however, social, cultural and economical differences between Roma and non-Roma appear to affect their regular school attendance.[57] Bottlenecks include language barriers, the expense

---

51 Koen Geurts, DE ROMA VAN BRUSSEL (2004).

52 Centre de Médiation des Gens du Voyage en Wallonie A.S.B.L. (note 44), 8. Minderhedenforum, Voyage Bouwstenen voor een Effectief Minderheidbeleid. Ons Verleden, Onze Toekomst, 78-81 (2010). Regionaal Integratiecentrum Foyer, Nota Situatie Woonwagenterreinen in het Brussels Hoofstedelijk Gewest, 1-15 (2006).

53 Regionaal Integratiecentrum Foyer, *id.*, 9-12.

54 Regionaal Integratiecentrum Foyer, *id.*, 5-8.

55 Stamper (note 47), 6, 23, 36.

56 STIJN DE REU, GEERT MATTHYS, BENEDICTE VANDERHAEGEN, CHRISTOPHE JANSSENS AND DAVID TALLOEN, IDENTITEIT: OOST-VLAMING. ETNISCH-CULTURELE DIVERSITEIT IN ONZE PROVINCIE, 48 (2010).

57 Stamper (note 47), 12, 36; Koen Geurts, Natasja Naegels en Norah Van den Daele, *Roma kinderen op de schoolbanken*, 21/1 WELWIJS 11-12 (2010). Koning Boudewijnstichting, Scholing van Roma Kinderen in België (2009), 41-64. Natasja Regionaal Integratiecentrum Foyer, Scholarisatie van Roma in Brussel. Analyse en Aanbevelingen (2006), 1-7.

connected with school activities, their semi-sedentary or itinerant lifestyle, and attitude.[58] Despite the absence of official education statistics on Roma in Belgium, available research demonstrates "striking differences in the level of school participation between the different groups with Rom and Roma pupils' enrolment rates at very low levels".[59] In addition, truant behaviour, irregular attendance, early dropout rates and poor flow-through to secondary education are remarkably higher among Roma children than among other groups.[60]

3. EMPLOYMENT

Unemployment amongst Roma is high.[61] Only a small number of Roma are employed through a standard employment contract; instead, most Roma are self-employed within the informal economy and have only irregular work.[62] From the later it follows that many Roma depend on themselves and their social network – which is often limited to their own Roma community – for their income and maintenance.[63] This is also true for Romani beggars who often live in extreme poverty.[64] Social services and the general public are insufficiently informed and sensitized about the existence, causes and needs of (minor) Roma beggars, which is demonstrated by the lack of coordinated and adapted long-term initiatives tackling the causes of poverty.[65]

4. SOCIAL SERVICES AND HEALTH CARE

Roma often have insufficient knowledge about the availability, functioning and cost of social services and health care services in Belgium.[66] For many

---

58 *Id.*

59 European Monitoring Centre On Racism And Xenophobia, Roma And Travellers In Public Education. An Overview Of The Situation In The Eu Member States, 22 (2006).

60 *Id.*

61 Nationale Strategie Voor De Integratie Van De Roma (2012) (Note 41), 10.

62 *Id.*

63 GEURTS, DE ROMA VAN BRUSSEL (2004).

64 ANN CLÉ, BEDELARIJ ONDERZOCHT, 6,7 (2007). FRÉDÉRIQUE VAN HOUCKE, RECHERCHE D'UNE RÉPONSE SOCIALE À LA MENDICITÉ DES MINEURS, 5 (2005).

65 CATHERINE JOPPART, RECHERCHE RELATIVE AU DÉVELOPPEMENT D'UNE RÉPONSE SOCIALE À LA QUESTION DE LA MENDICITÉ DES ENFANTS EN BELIGIQUE, 55, 60 and 61 (2003), Van Houcke, *id.*, 4-5.

66 Vlaams Minderhedencentrum, Werknota: Roma In Vlaanderen. Knelpunten En Aanbevelingen, 8 (2010).

Roma, the focus appears to be on short-term health issues rather than on long-term health concerns.[67] A lack of education means that many Roma are also insufficiently familiar with preventative health care and lack knowledge about disease symptoms, both of which result in the much greater likelihood that members of this community fail to receive the appropriate care in a timely fashion.[68] In addition, underage marriages and teen pregnancies frequently lead to an early school exit for girls, which in turn negatively influences the position of Roma women in Belgian society.[69]

5. Integration

In addition to culturally specific elements, the illegal and insecure residency status of Roma who are not Belgian nationals thwarts their integration process into Belgian society.[70] For some, this insecure situation leads to poverty.[71] Intercultural communication and intermediary structures can help to built trust and bridge the cultural difference between Roma, wider society and public and health services, thereby leading to more effective cooperation.[72] Mediators and outreach have proved to be a successful approach to Romani integration, be it so far only on a very small, local scale.[73]

This quick look at the abovementioned problems shows that they are interrelated and mutually reinforcing. It is therefore of crucial importance for all policy domains and policy levels to cooperate and align their efforts so as to achieve effective long-term gains and full equality for Roma in Belgium. Only an integrated, vertical *and* horizontal approach – including

---

67   *Id.*, 14, 15, 17, 18. Frauke Decoodt and Stijn De Reu, kosovaarse roma in het waasland, 27 (2009). Geurts, de Roma van Brussel (Note 63).

68   Walter Leenders, Jaarboen 2007 Oost-Vlaams Diversiteitscentrum VZW (2008), 23.

69   Decoodt and De Reu, kosovaarse roma in het waasland (Note 67), 52, 54, 57, 59-60, 89.

70   Geurts, de Roma van Brussel (Note 63).

71   Geurts, *id.* Bruggen, Roma in Vlaandern. Minderheid onder de Minderheden? 20, (2003).

72   Koen Geurts, *"Met één achterste kan je niet op twee paarden zitten" Roma-leerlingen op de schoolbanken*, Handboek Leerlingenbegeleiding (2010). Vlaams Minderhedencentrum, Werknota: Roma in Vlaanderen. Knelpunten en Aanbevelingen (2010), 20-21. Federale Overheid, Nationale Strategie voor de Integratie van de Roma (2012) (Note 41), 17, 22.

73   Vlaamse vereniging voor Voyageurs, Roms, Roma en Manoesjen. Laat maar zitten ... Integratie van Roma is een Doe-Woord (2009).

coordinated, consistent and structured policy responses – to the multi-faceted context of Roma in Belgium is likely to lead to real change.[74] In this process, the recognition of Romani cultural identity is a precondition for effective assistance and a meaningful integration policy adapted to the specific situation and needs of Roma in Belgium.[75]

IV. Positive Action for Roma in Belgium

A. Legislation

As mentioned in the introduction to this chapter, Directive 2000/43/EC allows for the implementation of positive action measures to eliminate the consequences of (past) inequalities linked to race or ethnic origin, provided such measures are limited in time and targeted at members of the excluded or underrepresented minorities.[76] In practice, this can be the provision of additional information to or training for ethnic minorities to stimulate members of such minorities to apply for jobs in which they are underrepresented.[77] In 2007, the EU Fundamental Rights Agency reported that only a limited number of Member states had utilized the possibility of taking positive action in relation to ethnic minorities.[78] Some Member states have experimented with public procurement contracts that place conditions concerning equal opportunity criteria upon recruitment in companies with which they contract for the delivery of goods and services.[79] In 2011, the European Commission stressed in its "EU Framework for National Roma Integration Strategies up to 2020"[80] (hereinafter EU Roma Framework) the importance of focus in integration policies at all levels for Roma. Such policies and implementing measures must be clearly, specifically

---

74　Federale Overheid, Nationale Strategie voor de Integratie van de Roma (Note 41), 4, 31.

75　Geurts, de Roma van Brussel (Note 63).

76　EU Agency for Fundamental Rights, Report On Racism And Xenophobia In The Memebr States Of The Eu (2007), 156.

77　Id.

78　Germany, Finland and Austria are identified in the report as Member states that implemented positive action measures at the recruitment stage in the course of 2006. EU Agency for Fundamental Rights, id., 67, 68, 156; European Monitoring Centre on Racism and Xenophobia, (Note 59) 60.

79　EU Agency for Fundamental Rights, (Note 76), 10.

80　COM(2011) 173 final, 5 April 2011, 4.

and explicitly focused on Roma and their needs in order to "prevent and compensate for disadvantages they face".[81] Such a targeted approach – which the European Commission frames within "the broader strategy to fight ... poverty and exclusion"[82] – is in line with the non-discrimination principle and is key to making real progress towards Romani integration.[83] In the EU Roma Framework, the European Commission reminded Member states of the possibility of taking positive action for ethnic minorities in Directive 2000/43/EC,[84] and noted that – prior to the implementation of the EU Roma Framework – only a few Member states, including the UK, Hungary and Bulgaria, had implemented measures to promote Romani rights, despite finding existing classical social inclusion measures insufficient to meet the specific needs of Roma.[85]

In implementation of Directive 2000/43/EC, the Belgian Antiracism Law defines positive action as "*specifieke maatregelen om de nadelen verband houdende met een van de beschermde criteria te voorkomen of te compenseren, met het oog op het waarborgen van een volledige gelijkheid in de praktijk*" (specific measures to prevent or compensate for the disadvantages related to one of the protected criteria, with the aim of warranting a full equality in practice).[86] Under the law, national or ethnic origin is considered a protected criterion alongside nationality, so-called race, complexion and descent.[87] The Antiracism Law provides that "*[e]en direct of indirect onderscheid op grond van een van de beschermde criteria geeft nooit aanleiding tot de vaststelling van enige vorm van discriminatie wanneer dit directe of indirecte onderscheid een maatregel van positieve actie inhoudt*" ([a] direct or indirect difference on the basis of one of the protected criteria never leads to the determination of any form of discrimination when this direct or indirect difference consists in a positive action measure).[88] For positive action measures to be implemented in Belgium, four cumulative conditions must be fulfilled, namely (1) there needs to be an obvious inequality; (2) the removal of such inequality must be

---

81   *Id.*
82   *Id.*
83   *Id.*
84   Directive 2000/43, 4.
85   COM(2011) 173 final, 4.
86   Wet van 30 juli 1981 tot bestraffing van bepaalde door racisme of xenofobie ingegeven daden, Article 4(11°), B.S. 8 August 81 (last modified on 10 May 2007 (B.S. 30 May 2007)) (herinafter 'Belgian Antiracism Law').
87   Belgian Antiracism Law, Art. 4(4°).
88   Belgian Antiracism Law, Art. 10(1).

defined as a promoted objective; (3) the measure of positive action must be of a temporary nature and disappear as soon as the promoted objective has been reached; and (4) the rights of others cannot be unnecessarily limited.[89] Positive actions must thus be implemented in order to ensure that everyone is treated equally in practice. As with Directive 2000/43/EC, the Antiracism Law only provides for the possibility of positive action in the public sphere and not in private relations.[90]

B. Policy levels

1. The Federal level and Brussels

Having legislation providing for the possibility of adopting positive action measures for the reparation or elimination of obvious inequalities of ethnic minorities is one thing; making use of such a possibility is another. At the federal level in Belgium, there are thus far no positive actions specifically targeting Roma. The National Roma Strategy, which was submitted in March 2012 by the Federal Government to the European Commission,[91] does not provide for specific positive action measures for Roma either. Instead it contains merely a grouping of previously existing actions not specifically targeting Roma, which are thus not adjusted to the specific needs of this minority.

At the level of the Brussels-Capital Region, there are also no positive action measures that specifically target Roma. Throughout the years, small-scale projects have been implemented – among others, initiatives by the Brussels-based organisation Foyer to promote education and schooling of Roma children in Brussels – to promote the education of Romani minors in Brussels. Such projects are financed both by the federal State and the Brussels-Capital Region.[92] Such projects usually include mediators of Romani origin, who function as intermediaries and exercise a bridge function between Romani families and educational facilities.[93]

---

89 Belgian Antiracism Law, Art. 10(2).

90 The rules and conditions of application of positive action measures in Belgium must be fixed in a Royal Decree. Belgian Antiracism Law, Art. 10(3).

91 Federale Overheid, (Note 41), 40.

92 Emmanuelle Bribosia and Isabelle Rorive, Report on Measures to Combat Discrimination. Country Report 2010 Belgium, 145 (2011).

93 Koning Boudewijnstichting, Scholing van Roma Kinderen in België (Note 57) 34-38 (2009). Geurts, de Roma van Brussel (Note 63). Geurts, Naegels and Van den Daele, *Roma kinderen op de schoolbanken* (note 57), 14-15.

2. Flanders

On 28 April 1998, the Flemish government adopted a Decree on Flemish policy concerning ethnic-cultural minorities (hereinafter Flemish Decree 1998), which brought Roma and Travellers – defined as "the traveling population" ("*de trekkende bevolking*") – under the scope of application of legislation promoting the participation of ethnic-cultural minorities as fully-fledged citizens of the Flemish Community.[94] Prior to this date, Roma and Travellers were not included under the scope of Flemish positive action in employment.[95] In application of the Decree, the Flemish Minorities Centre ("Vlaams Minderhedencentrum") was set up as a semi-public institution to monitor the situation of Roma and Travellers in Flanders, and to mediate between these minorities and the authorities where necessary.[96] In addition, a division for caravan work has been set up in each of the five integration centres in Flanders, which are recognized and subsidised by the Flemish Government, and which have the aim of stimulating, supporting and monitoring the Flemish minority policy.[97] Since 30 April 2009, Flemish Decree 1998 has encompassed the whole of Flemish integration policy,[98] which is defined as an inclusive emancipation policy directed at (1) the proportional participation of specific groups (see below), (2) the accessibility of all provisions by all and (3) a policy based on coexistence within diversity.[99] Since then, the Decree has focused on three groups of people, namely (1) people who reside legally in Belgium and who live or used to live in a trailer or whose parents did – with the exception of people living on a camping site or a weekend house;[100] (2) people who reside in Belgium legally and permanently and who do not possess Belgian nationality as a birthright, as well as people with Belgian nationality whose parents were not Belgian nationals from birth;[101] and

---

94 Decreet van 28 april 1998 van de Vlaamse Overheid inzake het Vlaamse beleid ten aanzien van etnisch-culturele minderheden, *B.S.* 19 juni 1998 (hereinafter Flemish Decree 1998).

95 Bribosia and Rorive, (Note 92), 143

96 Flemish Decree 1998, Art. 2, 8°, 10, 12, 13.

97 Flemish Decree 1998, Art. 2 (9° and 11°), 10, 27.

98 Decreet van 30 april 2009 van de Vlaamse Overheid betreffende het Vlaamse Integratiebeleid, B.S. 2 July 2009, p. 45282 (partly in force since 1 January 2011) (hereinafter Flemish Decree 2009).

99 Flemish Decree 2009, Art. 4(1).

100 Flemish Decree 2009, Art. 3(1), 2°.

101 Flemish Decree 2009, Art. 3(1), 1°.

(3) illegal immigrants, especially those in need of guidance because of an emergency situation.[102]

The educational policy of the Flemish Community, while nodding its head to interculturalism, has no positive action measures specifically targeting the poor participation of Roma children in education.[103] The Decree of 28 June 2002 on equal opportunities in education (hereinafter Flemish Decree 2002) is an exception, as it determines that schools enrolling children of Roma and Travellers can receive additional financial assistance.[104] The Decree also provides for the possibility of children of 'the travelling population' – which includes Romani children in addition to the children of bargees, circus artists and the children of families running fairground attractions[105] – to receive priority upon enrolment in schools.[106] So far, these actions have had little impact, as only a very limited numbers of schools have taken up this option, usually after receiving active support from civil society organisations.[107] Another exception is contained in a Circular of 16 August 2002 concerning the absence of pupils in primary education, which allows children of traveling families to be absent from school during the so-called 'travel periods' on the basis of a specific agreement that contains measures for monitoring their academic progress.[108] There is as yet no evidence for the effectiveness of this measure in reducing school dropout rates.[109]

The Flemish Community has also undertaken steps to improve the housing situation of the Roma in Flanders. Since 1990, local governments that decide to open a caravan site for Travellers can receive financial support of up to 90% of the total cost of the site from the Flemish government.[110] Partly thanks to this initiative, there are approximately thirty caravan sites in Flanders today; together these sites are able to satisfy approximately half

---

102 Flemish Decree 2009, Art. 3(2).
103 European Monitoring Centre on Racism and Xenophobia, Roma and Travellers in Public Education, 69.
104 Decreet van 28 juni 2002 van de Vlaamse Gemeenschap betreffende gelijke onderwijskansen, B.S. 14 september 2002 (hereinafter Flemish Decree 2002).
105 Flemish Decree 2002, Art. II.1, 21°.
106 Flemish Decree 2002, Art. III.4, 3°, III.5, III.6.
107 Bribosia and Rorive, Report on Measures to Combat Discrimination, 144. European Monitoring Centre on Racism and Xenophobia, (note 103) 69.
108 Omzendbrief BaO/2002/11 van 16 augustus 2002 van de Vlaamse Overheid inzake de afwezigheid van leerlingen in het basisonderwijs, point 3.5.
109 Bribosia and Rorive, (Note 92), 144.
110 *Id.*

of the requests for caravan stands by Roma in Belgium.[111] Despite these efforts, there is still a serious lack of affordable and adequately equipped caravan sites to accommodate the other half of the Travellers in Belgium, who are sometimes forced to live in houses or apartments as a consequence. Moreover, the quality of water, electricity and sanitary provisions on the existing sites are often insufficient and unacceptable. Since 2004, the Flemish Housing Code ("Vlaamse Wooncode") recognizes caravans – defined as "*[e]en woongelegenheid, gekenmerkt door flexibiliteit en verplaatsbaarheid, bestemd voor permanente en niet-recreatieve bewoning*" ([a] living quarter, characterised by flexibility and mobility, designated for permanent and non-recreational habitation) – explicitly as a form of housing and they thus afford protection from, for example, eviction.[112] Also since 2004, improving the housing conditions of caravan inhabitants became one of the goals of Flemish housing policy.[113]

3. WALLONIA

Since 1 July 1982, the French-speaking Community has had rules providing means of up to 60% of the total cost for local governments that install a site for mobile housing financial.[114] The Walloon Housing Code provides that the Walloon Region will take care of the costs of the sewage, lighting and water provisions when local governments install caravan sites.[115] Despite these regulations, Wallonia has only one caravan site for Travellers.[116]

In addition to these measures on housing, the French-speaking Community is also making efforts to improve the integration of Roma into the community. The Walloon Declaration of Regional Policy 2009-2014 stipulates support for communal projects promoting the integration of and coexistence

---

111 *Id.*, 145.

112 Decreet van 15 juli 1997 van de Vlaamse Overheid houdende de Vlaamse Wooncode, Article 2, 33°, B.S. 19 augustus 1997 (as modified by Decreet of 19 March 2004) (hereinafter Flemish Housing Code).

113 Flemish Housing Code, Art. 4, 4° (c).

114 Arrêté de l'Exécutif de la Communauté française de 1 juillet 1982 fixant les conditions auxquelles des subsides peuvent être octroyés aux provinces, aux communes, agglomérations, fédérations et associations de communes et aux pouvoirs subordonnés, en vue de l'acquisition, de l'aménagement et de l'extension de terrains de campement en faveur des nomades, *M.B.*10 Septembre 1982.

115 Décret du 29 octobre 1998 de la Communauté française sur la Code Wallon du Logement, article 44, *M.B.* 04 Décembre 1998, p. 38965.

116 Bribosia and Rorive, (Note 92), 144.

with Travellers, for the fight against stigmatisation of this ethnic minority and the development of additional regulations to organise the temporary stay of Travellers on the territory of Municipalities.[117] Since 2001, Wallonia has its own Minorities Centre – the Mediation Centre of Travellers of the Walloon Region ("Centre de Médiation des Gens du Voyage de la Région wallonne") – that is responsible for organising dialogue between Travellers, wider society, regional and local governments.[118]

Moreover, the French-speaking Community has also adopted positive action measures that are targeted at an excluded group that includes many more than only Roma, namely newly arrived migrants.[119] A Decree of 30 April 2009 introduced a differentiated supervision scheme within schools allowing for differentiated attribution of means – especially personnel – to schools that take in socially disadvantaged children.[120] The number of supervision personnel at schools in the French-speaking Community is thus connected to the socio-economic origin of the pupils in the school.[121]

V. The Importance of Ethnic Data

It is widely accepted that for positive action measures to be implemented and executed effectively, there is a need for precise and accurate data on the situation – for example in employment or education – of the group(s) for whom the positive action measures are to be introduced.[122] The collection of such equality data serves different purposes. In the context of Roma in Belgium, the collection of data on ethnicity would finally (1) provide a decisive answer as to the number of Roma residing in Belgium; (2) allow for the clear identification of the nature and extent of the problems and

---

117 Déclaration de politique régionale wallone 2009-2014 du Government wallone (2009), 219, available at: http://easi.wallonie.be/servlet/Repository/DPR_wallonne_2009. PDF?IDR=9295.

118 BRIBOSIA AND RORIVE, (Note 92), 144.

119 *Id.*, 145.

120 Décret de 30 avril 2009 de la Communauté française organisant un encadrement différencié au sein des établissements scolaires de la Communauté française afin d'assurer à chaque élève des chances égales d'émancipation sociale dans un environnement pédagogique de qualité, *B.S.* 9 juillet 2009, 47476.

121 This legislation adds to the Decree of 14 June 2001 concerning the reception of newly arrived children in the educational system organised or subsidised by the French speaking Community. Décret de 14 juin 2001 visant à l'insertion des élèves primo-arrivants dans l'enseignement organize ou subventionné par la Communauté française, B.S. 17 juillet 2001, 24355. Bribosia and Rorive, (Note 109), 145.

122 EU Agency for Fundamental Rights, (Note 76) 1.

discrimination that Roma face in Belgian society and thus the identification of policy domains and levels where positive action is most needed.[123] Directive 2000/43/EC does not oblige Member states to employ statistics when proving discrimination, but the use of statistics are recognised as being of particular importance in proving indirect discrimination, in which a seemingly neutral practice or rule disproportionately impacts individuals of a certain group.[124] Moreover, equality data would make it possible to (3) effectively implement positive action measures as well as evaluate the effect of the measures;[125] finally (4) the data would allow policy makers to know when a discriminatory situation has been eliminated and thus when positive action measures should cease.[126]

However, the Belgium census collects information about individuals' nationality but never about their ethnicity, because such a question is considered to be contrary to data protection rules and the right to privacy. Although, as noted above, nationality can be an indication of ethnicity, it does not provide certainty or any of the fine distinctions that make such data so useful in directing anti-discrimination policies. Assuming – without any nuances – that the collection and use of ethnic data constitutes a violation of privacy and data protection rules is incorrect. Provided certain conditions are met – including consent and the right to self-identification – the collection and use of such data is possible – and even required – in a pro-active policy fighting discrimination. In November 2006, the European Commission published the *European Handbook on Equality Data* in which it explains why and how Member states should build "a national knowledge base on equality and discrimination on the grounds of racial and ethnic origin, religion and belief, disability, age and sexual orientation".[127] Member states have thus been encouraged by the European Commission to collect sensitive data on ethnicity and use it in order to render their equality policies fully effective. For example, if racist and discriminatory incidents in Belgian public educational institutions, as well as data on the school performance of ethnic minorities, were to be systematically recorded, it would become possible to identify the required analytical tools to tackle and remove the practices and structures

---

123 *Id.*, 156.
124 Bribosia and Rorive, (Note 92), 34.
125 EU Agency for Fundamental Rights, (Note 122) 156.
126 *Id.*
127 European Commission, European Handbook on Equality Data (2006), 105.

that lead to systemic inequality in Belgian education.[128] Such reasoning can also be applied to other domains, such as housing.

In the course of 2006, consultations were held in Belgium at different levels about ethnic monitoring. While at the federal level the topic was merely discussed, at the Flemish level a data management tool was implemented within the Flemish Service for Employment Mediation and Professional Training (VDAB), which made a distinction between ethnic categories on the basis of first and last names.[129] The Flemish Service admitted the system was not flawless but that for the groups it targets – namely the labour market position of the two largest groups of non-EU migrants in Belgium – it suffices to look at the name as effective proxy.[130] Even though this tool mainly targets people of Maghreb and Turkish origin, and not Roma, it could be a forerunner of a future system in which data on ethnic origin is collected and statistically processed for use in the fight against discrimination of Roma and to promote their integration into Belgian society as full-fledged citizens.

VI. Conclusion

The road towards equality for the Roma in Belgium – and across the EU – is slow and the end is still far from sight. A serious step towards better integration of and life for Roma in Europe was taken last year when Romani issues were finally put high on the EU agenda. The EU Roma Framework forces Member states to confront the problems that Roma in their country struggle with on a daily basis. The Framework reaffirms that the prohibition of discrimination alone does not suffice to tackle the complexity of problems facing Romani communities, but that active employment, housing, and other policies are required to fight inequalities and to realize the full integration of Roma into society. Another – be it very small – step to tackle Roma issues was taken with the submission of the EU Member states of their National Roma Strategy to the European Commission. Both the European Commission and civil society strongly insist that much more needs to be done by Member states, including the adoption of "more concrete measures, explicit targets

---

128 EU Agency for Fundamental Rights, (Note 122), 157.

129 *Id.*, 50.

130 The VDAB publishes monthly statistics on the unemployment rate of persons labelled to belong to the non-active ethnic category based on name recognition. The statistics can be consulted at http://arvastat.vdab.be/arvastat/index.html. EU Agency for Fundamental Rights, *id.*, 50-51.

for measurable deliverables, clearly earmarked funding at national level and a sound national monitoring and evaluation system".[131] In the Belgian Roma Strategy, for example, no effort was made to introduce new positive action measures specifically targeted at the needs of the Roma population; instead, the Strategy collects already existing, general measures that clearly have not had the desired impact on the situation of Roma in Belgium into a single document. It is true there have been local initiatives and successes in fostering Romani integration, but they have been too small and too local to tackle the bigger issues at hand. Tackling Romani marginalisation needs to be put high up on the Belgian political agenda. The complex issues call for firm cooperation across policy borders and levels. Long-term, explicitly targeted, structured, coordinated, integrated initiatives are needed, both horizontally between different policy domains and vertically, between different competence levels, as well as at the local, provincial, national and European level.

Belgium needs to invest more in positive action measures for Roma, as well as in information and awareness campaigns of the complex situation of Roma and the need for positive action. In this process of fighting inequality and discrimination, ethnic data is indispensable. Despite encouragement and guidance by the European Commission, Belgium – along with many other EU Member states – is still far from collecting and using such sensitive data. The debate on this topic should be revived and stimulated instead of being shunned. Stated quite clearly, the lack of ethnic data forms a huge barrier to the identification of problem areas in which inequalities exist, to the implementation of effective measures to eliminate such inequalities and discrimination, as well as to the monitoring of the impact of these measures. It is clear Belgium still has a long way to go, which is precisely why serious action should be taken now.

---

131 COM(2012) 226 final, 21 May 2012, 16-18. European Roma Policy Coalition, *ERPC welcomes European Commission's negative assessment of the National Roma Integration Strategies* (2012).

Annex

Extract From
The Situation Of Roma In 11 EU Member States: Survey Results At A Glance

Fundamental Rights Agency

In May 2012, the European Union Agency for Fundamental Rights (FRA), together with the United Nations Development Programme (UNDP), published a report on *The Situation of Roma in 11 EU Member States – Survey results at a glance.*[1] This publication contains the first results of two surveys carried out in the course of 2011, namely the FRA Roma pilot survey and the UNDP/World Bank/European Commission regional Roma survey. The first survey covered eleven EU Member States, namely Bulgaria, the Czech Republic, France, Greece, Italy, Hungary, Poland, Portugal, Romania, Slovakia and Spain, whereas the second survey covered five of these EU Member States, namely Bulgaria, the Czech Republic, Hungary, Romania and Slovakia, as well as six countries outside the EU in the western Balkans and the Republic of Moldova. The FRA Roma pilot survey was conducted via face-to-face interviews with 22,203 Roma and non-Roma, through which information was collected on 84,287 household members.

The FRA report covers education, health, employment, housing, poverty, and discrimination and rights awareness. The research results show a negative picture of the socio-economic situation of Roma in the 11 EU Member States. As the report states, "[…] in the 11 EU Member States covered by the surveys the socio-economic situation of the Roma in the four key areas of employment, education, housing and health is not satisfactory and is worse, on average, than the situation of the non-Roma living in close proximity. They also show that Roma continue to experience discrimination and are not sufficiently

---

1   European Union Agency for Fundamental Rights (FRA), *The situation of Roma in 11 EU Member States. Survey results at a glance* (Luxembourg: Publications Office of the European Union, 2012).

aware of their rights guaranteed by EU law, such as the Racial Equality Directive (2000/43/EC)".[2] Four parts of the report are reproduced here with the kind permission of the FRA, namely (I) education, (II) employment, (III) poverty and (IV) discrimination and rights awareness. The full report can be found on FRA's website.[3]

I. Education

> Education determines future life chances, and is crucial for finding stable and decently paid employment. The results of the surveys confirm that largely Roma children lag behind in educational achievement. Nevertheless, the right to education is a fundamental human right protected under Article 28 of the United Nations (UN) Convention on the Rights of the Child (CRC) ratified by all EU Member States and under Article 14 of the European Union Charter of Fundamental Rights. EU Member States have thus a duty to ensure that all children enjoy equal access to education, in particular to compulsory education. According to the United Nations Educational, Scientific and Cultural Organization (UNESCO),[4] those who do not complete at least compulsory education face high risks of living in poverty and have limited chances to develop learning skills and reach their full potential.
>
> This section examines school participation, attendance and completion rates comparing Roma and non-Roma. The results confirm the findings of past research[5] that Roma children lag behind in educational achievement.

© FRA, *The Situation of Roma in 11 EU Member States. Survey results at a glance*, p. 12-13 (Luxembourg: Publications Office of the European Union, 2012).

---

2   FRA, *The Situation of Roma in 11 EU Member States. Survey results at a glance* (Luxembourg: Publications Office of the European Union, 2012), p. 12.

3   http://fra.europa.eu/en/publication/2012/situation-roma-11-eu-member-states-survey-results-glance.

4   UNESCO (2010) Education for all Global Monitoring Report 2010. Reaching the marginalized, Paris, UNESCO, p. 155.

5   EUMC (2006) Roma and Travellers in public education, Vienna, EUMC; Ivanov, A., Collins, M., Grosu, C., Kling, J., Milcher, S., O'Higgins, N., Slay, B. and Zhelyazkova, A. (2006) At risk: Roma and the displaced in Southeast Europe, Bratislava, UNDP/World Bank/EC Regional Bureau for Europe and the CIS; Revenga, A., Ringold, D. and Tracy, W.M. (2002) Poverty and ethnicity. A cross-country study of Roma poverty in central Europe, Washington D.C., The World Bank.

PARTICIPATION IN PRE-SCHOOL AND KINDERGARTEN

Early childhood education is crucial for subsequent successful school participation. In its 2011 Communication on early childhood education and care, the European Commission highlighted that "early childhood is the stage where education can most effectively influence the development of children and help reverse disadvantage".[6] In this light, the European Commission Communication on an EU Framework for national Roma integration strategies asked EU Member States specifically to "widen access to quality early childhood education and care"[7] for the Roma. The results show that this is indeed a significant priority.

Figure 2: Children aged 4 to starting age of compulsory education attending preschool or kindergarten (pooled data) (%)

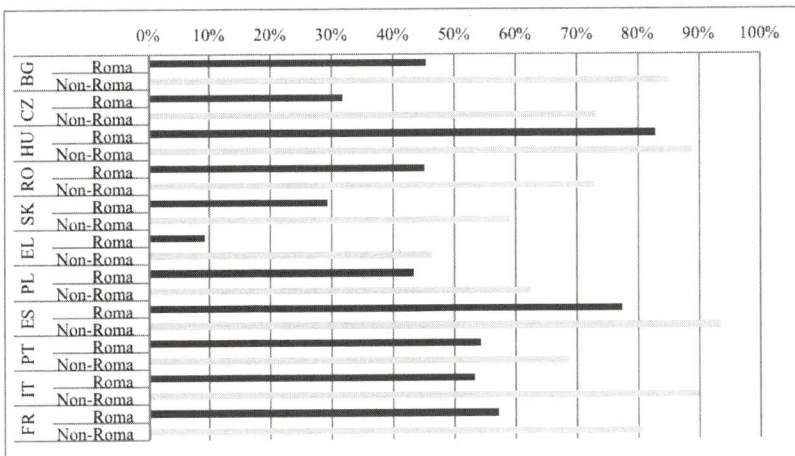

In nine of the 11 EU Member States surveyed, the results show a considerable gap between Roma and non-Roma children attending pre-school and kindergarten (*see Figure 2*). However, significant differences exist between EU Member States: in Hungary and Spain, for instance, at least seven out of 10 Roma and non-Roma children surveyed are reported to attend pre-school or kindergarten. In stark contrast, in

---

6   European Commission (2011) Early childhood education and care: Providing all our children with the best start for the world of tomorrow, COM(2011) 66 final, Brussels, 17 February 2011, p. 3, http://ec.europa.eu/education/school-education/doc/ childhoodcom_en.pdf.

7   European Commission COM(2011) 173 final, 5 April 2011, 6.

Greece, less than 10% of Roma children are reported to be in pre-school or kindergarten compared with less than 50% of non-Roma children. The lowest participation rates in pre-school and kindergarten education for both Roma and non-Roma children are reported in Greece and Slovakia. The results do not show any significant gender differences overall.

© FRA, *The Situation of Roma in 11 EU Member States. Survey results at a glance*, p. 13 (Luxembourg: Publications Office of the European Union, 2012).

SCHOOL ATTENDANCE OF CHILDREN OF COMPULSORY SCHOOL AGE

The completion of compulsory education is a precondition for decent employment and access to further and higher education. The percentage of children who are not in school at the age of 7 to 15[8] is not only an indicator for the future chances of this generation, but also a warning sign for the education systems. It should be noted that these results do not distinguish between different school types, for example, schools intended for children with mental or physical disabilities, which exist in certain EU Member States and to which Roma children are often assigned, according to previous research.[9]

Figure 3: Children aged 7 to 15 not in school (%)

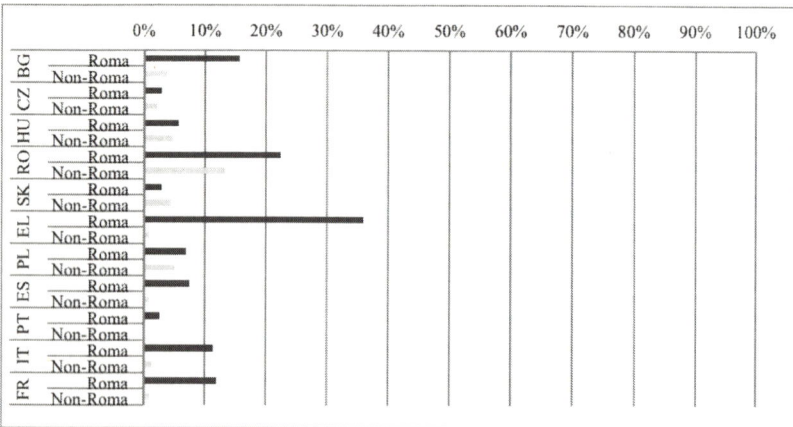

---

8   In Bulgaria, Hungary, Poland and Romania, many children enter primary education at the age of 7, elsewhere at 6. In the Czech Republic and Greece, compulsory school ends at the age of 15, elsewhere at a later age.

9   EUMC (2006) Roma and Travellers in public education, Vienna, EUMC.

The results show important differences in school attendance between Roma and non-Roma children (*see Figure 3*). The situation, however, differs considerably between EU Member States. At least 10% of Roma children aged 7 to 15 in Greece, Romania, Bulgaria, France and Italy are identified in the FRA survey as not attending school, meaning that they are either still in preschool, not yet in education, skipped the year, stopped school completely or are already working. This proportion is highest in Greece with more than 35% of Roma children not attending school.

© FRA, *The Situation of Roma in 11 EU Member States. Survey results at a glance*, p. 14 (Luxembourg: Publications Office of the European Union, 2012).

COMPLETED GENERAL AND VOCATIONAL UPPER-SECONDARY EDUCATION

Completing any type of upper-secondary general or vocational education is a prerequisite for skilled employment and access to higher education. The higher the education level attained, the greater the chances to access secure, decent and well-paid employment. Results for young adults aged 20 to 24, who are entering the labour market, show significant differences between Roma and non-Roma in all EU Member States (*see Figure 4*). In five out of 11 EU Member States, Portugal, Greece, Spain, France and Romania, fewer than one out of 10 Roma is reported to have completed

Figure 4: Household members aged 20 to 24 with at least completed general or vocational upper-secondary education (pooled data) (%)

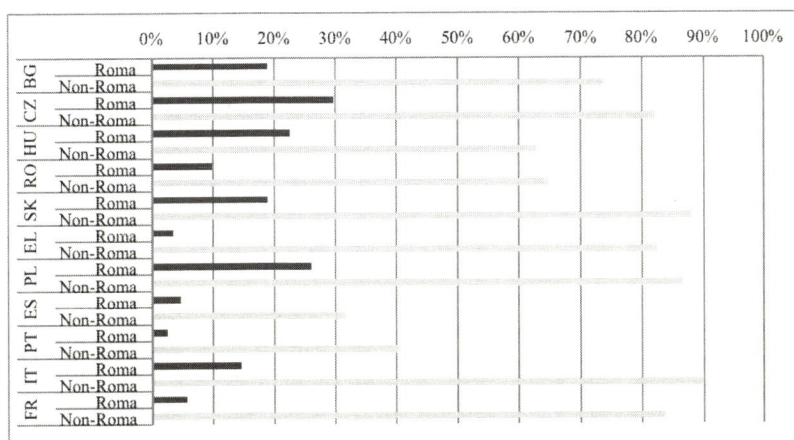

upper-secondary education. In the Czech Republic and Poland, the results are better but still fewer than one out of three young Roma is reported to have completed this level of education.

In Portugal and Spain, the proportion of non-Roma who are reported to have completed upper-secondary education is much lower than in other EU Member States, possibly reflecting local or regional structural disadvantages that affect both groups living in close proximity. The results showed small gender differences among Roma for this level of education, except in Poland where Roma women more often than Roma men report to have completed upper secondary education.

© FRA, *The Situation of Roma in 11 EU Member States. Survey results at a glance*, p. 15 (Luxembourg: Publications Office of the European Union, 2012).

II. Employment

According to Eurostat figures, the paid employment rate[10] in the EU for those aged 20 to 64 amounted, on average, to 68,6% in 2010; the Europe 2020 strategy sets a headline target of 75%. In the context of the economic crisis, however, it is reasonable to assume that competition for jobs, especially low-skilled jobs, will increasingly put many Roma at a disadvantaged position when competing for employment. This is not only due to their lack of adequate education and marketable skills, but also because they are often discriminated against: in 2009, EU-MIDIS data showed that one in five of the Roma surveyed reported discriminatory experiences when looking for work.

© FRA, *The Situation of Roma in 11 EU Member States. Survey results at a glance*, p. 16 (Luxembourg: Publications Office of the European Union, 2012).

---

10 This indicator is not directly comparable with the results of the surveys since it is based on a different definition. For Eurostat data, see: http://epp.eurostat.ec.europa.eu/tgm/table.do?tab=table&init= 1&plugin=1&language=en&pcode=t2020_10.

PAID EMPLOYMENT RATE

The term 'paid employment'[11] includes paid work (full time, part time and ad hoc) as well as paid parental leave, while excluding self-employment. In certain EU Member States, the self-employment rate is quite high, as explained below. It should also be noted that the non-Roma surveyed are not representative of the general population; the results for this group will therefore differ from data on general population statistics, such as the Labour Force Survey (LFS).

Overall, the results show that the headline target of Europe 2020 poses a considerable challenge. In this regard, the EU Framework target for "cutting the employment gap between Roma and the rest of the population" will require substantial efforts by EU Member States.

Figure 5: Household members aged 20 to 64 in paid employment (pooled data) (%) – excluding self-employment

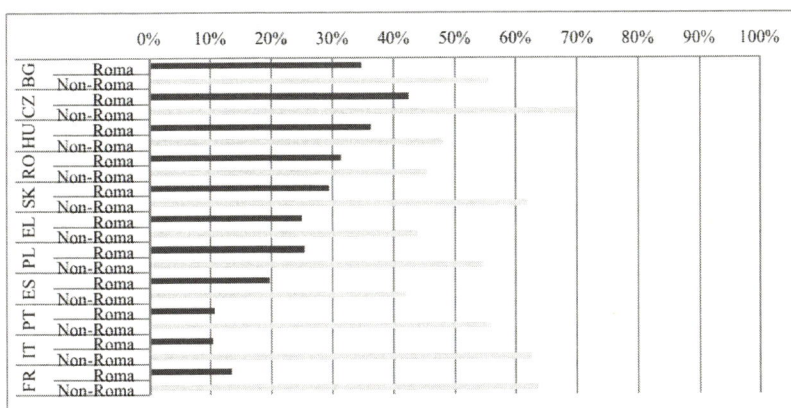

The surveys found important differences between the Roma and non-Roma surveyed in France, Italy and Portugal, where only about one out of 10 Roma aged 20 to 64 is reported as being in paid employment (*see Figure 5*). This is in stark contrast to the non-Roma surveyed, who report much higher employment rates. These low employment rates of Roma require further investigation as several explanations for these findings

---

11   The surveys asked respondents to identify the work situation of each household member.

are possible: it may, for example, be related to the varying extent of self-employment across the countries surveyed – about 20% of the Roma surveyed in France, but also in Greece, and about 25% in Italy said that they are self-employed. In this regard, the European Commission Communication on an EU Framework for national Roma integration strategies asks EU Member States to grant Roma people full access in a non-discriminatory way to self-employment tools and initiatives, as well as access to micro-credit.

The highest rates in paid employment for both Roma and non-Roma are reported in the Czech Republic, while the smallest differences in employment rates between Roma and non-Roma are reported in Hungary.

The employment rates, which were calculated based on the UNDP/World Bank/EC data using the LFS methodology, show a similar picture, while also revealing additional important details in the five EU Member States – Bulgaria, Czech Republic, Hungary and Slovakia – covered by both surveys. For both Roma and non-Roma, employment rates for women are lower than for men, in particular for Roma.

© FRA, *The Situation of Roma in 11 EU Member States. Survey results at a glance*, p. 16 (Luxembourg: Publications Office of the European Union, 2012).

SELF-REPORTED UNEMPLOYMENT

Measuring unemployment in surveys is complex as respondents may interpret their situation differently. For example, persons who work only occasionally or in the informal economy may prefer to classify themselves in a survey as unemployed. With this in mind, the findings under the indicator 'self-reported unemployment'[12] should be read in connection with other indicators, such as paid employment presented in the previous section.

---

12 This indicator is not comparable to the LFS indicators for unemployment, which defines unemployed persons as those without work during a reference week but currently available for work, and who were either actively seeking work in the past four weeks or who had already found a job to start within the next three months. The FRA Roma pilot survey, unlike the UNDP/World Bank/EC regional Roma survey, did not limit the definition to any specific time period, reference week or availability and/or willingness to work in order to capture also those persons who may have been unemployed for longer periods and were not actively seeking work.

Figure 6: Respondents aged 20 to 64 who considered themselves as unemployed (%)

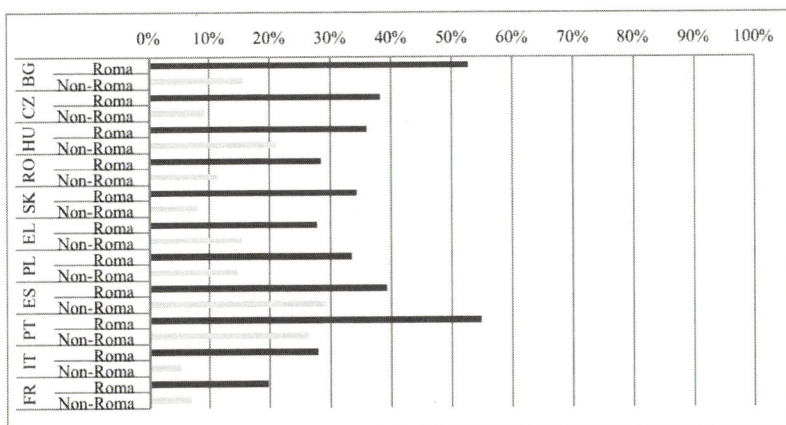

The survey finds high unemployment rates for the Roma across all EU Member States where they were surveyed (*see Figure 6*). In most Member States, the number of Roma saying that they are unemployed is at least double than the number of non-Roma; in Italy, the Czech Republic and Slovakia, up to 4 to 5 times more Roma than non-Roma said they are unemployed.

UNDP/World Bank/EC data on unemployment calculated using the LFS methodology show a similar picture and reveal additional important details in the five Member States covered by both surveys in regard to gender and age. For instance, the unemployment rates reported for Roma women is on average one third higher than those for Roma men, while in the case of non-Roma the gap between female and male unemployment rates is much lower. In addition, of those young Roma aged 15 to 24, who said that they are unemployed, a worrying share – ranging from about 58% in Hungary to 77% in the Czech Republic – have no previous work experience.

© FRA, *The Situation of Roma in 11 EU Member States. Survey results at a glance*, p. 17 (Luxembourg: Publications Office of the European Union, 2012).

PENSION

The FRA survey also asked respondents whether they are or will be entitled to a private or state pension.[13] In all EU Member States, fewer Roma than non-Roma respondents said that they are or will be eligible for such pension (*see Figure 7*). Nevertheless, more than half of the Roma surveyed said they are or will be entitled to a pension in the Czech Republic, Hungary and Slovakia, and two out of three Roma indicated this in Portugal. The results show small gender differences overall; in Greece and Spain, however, Roma men indicated more often than Roma women that they are or will be entitled to a pension.

Figure 7: Respondents aged 18 and above stating that they are or will be entitled to private or state pension (%)

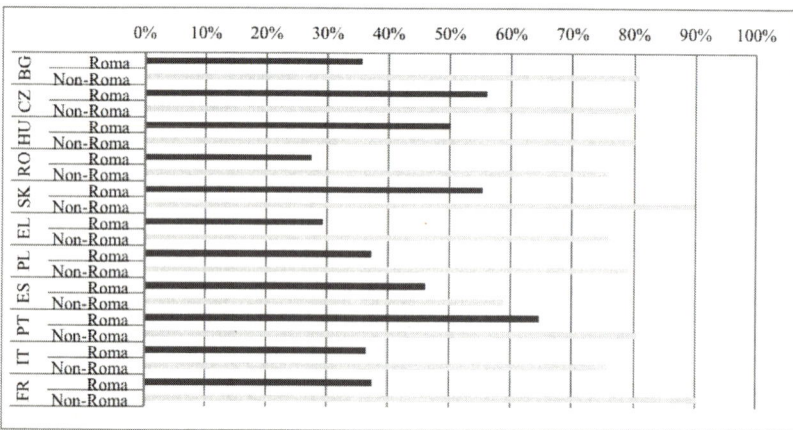

© FRA, *The Situation of Roma in 11 EU Member States. Survey results at a glance,* p. 18-19 (Luxembourg: Publications Office of the European Union, 2012).

---

13   This question was not included in the common core questionnaire or the UNDP questionnaire.

CHILD LABOUR

The proportion of children aged 7 to 15 who are reported as working outside the home is very low in most EU Member States (*see Figure 8*); for non-Roma children, it is almost non existent.

Figure 8: Roma children aged 7 to 15 that work outside the home (%)

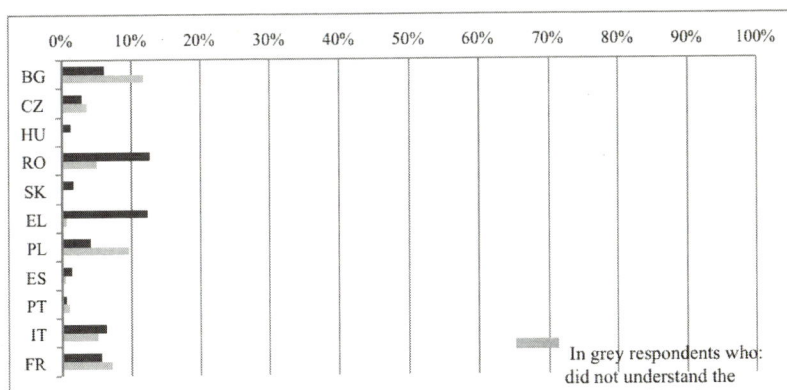

However, in Greece and Romania more than one out of 10 Roma children are reported to be working outside the home, while in Italy, France and Bulgaria the proportion is about 6%. When asked which type of work children do outside the home, respondents said either that they are collecting objects for reselling or recycling, or they are begging on the street for money. Other activities of Roma children working outside the home include working in a shop, on a farm, in a market or selling things in the streets, running errands or guarding cars.

A significant number of respondents said that they do not understand the question, do not know or refuse to answer, which possibly indicates their reluctance to say that the children are working, or because the children's work did not fit any of the above categories.

© FRA, *The Situation of Roma in 11 EU Member States. Survey results at a glance*, p. 18-19 (Luxembourg: Publications Office of the European Union, 2012).

DISCRIMINATION ON GROUNDS OF ETHNIC ORIGIN WHEN LOOKING FOR WORK

The survey results of perceived experiences of discrimination when looking for work in the past five years largely corroborate the findings of the EU-MIDIS survey in 2009. Eleven years after the adoption of the EU's Racial Equality Directive, more than half of the Roma respondents looking for work said that they have experienced discrimination because they are Roma (*see Figure 9*). The largest shares of discrimination experiences are among Roma in Italy and the Czech Republic. However, discrimination experiences are reported less in Bulgaria and Romania confirming earlier EU-MIDIS findings.

Figure 9: Roma respondents aged 16 and above looking for work during the past 5 years, who said that they experienced discrimination because of their Roma background (pooled data) (%)

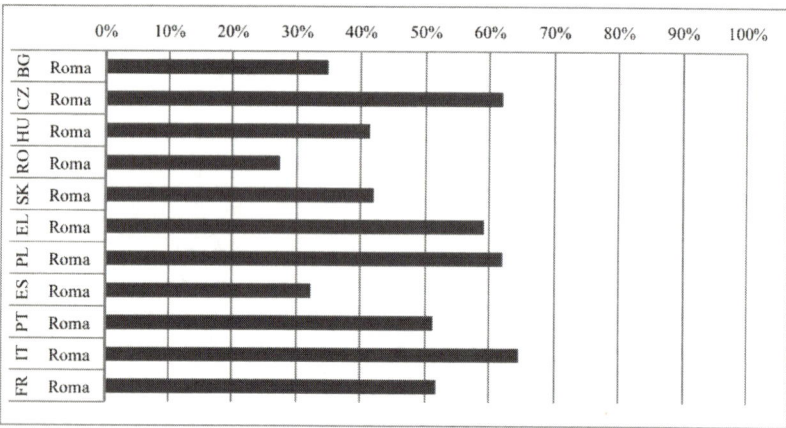

© FRA, *The Situation of Roma in 11 EU Member States. Survey results at a glance,* p. 19 (Luxembourg: Publications Office of the European Union, 2012).

III. Poverty

This section focuses specifically on income poverty measured in relation to the distribution of income within each country. However, poverty or the lack of what is essential for a minimum standard of life is a wider concept than monetary poverty. It also includes access to essential social resources, such as education and healthcare. The situation regarding the four key areas, namely employment, education, health and housing described in the previous sections, thus forms an essential part of a broader understanding of the deprivation levels of the Roma and non-Roma household members surveyed.

© FRA, *The Situation of Roma in 11 EU Member States. Survey results at a glance*, p. 25 (Luxembourg: Publications Office of the European Union, 2012).

'AT-RISK-OF-POVERTY'

Households 'at-risk-of-poverty' are those with an equivalised[14] income below 60% of the national median equivalised disposable income. The FRA Roma pilot survey results show that in all EU Member States covered significant differences exist in the proportion of Roma and non-Roma living in households that are at-risk-of-poverty, according to the household income reported by the respondents. In all EU Member States, at least eight out of 10 of the Roma surveyed are at risk of poverty with the highest levels reported in Portugal, Italy and France (*see Figure 14*).

The differences between Roma and non-Roma are more pronounced in France and in Italy, where the proportion of Roma living in households at risk of poverty is more than twice as high as for the non-Roma.

When analysing the results of the UNDP/World Bank/ EC regional Roma survey, it is interesting to note income inequalities within both the Roma and the non-Roma surveyed. In the Czech Republic, Hungary and Slovakia, for instance, such inequalities are small. However, in the case of Romania and Bulgaria for example, the average income of the

---

14   Equivalised income is a measure of household income that takes account of the differences in a household's size and composition. For more information, see http:// epp. eurostat.ec.europa.eu/statistics_explained/index.php/ Glossary:Equivalised_ income.

Figure 14: Persons living in households at risk of poverty (%)

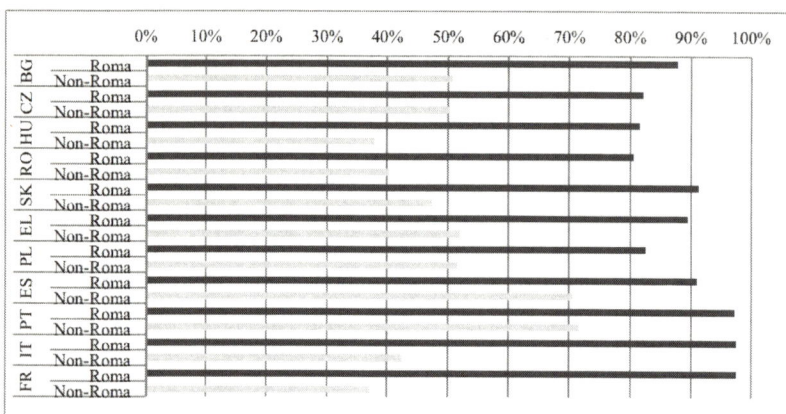

---

richest 20% of the Roma surveyed was reported to be respectively 13 and 12 times higher than the income reported by the poorest 20% of Roma. These differences point to the complex composition of the populations surveyed and underscore the need for more in-depth qualitative research to better understand the nature and consequences of these differences.

© FRA, *The Situation of Roma in 11 EU Member States. Survey results at a glance*, p. 24-25 (Luxembourg: Publications Office of the European Union, 2012).

HOUSEHOLDS THAT COULD NOT ALWAYS AFFORD TO BUY FOOD

The 2003 UNDP *report Avoiding the dependency trap* highlighted that many Roma endure severe challenges in terms of illiteracy, infant mortality and malnutrition. The surveys tried to assess again the validity of this claim by asking respondents whether they or somebody else in their household "went to bed hungry in the past month because there was not enough money to buy food".

In all EU Member States, Roma and non-Roma respondents said that they have experienced a situation where at least once during the previous month somebody went to bed hungry because they could not afford to buy food (*see Figure 15*). With the exception of France and Spain, where around one in 10 Roma respondents experience this level of deprivation, in the other Member States this proportion rises markedly from around

Figure 15: Persons living in households in which someone went to bed hungry at least once in the past month (pooled data) (%)

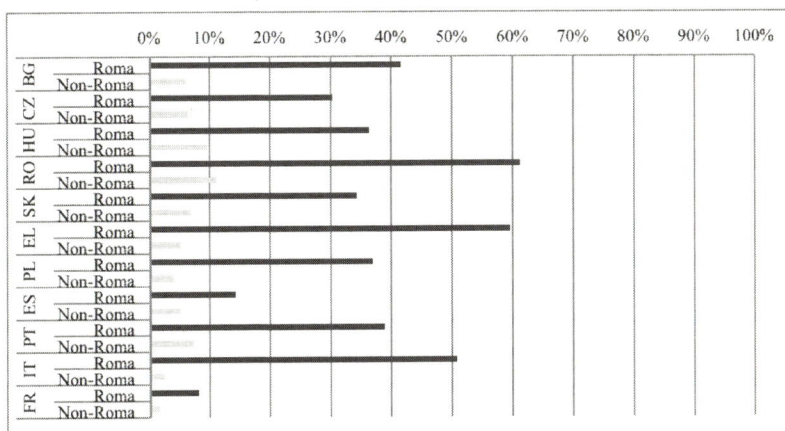

30% in the Czech Republic to around 60% in Greece and Romania. While the percentages of households in which someone went to bed hungry at least once in the past month are high for the Roma, it is noteworthy that hunger constitutes also a factor in the lives of some persons in non-Roma households.

© FRA, *The Situation of Roma in 11 EU Member States. Survey results at a glance*, p. 24-25 (Luxembourg: Publications Office of the European Union, 2012).

SEVERE MATERIAL DEPRIVATION

Severe material deprivation is one of the key indicators for Europe 2020. It is a composite indicator[15] incorporating housing and economic deprivation. According to Eurostat, deprivation covers indicators relating to economic strain, durables, housing and environment of the dwelling. Persons who are 'severely materially deprived' live under conditions constrained by a severe lack of resources, that is, they cannot afford at least four of the following items:

- to pay rent or utility bills;
- to keep their home adequately warm;

15   For more information, see: http://epp.eurostat.ec.europa.eu/ tgm/table.do?tab=table &init=1&language=en&pcode=t2020_5 3&plugin=1.

- to face unexpected expenses;
- to eat meat, fish or a protein equivalent every second day;
- to have a week's holiday away from home;
- a car;
- a washing machine;
- a colour TV;
- a telephone.

According to the UNDP/World Bank/EC regional Roma survey data, between 70% and 90% of the Roma surveyed report living in conditions of severe material deprivation. The proportion of non-Roma in such conditions is significantly lower with substantive differences between the EU Member States (*see Figure 16*).

Figure 16: Households with severe material deprivation (UNDP/World Bank/EC data) (%)

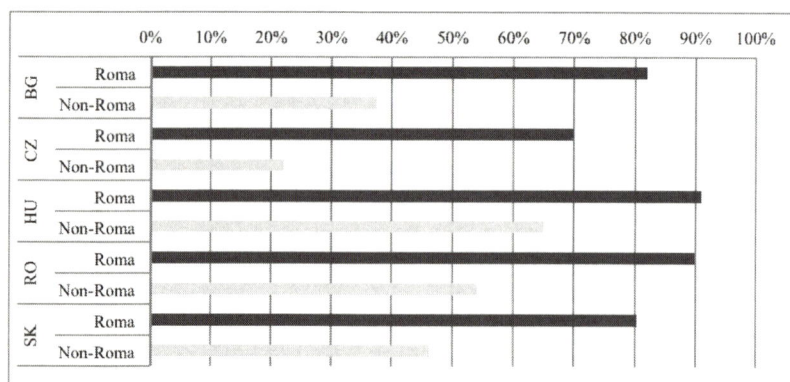

According to the UNDP/World Bank/EC regional Roma survey data, between 70% and 90% of the Roma surveyed report living in conditions of severe material deprivation. The proportion of non-Roma in such conditions is significantly lower with substantive differences between the EU Member States (*see Figure 16*).

IV. Discrimination and Rights Awareness

The survey asked Roma respondents about their experiences of discriminatory treatment in employment, housing, health and education because of their ethnic origin. The results show high numbers of respondents indicating that they have experienced discrimination, as was also the case in the FRA EU-MIDIS survey.

© FRA, *The Situation of Roma in 11 EU Member States. Survey results at a glance*, p. 27 (Luxembourg: Publications Office of the European Union, 2012).

DISCRIMINATION ON GROUNDS OF ETHNIC ORIGIN

In all EU Member States, a significant proportion of Roma respondents said that they have experienced discriminatory treatment because of their ethnic origin in the 12 months preceding the survey. The proportions range from more than 25% in Romania to around 60% in the Czech Republic, Greece, Italy and Poland (*see Figure 17*). In consistency with the findings of EU-MIDIS,[16] the levels of discrimination experiences in

Figure 17: Roma respondents aged 16 and above who experienced discrimination because of their Roma background in the past 12 months (pooled data) (%)

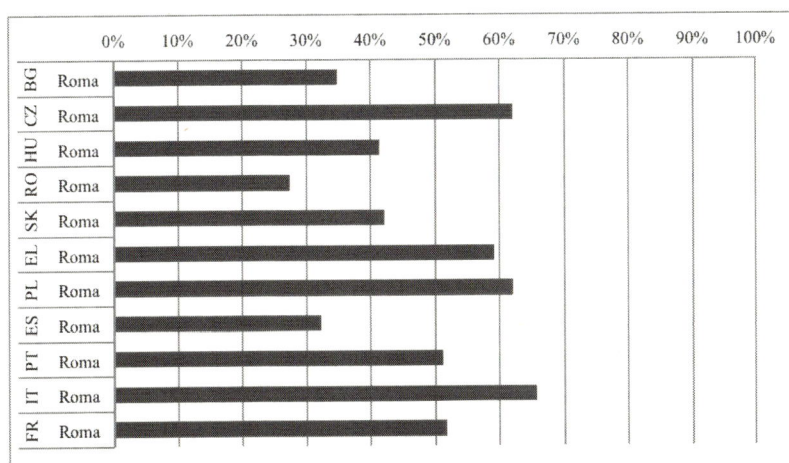

---

16   FRA (2009) 'The Roma', Data in focus report, Luxembourg, Publications Office, p. 12, http://fra.europa.eu/fraWebsite/ attachments/EU-MIDIS_ROMA_EN.pdf.

> Romania and Bulgaria are relatively low compared with the other EU
> Member States.

© FRA, *The situation of Roma in 11 EU Member States. Survey results at a glance*,
p. 26-27 (Luxembourg: Publications Office of the European Union, 2012).

AWARENESS OF ANTI-DISCRIMINATION LEGISLATION IN
EMPLOYMENT

Figure 18: Respondents aged 16 and above who knew about a law forbidding
discrimination against ethnic minority people when applying for a job
(pooled data) (%)

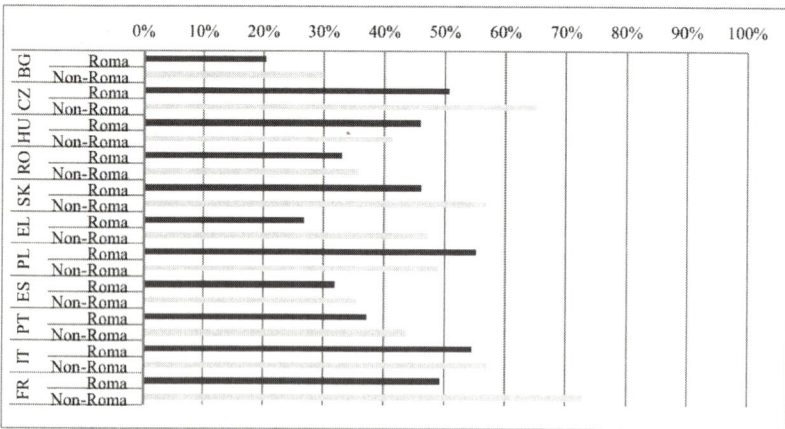

The respondents were asked if they knew of any law that forbids
discrimination against ethnic minority people when applying for a job.
The results reveal important differences between EU Member States (*see*
Figure 18). In general, a larger proportion of non-Roma is aware of such
laws. Differences between Roma and non-Roma are highest in Greece,
France and Bulgaria.

About half of the Roma respondents are aware of anti-discrimination
legislation in Poland, the Czech Republic, Italy, and France. The Member
States showing the lowest awareness levels among Roma respondents are
Bulgaria and Greece.

In all EU Member States, Roma men show greater awareness of anti-
discrimination laws than Roma women, in particular in Italy and Poland.

© FRA, *The Situation of Roma in 11 EU Member States. Survey results at a glance*,
p. 27 (Luxembourg: Publications Office of the European Union, 2012).

Other titles available in the IES Publication Series

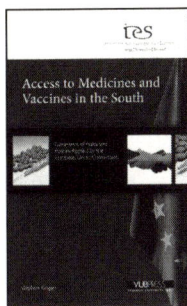

ACCESS TO MEDICINES AND VACCINES IN THE SOUTH
Coherence of Rules and Policies Applied by the European Union Commission
Stephen Kingah

978 90 5487 976 3 – 282 pp. – € 36,00

How can developing countries maximize some of the beneficial rules and policies provided to them by the EU and international organizations to reduce public health plight in terms of inadequate access to medicines and vaccines? By navigating some of the complex European and international rules and policies that have hitherto been put in place to ease access to affordable healthcare, the author identifies ways in which policy makers and legislators can optimally use extant rules to enhance healthcare provision.
Access to affordable healthcare is a matter that is undergirded by many policy fields. These include intellectual property, research, migration and infrastructure. It equally encompasses a genuine sense of awareness that available healthcare is the decent minimum from which people should not be deprived. This is more so because there are rules and policies which countries of the South can avail themselves of to improve access for their populations.
This book uses the idea of coherence to indicate how policies and rules at the European and international pedestals could be adapted and adopted to assuage the access problems faced by developing countries.

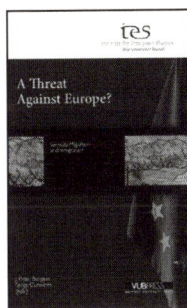

A THREAT AGAINST EUROPE?
Security, Migration and Integration
Peter Burgess, Serge Gutwirth

978 90 5487 929 9 – 224 pp. – g 32,00

The concept of security has traditionally referred to the status of sovereign states in a closed international system. In this system the state is assumed to be both the object of security and the primary provider of security. Threats to the state's security are understood as threats to its political autonomy in the system. The major international institutions that emerged after the Second World War were built around this idea. When the founders of the United Nations spoke of collective security, they were referring primarily to state security and to the coordinated system that would be necessary in order to avoid the 'scourge of war'. But today, a wide range of security threats, both new and traditional, confront Europe, or at least as some would say. New forms of nationalism, ethnic conflict and civil war, information technology, biological and chemical warfare, resource conflicts, pandemics, mass migrations, transnational terrorism, and environmental dangers challenge, according to many, the limits of our ability to safeguard the values upon which European society is based.

res

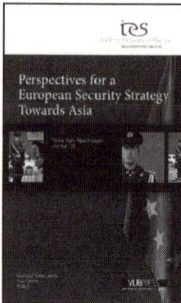

PERSPECTIVES FOR A EUROPEAN SECURITY STRATEGY TOWARDS ASIA

Views from Asia, Europe and the US
Gustaaf Geeraerts, Eva Gross (eds.)

978 90 5487 776 9 – 250 pp. – g 36,00

EU-Asia relations have steadily moved up the Brussels policy agenda. At the same time, EU-Asia relations remain beset by a lack of strategic thinking as to the EU's policy interests in Asia as well as the most appropriate tools to pursue them. This volume seeks to address the gap. First, contributors provide assessments of the EU's strategic interests in Asia, its capacity for action as well as clarity as to the options to address various policy challenges. Second, individual chapters also address Asian views of the EU as well as ways in which the EU can and should bolster its bilateral and regional engagement in the field of security. Taking account of EU as well as Asian interests and perceptions, this book offers concrete recommendations of how to strengthen EU engagement with Asia in a changing global context.

ON THE ROAD TO EU MEMBERSHIP

The Economic Transformation of Turkey
Selen Sarisoy Guerin, Yannis Stivachtis (eds.)

978 90 5487 861 2 – 302 pp. – g 40,00

This book focuses on the experience of Turkey to date in fulfilling its EU membership requirements and its impact on Turkish economy. It begins by evaluating the economic dimension of the EU-Turkey enlargement negotiations process; it follows by assessing the current strengths and weaknesses of the Turkish candidature by outlining how well Turkey has fared so far and finally, it details the implications of the accession negotiations for various sectors of the Turkish economy.

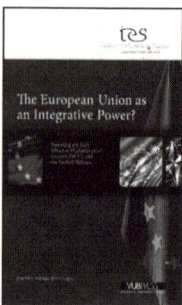

THE EUROPEAN UNION AS AN INTEGRATIVE POWER?

Assessing the EU's 'Effective Multilateralism' towards NATO and the United Nations
Joachim Alexander Koops

978 90 5487 772 1 – 500 pp. – g 48,00

This book offers a comprehensive analysis of the European Union as an International Actor and of its foreign policy of 'effective multilateralism' in both theory and practice. The core argument is that the EU has fostered integrative links - not only between states, but more recently also among international organisations. The study highlights the successes and critically examines the weaknesses of the EU's effective multilateralism with NATO and the United Nations and offers concrete proposals for strengthening the EU as an inter-organisational security actor and Integrative Power in the short- and long-term.

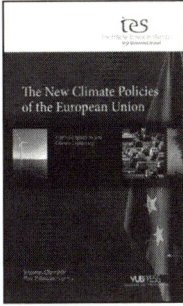

THE NEW CLIMATE POLICIES OF THE EUROPEAN UNION
Internal Legislation and Climate Diplomacy
Sebastian Oberthür, Marc Pallemaerts (eds.)

978 90 5487 607 6 – 340 pp. – g 40,00

This book provides a timely overview and assessment of the development of the new EU climate policies with a focus on the new climate and energy package. Are EU climate policies sufficient to meet the environmental, economic and political challenge posed by global climate change? How do international and domestic climate policies of the EU interact and are they mutually supportive? What are the prospects for the EU keeping its international leadership in the face of a more engaged US and increasingly assertive emerging economies? In addressing these questions, the volume aims to enhance understanding and contribute to further discussions on the current and potential role of the EU in the fight against climate change.

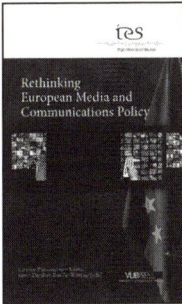

RETHINKING EUROPEAN MEDIA AND COMMUNICATIONS POLICY
Caroline Pauwels, Harri Kalimo, Karen Donders and Ben Van Rompuy (eds.)

978 90 5487 603 8 – 370 pp. – g 42,00

This book is a collection of expert insights on EU media and communications policies in the era of convergence. The media and ICT (Information and Communications Technology) sectors are at the heart of a competitive and inclusive European knowledge society. Since the late 1980s, the boundaries between these sectors have been blurring. It appears therefore necessary to fundamentally reconsider the existing legal and policy frameworks. Have they become completely outdated? What are the main problems, and how should they be addressed? These are the very questions that top experts address in this book.

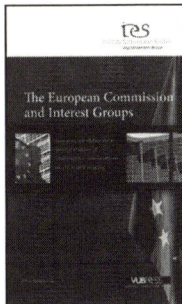

THE EUROPEAN COMMISSION AND INTEREST GROUPS
Towards a Deliberative Interpretation of Stakeholder Involvement in EU Policy-Making
Irina Tanasescu

978 90 5487 546 8 – 286 pp. – g 36,00

The analysis and understanding of the particular nature of the interactions between organized interests and the European Union institutions has had a prominent place on the research agenda of the past decade. This volume seeks to contribute to the debate by providing an in-depth assessment of European Commission consultation exercises from a novel perspective, namely a set of criteria inspired from deliberative democracy theories. While previous studies have explained how interest groups are organized at the EU level, which strategies they use and what the different access points to the EU institutions are, this book analyzes what happens in concrete instances of consultation.

res
Institute for European Studies
Vrije Universiteit Brussel

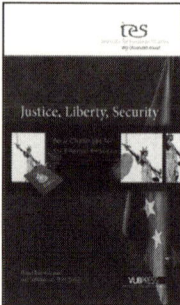

JUSTICE, LIBERTY, SECURITY
New Challenges for EU External Relations
Bernd Martenczuk and Servaas van Thiel (eds.)

978 90 5487 472 0 – 524 pp. – g 48,00

The European Union is rapidly creating a European space in which citizens can live in Justice, Liberty and Security. This bold push forward in the European integration process touches on three highly sensitive societal subjects: immigration and asylum, civil law, and criminal law. This book gives an excellent overview over the many current topics in these sensitive areas. Justice, Liberty, Security is structured in a user-friendly way and should be easily accessible to a broad audience of students, teachers, practitioners and the interested public. It is warmly recommended to anybody who wants to broaden his or her understanding of the increasing importance of the external side of European policies on Justice, Liberty and Security.

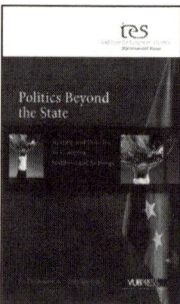

POLITICS BEYOND THE STATE
Actors and Policies in Complex Institutional Settings
Kris Deschouwer and M. Theo Jans (eds.)

978 90 5487 436 2 – 295 pp. – € 36,00

Politics Beyond the State seeks to capture the changing nature of politics both within and beyond the state. Its analysis clarifies that the central state continues to guide our understanding of politics but that it needs to be complemented with ample attention to both the sub- and the supranational tiers of government.

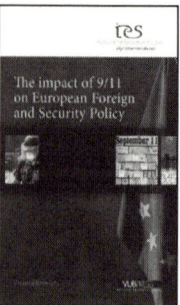

THE IMPACT OF 9/11 ON EUROPEAN FOREIGN AND SECURITY POLICY
Giovanna Bono (ed.)

978 90 5487 409 6 – 295 pp. – € 35,87

The contributors to this book argue that the events of 9/11 and the 'war on terror' are having a significant transformative impact on European Foreign and Security Policy. This is demonstrated through an analysis of changes in the attitudes of EU officials and politicians towards the laws and norms governing the use of force and through an analysis of changes in strategies towards the Balkans, sub-Saharan Africa, the Middle East and the United States.

Institute for European Studies
Vrije Universiteit Brussel

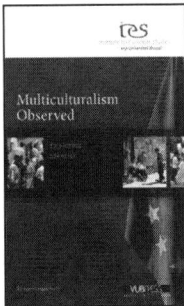

MULTICULTURALISM OBSERVED
Exploring Identity
Richard Lewis (ed.)

978 90 5487 330 3 – 156 pp. – € 28,00

This book offers a timely and unique perspective on a phenomenon which is highly divisive and splits academic and public opinion alike. In the wake of the terrorist attacks in New York, Madrid and London, the question how western society integrates its minorities has become one of the most crucial issues facing government today and excites media attention and frequent public controversy. This volume presents a number of points of view both from Europe and North America by academic, religious and political authors from a variety of cultures, all with a very different perspective on whether multiculturalism is a valid answer to ensuring harmony in our societies.

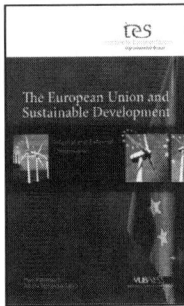

THE EUROPEAN UNION AND SUSTAINABLE DEVELOPMENT
Internal and External Dimensions
Marc Pallemaerts and Albena Azmanova (eds.)

978 90 5487 247 4 – 342 pp. – € 40,00

Since the Treaty of Amsterdam, sustainable development is legally enshrined among the fundamental objectives of European integration. But how has the European Union addressed this issue? Is sustainable development a truly innovative policy paradigm which will revolutionize the way Europe approaches economic, social and environmental issues, or is it little more than a fashionable but vacuous political buzzword? These are some of the questions addressed by the contributors to this volume, who bring a diversity of perspectives to bear on both the internal and external dimensions of the EU's ambiguous relationship with sustainable development.

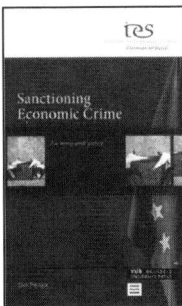

SANCTIONING ECONOMIC CRIME
An Integrated Policy
Dirk Merckx

978 90 5487 360 0 – 445 pp. – € 44,00

The sanctioning of economic crime has traditionally been a part of general criminal law. However, an economic criminal law appears to have been developed in modern economic systems as well. Administrative penal law and punitive civil law are also becoming increasingly important. The key question in this study concerns the use of sanctioning systems in combating economic crime. To this end, four central themes have been studied: the social definition of the issue of fraud, the legal techniques for sanctioning, the characterisation of the notion of sanction and the concrete implementation of sanctions as far as modalities and severity are concerned.

Institute for European Studies
Vrije Universiteit Brussel

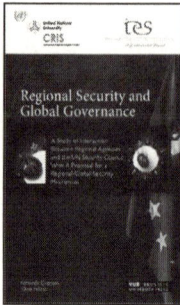

REGIONAL SECURITY AND GLOBAL GOVERNANCE
A Study of Interaction between Regional Agencies and the UN Security Council with a Proposal for a Regional-Global Security Mechanism
Kennedy Graham and Tânia Felício

978 90 5487 404 1 – 362 pp. – € 42,00

This ground-breaking book explores, for policy-makers worldwide, how peace and security might best be attained in the 21st century. Its central message is the importance of realizing UN Secretary-General Kofi Annan's vision of a "regional-global security mechanism" within the next decade. The book reviews the historical tussle between universalism and regionalism as the cornerstone of international security over the past century, culminating in the "new regionalism" that has characterized international relations in recent decades.

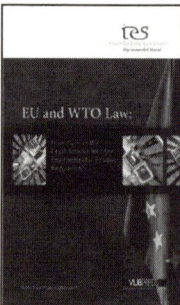

EU AND WTO LAW
How Tight is the Legal Straitjacket for Environmental Product Regulation?
Marc Pallemaerts (ed.)

978 90 5487 403 4 – 327 pp. – € 40,00

Do free trade rules impose a legal straitjacket on product-oriented environmental measures? While environmental law increasingly relies on product regulations as an important policy instrument, supranational economic law, as laid down within the framework of the EU and the WTO, tends to view such regulations as trade barriers which are to be removed as far as possible. This book aims, to help clarify the legal boundaries of the policy space that remains open to public authorities at the national and supranational level to regulate trade in products in pursuit of legitimate objectives of environmental protection and sustainable development.

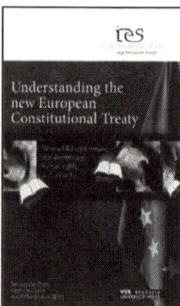

UNDERSTANDING THE EUROPEAN CONSTITUTIONAL TREATY
Why a NO Vote Means Less Democracy, Human Rights and Security
Servaas van Thiel, Richard Lewis and Karel De Gucht (eds.)

978 90 5487 390 7 – 316 pp. – € 40,00

In this book, a selection of well placed authors, who as political and judicial leaders (Belgian Prime Minister Verhofstadt and Foreign Affairs Minister De Gucht, former Commissioner Vitorino, European Court Judge Lenaerts), Union officials (Devuyst, van Thiel, Martenczuk, Lewis) and academics (De Schouwer, De Hert, Biscop, Gerard), know Europe from the inside, analyse and explain how the Constitution would contribute to a more efficient and democratic Europe that would be better equipped to face the challenges of a globalising world.

Institute for European Studies
Vrije Universiteit Brussel

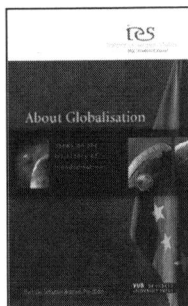

ABOUT GLOBALISATION
Views on the Trajectory of Mondialisation
Bart De Schutter and Johan Pas (eds.)

978 90 5487 360 0 – 344 pp. – € 40,00

Globalisation is probably one of the most controversial issues of the last decade, but too often it has been looked at from within one discipline only. The present book particularly wishes to point out to the reader that, due to its different aspects, globalisation can only be grasped from within a multi-disciplinary approach. Therefore the different authors look at the issue from a politics, law, philosophy ... point of view.

The book also sheds a light on various contested topics relating to globalisation, such as information and communication technology, intellectual property rights and currency transaction taxation.

res

Institute for European Studies
Vrije Universiteit Brussel

BOOKS IN DUTCH

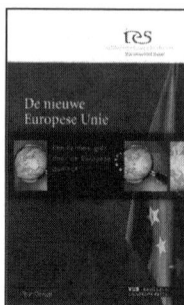

DE NIEUWE EUROPESE UNIE
Een heldere gids door de Europese doolhof
Youri Devuyst

978 90 5487 370 9 – 296 pp. – € 36,00

Voor de gewone burger is de Europese Unie bijzonder ondoorzichtig. Ons dagelijks leven wordt nochtans voortdurend door de EU beïnvloed. Het nodige inzicht in de besluitvorming en het beleid van de EU is daarom van belang. Enkel diegenen die op de hoogte zijn kunnen immers de werking van de EU bijsturen. Wie bijvoorbeeld naar sociale vooruitgang streeft, kan vandaag niet anders dan strijd voeren op Europees niveau. Maar dit vergt de nodige kennis van de Europese besluitvorming. Vanuit dit perspectief tracht dit boek een heldere gids te zijn die belangstellenden op een eenvoudige wijze doorheen de Europese doolhof loodst. Het bevat daarbij de meest recente informatie over de ontwikkeling van de Europese Unie.

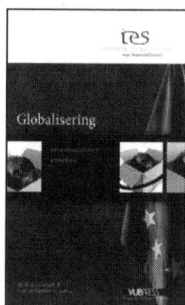

GLOBALISERING: INTERDISCIPLINAIR BEKEKEN
Jacobus Delwaide and Gustaaf Geeraerts (eds.)

978 90 5487 490 4 – 336 pp. – € 40,00

De globalisering raakt aan alle aspecten van ons dagelijks leven. Ze is meer dan alleen maar een economisch fenomeen. Daarom moet ze vanuit verschillende disciplines worden belicht. Deze bundel brengt vijftien auteurs samen die vanuit vijf disciplines - communicatiewetenschap, economie, geschiedenis, politieke wetenschap en rechten - de oorsprongen, vormen en gevolgen van de globalisering analyseren.